450 MONEY QUESTIC

About the author

Jonquil Lowe is a freelance journalist and former head of the Money Group at *Which?* magazine. She is author of several other books on personal finance including *The Which? Guide to Pensions* and *The Which? Guide to Giving and Inheriting*, published by Consumers' Association.

450 MONEY QUESTIONS ANSWERED

JONQUIL LOWE

CONSUMERS' ASSOCIATION

Which? Books are commissioned and researched by
The Association for Consumer Research
and published by Consumers' Association,
2 Marylebone Road, NW1 4DF

Distributed by The Penguin Group:
Penguin Books Ltd, 27 Wrights Lane, London W8 5TZ

First edition September 1994

Copyright © 1994 Consumers' Association Ltd

British Library Cataloguing in Publication Data

Lowe, Jonquil
  450 Money Questions Answered. –
  (Which? Consumer Guides)
  1. Title II Series
  344.10682

  ISBN 0–85202–508–4

No part of this publication may be reproduced or transmitted in any form or by
any means, electronically or mechanically, including photocopying, recording or
any information storage or retrieval system, without prior permission in writing
from the publisher. This publication is not included under licences issued by the
Copyright Agency.

Cover photographs by ACE Photo Agency

Typeset by Litho Link Limited, Welshpool, Powys, Wales
Printed and bound by Firmin-Didot (France), 27860
Groupe Herissey

CONTENTS

Introduction

In today's busy and complex world few of us have the time to become expert in areas outside our normal careers or special interests. Yet everyone is expected to have at least a passing knowledge of the tax system, handling savings, running bank accounts, organising a pension and a whole host of other personal financial matters.

It's not easy to keep abreast of the new financial products, be able to evaluate them and compare them with others. Do you know what critical illness insurance covers? Can you judge whether premium bonds are an investment or simply a gamble? How do you choose the best home for your current account, or the most suitable credit card? Is mail-order shopping an expensive convenience? Should you take out an extended guarantee on your new washing machine? Is an E111 a reasonable substitute for holiday insurance? How do you evaluate the pros and cons of different savings schemes? How can you avoid the sharks if you want to buy a timeshare? Do TESSAs make a good short-term investment? What are your options when you leave a pension scheme? And what are the best ways to save for school fees?

In many areas, advice is available, but would you know where to find out about housing benefit, or to get help in choosing permanent health insurance? Can you tell if you're being given good advice about investing in an endowment insurance or personal equity plan? Are you sure you know the difference between an independent financial adviser and a tied agent?

Now you have a guide to point out what's available, explain the key factors and set you on the right track: *450 Money Questions Answered*. You can use it for reference when you need to know about a particular area of personal finance, such as mortgages, maintenance payments,

TESSAs or no-claims discounts for car insurance. It will also give you a useful overview of matters such as income tax, investment planning and personal banking. And it will ensure that you have the knowledge to make confident use of service providers and advisers.

The book draws on the wealth of information published in *Which?* magazine and on the postbag it receives, as well as the many and varied questions which have been put to me over the years by readers, friends and family. My thanks to all those who provided inspiration for the questions and answers presented here.

CHAPTER 1

YOUR FAMILY

FAMILIES are at the heart of many finance matters. Sometimes they play a passive role – for example, your tax position will be different if you are married from that of someone who is single or cohabiting, and different again if you are going through a separation or divorce. Similarly, your entitlement to state benefits and the amount you can claim will often be affected by your family situation.

In other respects, the family is the driving force behind your financial planning, dictating your need for insurance, the way you arrange your investments and the steps you take to pass possessions from one generation to the next.

Marriage

Q *Our daughter has just announced her engagement. She and her fiancé plan to save up for a home and get married in about two years' time. What's the best way for us to save to pay for the big day?*

A First, you need to work out roughly how much money you'll need in two years' time. As two years is not very long, your savings won't have much time to grow, so you might divide this sum by, say, twenty and aim to set aside that amount each month from now on. You should avoid investments whose value can fall as well as rise (such as unit trusts) because you cannot be sure of enough money being available when you need it. Your choice is restricted to various forms of deposit accounts offered by building societies, banks and National Savings. Shop around for the best returns given the amount you can save and your tax position. Once you have built up a reasonable sum of capital, you might be able to get a better return by switching to another account. For more about investments, turn to Chapter 7.

Q *For tax purposes, is there a 'best' time of year to get married?*

A The main tax change when you marry is that you become eligible for the married couple's allowance, which reduces your liability for income tax. In the 1994–5 tax year, the full year allowance is £1,720 and gives you tax relief at a rate of 20 per cent, saving you £344. From 6 April 1995, the rate of relief is due to fall to 15 per cent. If you marry on or after 6 April but before 6 May, you will get the full married couple's allowance during the tax year in which you marry. If you marry after 5 May, the allowance is reduced by one-twelfth for each complete month after 6 April that you remain unmarried – see Table 1.1. In this sense, you might consider it 'best' to marry early in the tax year.

To claim the married couple's allowance, contact your tax office as soon as possible after the wedding; if you pay tax, use form 11PA, which you can get from any tax office (see Addresses section).

Table 1.1: Married couple's allowance in the tax year[1] of marriage for those marrying in 1994–5

Date of marriage	Married couple's allowance £	Tax saving £
6 April-5 May	1,720	344.00
6 May-5 June	1,577	315.40
6 June-5 July	1,434	286.80
6 July-5 August	1,290	258.00
6 August-5 September	1,147	229.40
6 September-5 October	1,004	200.80
6 October-5 November	860	172.00
6 November-5 December	717	143.40
6 December-5 January	574	114.80
6 January-5 February	430	86.00
6 February-5 March	287	57.40
6 March-5 April	144	28.80

[1] A tax year runs from 6 April in one year to 5 April in the next.

Q *I'm remarrying soon and have a child from my previous marriage. Will I be able to carry on getting the additional personal allowance once I'm married?*

A Single people looking after a dependent child qualify for the additional personal allowance to reduce their income tax liability. It is set at the same level as the married couple's allowance – i.e. in the 1994–5 tax year it is £1,720 and gives you tax relief at a rate of 20 per cent (reducing to 15 per cent from 6 April 1995). If you marry, you cease to be eligible for the additional personal allowance, but you can carry on getting it just for the tax year in which you marry. A man must choose whether or not to keep the allowance; if he does, he cannot also claim the married couple's allowance for that year. If he marries after 5 May, it will be worth his keeping the additional personal allowance because it will be higher than the reduced married couple's allowance he could otherwise get (see opposite). A woman can carry on claiming the additional personal allowance for the remainder of the tax year in which she marries without this affecting the couple's claim for married couple's allowance.

After the end of the tax year of marriage, the additional personal allowance ceases, unless it can be claimed by the husband because his wife is totally mentally or physically incapacitated throughout the whole year and they have a dependent child.

Q *Why is it the husband who gets the married couple's allowance and not the wife?*

A Traditionally, the income tax laws have been sexist and assumed that the husband was the main breadwinner. But from April 1990 a system of 'independent taxation' was introduced (see Box) and the tax rules have treated men and women much more equally since then. Even under the new system, however, it was the husband who received the married couple's allowance unless he had too little income to make full use of it. On 6 April 1993 this changed: the married couple's allowance is still initially given to the husband, but the wife has a right to half the allowance and can make a claim for this to be given to her, rather than her husband. Alternatively, the husband and wife can jointly elect for the whole allowance to be given to the wife and, in this case, the husband then has the right to claim back half the allowance. To make these changes, fill in form 18 from your tax office. You must normally make your claim before the start of the tax year in which the change is to apply. Only the basic married couple's allowance (£1,720 in 1993–4) can be transferred in this way – not any extra age-related amounts (see pages 13–14).

In addition, if a husband or wife has too little income to make use of all or part of the married couple's allowance, the unused amount can be transferred to the other spouse. In this situation, age-related amounts can be transferred as well as the basic allowance. You must tell your tax office, within six years of the end of the tax year to which it applies, if you want to make this switch.

INDEPENDENT TAXATION

In the past, a married couple used to be regarded as one collective person for income tax purposes, with the wife's earnings normally treated as if they were her husband's. But from the 1990–1 tax year onwards, 'independent taxation' applies. This means that a husband or wife:

- is taxed solely on his or her own income
- has his or her own tax-free allowances
- is responsible for his or her own tax affairs.

Q *My daughter is getting married in two months' time. My father wants to give her the deposit for a house as a wedding present. My father is quite wealthy and I'm anxious that the present may cause tax problems.*

A There are two taxes you might need to consider: capital gains tax and inheritance tax. But, provided your father is making a gift of money (rather than things), you can ignore any question of capital gains tax. Inheritance tax is a tax on gifts you make during your lifetime and the estate you leave on your death. Most lifetime gifts are potentially exempt transfers (PETs) and are tax-free provided the giver survives for seven years. In addition, many gifts are tax-free for other reasons, and there is an exemption which applies specifically to wedding gifts:

- each parent of the bride and groom can give up to £5,000 tax-free
- each grandparent (and more distant ancestors) can give up to £2,500 tax-free
- anyone else can give up to £1,000 tax-free.

In addition, the first £3,000 of gifts in any tax-year is tax-free, so if your father has not made any other gifts this year, he could give your daughter up to £5,500 as a wedding present without incurring any tax problems either now or when his estate comes to be assessed.

Q *My husband is a student and has virtually no income at present. As I'm supporting us both, can I make use of his tax allowances?*

A The married couple's allowance can be transferred to you, as described on page 11. But you cannot make use of his personal allowance (see page 143) even if he has too little income to use it, because personal allowances can never be transferred from one person to another. If you have any investment income, you might be able to transfer part or all of this to him (see next question), so that he can set his personal allowance against it.

Q *My husband is a higher-rate taxpayer but I pay tax only at the basic rate. Is there any way we can transfer income or tax rates in order to cut our overall income tax bill?*

A There is no way in which you can transfer your lower tax rate to your husband, but you may be able to transfer income:

- if you have any investments which you own jointly with your husband. In the first instance, you will be treated as if you have equal shares in them. But you can ask for income from them to be split unequally between you for tax purposes – in your case, clearly, it would make sense for you to have a higher share of the income, since your top rate of tax is lower. But note that this split must reflect the *actual* shares which you and your husband have in the investments and will also apply in any assessment for capital gains tax when you sell them or give them away

13

- if your husband has income-producing investments in his own name. He could save tax either by transferring them into your joint names or by giving them to you outright, so that part or all of the income becomes yours.

Q *I've been told that, because I'm 65 next year, my husband can get a higher tax allowance. Is that right?*

A Your husband can claim a higher married couple's allowance from the start of the tax year in which either he or you (or both of you) reach age 65. In the 1994–5 tax year, the allowance is £2,665 if you or your husband are aged 64 to 73 on the first day of the tax year (6 April), and £2,705 if you or your husband is aged 74 or over on the first day. But the higher allowance will be reduced if your husband has income above a given level (see page 144) though never to less than the basic married couple's allowance (£1,720).

TAX RELIEF ON HOME LOANS

There is usually no help from the Inland Revenue with repaying loans, but an important exception is a mortgage or other loan you take out to buy your only or main home. You get tax relief on interest on up to £30,000 of such a loan. In the 1994–5 tax year, the relief is limited to a rate of 20 per cent, falling to 15 per cent from 6 April 1995. The £30,000 limit applies both per person and per property, so if you buy a home jointly with someone else, you will only get £30,000's worth of relief between you. Different rules apply if you bought your home before 1 August 1988, when you and an unmarried partner could both get mortgage relief on the same property. If you are still benefiting under the old rules, be wary of changing your mortgage or getting married because you'll lose the extra tax relief.

Q *My fiancé and I both have our own flats at present but are hoping to buy a house together when we marry. How much tax relief on the mortgages can we claim if we don't manage to sell both flats immediately?*

A If you and your fiancé both qualify for mortgage tax relief at present and will not be living together before buying the house, you can:

- continue to get tax relief on both the flats for up to 12 months after the date you move out, *and*
- jointly get tax relief on up to £30,000 of a mortgage on your new house.

If, instead, you decide to live together in one of the flats, you can continue to get tax relief on the flat you are trying to sell for up to 12 months as well as carrying on getting tax relief on the flat you live in.

Q *Our home is in the joint names of myself and my husband, as is the mortgage. Who gets the tax relief on the mortgage payments?*

A Initially, it is assumed that the mortgage is split evenly between you and your husband, but you can elect to have it split differently – called an **allocation of interest election**. Unlike the treatment of joint assets (see page 13), the way you choose to split the mortgage relief does not have to reflect how the mortgage or repayments are shared between you. You can choose whatever split is most beneficial to you and your husband. Even if the mortgage were just in your husband's name, you could choose that all the tax relief be given to you. If you are paying your mortgage through the Mortgage Interest Relief at Source (MIRAS) scheme, the interest you pay the lender will already have had the tax relief deducted from it, so the question of who gets the tax relief isn't usually relevant. But if you or your husband is aged 65 or more, who gets the relief could affect your personal age allowance or the age-related married couple's allowance (see page 144). If you are not paying through MIRAS, an allocation of interest election could be worth making if either you or your husband is a non-taxpayer. To make an election, you need to complete form 15 from any tax office. You must make the election within 12 months of the end of the tax year to which you want it to apply.

Q *Our solicitor has suggested that we should switch the way we own our home from a 'joint tenancy' to 'tenants in common'. What does this mean and why is it important?*

A There are two ways in which you can own a home – or, indeed, anything else – and this applies whether there are just two owners or more:

- under a **joint tenancy** all the owners have equal and identical shares in the home or other asset which give each owner the right to the full benefit or use of the whole asset. But these shares can't be separately identified and, on the death of one of the owners, his or her share automatically passes to the other owners
- **tenants in common** also share the home or other asset and enjoy the full benefit or whole use of it. But they have separately identifiable shares which need not be equal and, on the death of one of the owners, what happens to their share depends either on the terms of his or her will or on the intestacy rules, if there is no will (see page 43).

Married couples often own their home and assets as joint tenants, but owning them as tenants in common is more flexible, especially when it comes to tax and inheritance planning. And, given that many marriages end in divorce, tenancy in common may be preferred as a way of making the division of joint assets more straightforward, in the event of the marriage ending.

Q *I've spent most of my married life bringing up the children and taking care of the home, but now I've taken a part-time job and have a little income of my own. Should I be putting some of this into a pension plan, or is it o.k. to rely on my husband's pension arrangements?*

A The answer to this will depend on a variety of factors, including: what sort of pension arrangements your husband has, how much you can afford to save, how old you are now, and whether your marriage is stable. You will find information about pension planning in Chapter 8. But do bear in mind that women's role in society has changed greatly over the last few decades and all women are advised to take responsibility for financial affairs, not simply leave them to their husbands. You and your husband should jointly consider what financial resources you would have in the various situations which the future might hold. These include not just a shared retirement but also, for example, the possibility of either you or your husband being widowed.

(Younger couples, in particular, should also be realistic about the risk of divorce.) Look at how well your current financial arrangements might meet these situations and consider what extra provision you, your husband or both of you together could make to improve your ability to cope.

Living together

Q *My girlfriend and I are about to have a baby. I think there's an extra tax allowance we can get after it's born. How do we claim it?*

A The allowance you are thinking of is the **additional personal allowance**. In the 1994–5 tax year, this is £1,720 and gives you tax relief at a rate of 20 per cent (falling to 15 per cent from 1995–6) – i.e. the same as the married couple's allowance. You can claim the additional personal allowance if you have a dependent child and you are:

- a single person
- a married woman separated from your husband
- a married man whose wife will be totally incapacitated throughout the tax year
- a newly married man or woman, but only in the tax year of marriage – see page 11 for further information.

You can only get one additional personal allowance regardless of the number of children you have and, since 1989, an unmarried couple living together as man and wife has only been able to claim one allowance between them. However, the allowance can be given either to you or your girlfriend, or split between you in shares which you choose. To claim the allowance this year, contact your tax office which will send you a form 11PA. In subsequent years, claim through your tax return.

Q *As a single parent, I get the additional personal allowance to set against my income tax. Will I lose this if I move in with my boyfriend?*

A No. Provided you meet the conditions for the additional personal allowance, you receive it even if you are living with someone. But note that if your boyfriend is also currently getting additional personal allowance because he has a dependent child too, you can't *both* carry on getting the allowance once you live together as man and wife (see previous question).

Q *The Benefits Agency is threatening to cut my income support because, it claims, my boyfriend lives with me. But he has his own house and just stays here sometimes. How does the Agency define 'living together'?*

A If you and your partner live together as man and wife, you will be assessed jointly for income support and various other state benefits, and only one of you will be able to make a claim on behalf of both of you. In deciding whether you live together as man and wife, the rules are not hard and fast, but the following factors will be considered:

- do you share the same household?
- do you share household expenses?
- is your relationship stable?
- do you present yourself to the world as a couple?
- do you have children?

Answering 'yes' to any of these could be used as evidence that you do live together as man and wife. The fact that your boyfriend normally lives at a separate address should be strong evidence that you don't, but it's all the factors in combination which will determine your particular case. The onus is on the Benefits Agency to prove that you do live together and, if you feel it has decided wrongly, you can challenge the decision. Your local Benefits Agency will tell you what steps to take. See pages 106–7 for more about state benefits.

Children

Q *I've just learnt that I'm pregnant. I'm really delighted, but I do have a job which I'm determined to carry on with even after the baby's born. How long can I take off work without losing my job?*

A Provided you'll have worked for your current employer for at least two years up to the eleventh week before the baby is due, you have the right to take maternity leave and return to your job at any time up to

29 weeks after the baby's birth. If you've been in your job for less than two years, you don't have the *right* to go back to your job, but your employer may let you do this.

Q *Will I still get paid while I'm on maternity leave?*

A The law sets out a minimum level of pay which your employer must normally give you, for at least a specified period, while you're taking maternity leave: this is called Statutory Maternity Pay (SMP). Many employers run more generous schemes, so check with your personnel officer.

There are three main conditions you must meet in order to qualify for SMP:

* you must be working, even if only for one day, during the **qualifying week** (this is the fifteenth week before the week in which your baby is due)
* you must have been working for the same employer for at least 26 weeks up to the end of the qualifying week
* your average earnings (including overtime and bonuses) over the eight weeks before the qualifying week must be at least as much as the **lower earnings limit** (which is £57 a week in the 1994–5 tax year).

You will have to give your employer at least 21 days' notice of the date when you intend to start your leave, together with evidence of when your baby is due – this will usually be in the form of a certificate MATB1 provided by your GP or antenatal clinic.

Q *I've only been in my current job a couple of months. Although my boss has agreed to hold my job open for me while I'm on maternity leave, he says I can't get SMP. What should I do?*

A You may be able to get maternity allowance instead (see page 22). Make sure that your employer has given you a form, SMP1, saying why you are not eligible for SMP and returned your certificate MATB1 if you gave it to him, because you will need to give these to your local Benefits Agency along with your claim for maternity allowance.

Some employers run maternity pay schemes which provide an income during maternity leave even if you do not have a legal right to SMP.

Q *For how long will I get maternity pay?*

A SMP is paid for a core period of 13 weeks starting with the sixth week before the week in which the baby is due and ending with the sixth week after the week in which the baby was due. You can also get SMP for a further five weeks which can either be taken before the baby is due, after it is born or split between these as you decide. So the maximum SMP period is 18 weeks and the earliest it can start is 11 weeks before the baby is due – see Chart 1.1.

You have to stop work in order to get SMP. Your maternity leave does not have to be the same as the SMP period, but you lose the right to SMP for any of the core weeks in which you choose to carry on working.

Once again, your employer may run a more generous scheme than the statutory minimum.

Chart 1.1: Eligibility for Statutory Maternity Pay (SMP) or maternity allowance (MA)

CORE PERIOD		6 WEEKS	WEEK BABY DUE	6 WEEKS	
EARLIEST PERIOD FOR SMP/MA	5 WEEKS	6 WEEKS	WEEK BABY DUE	6 WEEKS	
LATEST PERIOD FOR SMP/MA		6 WEEKS	WEEK BABY DUE	6 WEEKS	5 WEEKS

Q *How much maternity pay can I expect while I'm on maternity leave?*

A SMP is paid at two levels. For women expecting their babies from 16 October 1994, these are:

- a higher rate payable for the first six weeks of your leave, provided you have worked for your employer for at least two years up to the qualifying week (see page 19). The higher rate is nine-tenths of your average weekly earnings
- a lower rate of £52.50 a week payable for the remaining 12 weeks or for the whole period if you do not qualify for the higher rate.

Your employer may operate a more generous maternity pay scheme.

Q *Will I have to pay tax on my maternity pay?*

A Yes. SMP and any other maternity pay provided by your employer is treated in exactly the same way as other earnings. This means that you are liable for both income tax and National Insurance on maternity pay, if it is high enough. Usually, your employer will deduct tax and National Insurance through PAYE (see pages 51–2) before you get the pay. But, if your pay during this time is too low for you to have to pay National Insurance (see page 56), you'll get National Insurance credits to protect your record. (You'll get these credits even if you normally pay National Insurance at the reduced rate – see page 57).

MORE INFORMATION ABOUT MATERNITY LEAVE AND PAY

Department of Employment booklet PL 710, *Employment Rights for Expectant Mothers,* from Benefits Agencies and Job Centres.

Department of Social Security booklet NI 17A, *A Guide to Maternity Benefits,* from Benefits Agencies, also some post offices and public libraries.

In March 1994, the government announced improvements to the system of maternity pay and benefit in order to bring UK benefits into line with the requirements of a European Union Directive. The new rules and benefits, which are described here, apply to women expecting their babies on or after 16 October 1994 (and thus become payable from July 1994 onwards).

Q *I'm expecting a baby in November and will have to take some time off from my business. Can I get any maternity pay from the state?*

A There are a number of reasons why you might not be entitled to get Statutory Maternity Pay (SMP). Two of the main ones are:

- you are self-employed
- you are an employee, but you do not meet the conditions set out on page 19 – for example, your pay is too low or you were not at work during the qualifying week (because you were off sick, say).

If you cannot get SMP, you may be able to get maternity allowance instead which is paid by the Department of Social Security (DSS). In order to qualify for it, you must have paid National Insurance contributions (at either the Class 2 or standard Class 1 rate – see page 55) for at least 26 weeks out of the 66 weeks up to the end of the fifteenth week before the baby is due.

If you think you might be eligible for maternity allowance, get form MA1 from your local Benefits Agency. You'll also have to provide the Agency with a certificate MATB1, from your GP or clinic, as proof of the date your baby's due. You can't make your claim until the fourteenth week before the baby's due.

Q *How much is maternity allowance?*

A Maternity allowance is paid at one of two flat rates. Most employees expecting babies on or after 16 October 1994 qualify for the higher rate, £52.50 a week in the 1994–5 tax year. Other women, e.g. those who are self-employed, get the lower rate, set at £44.55 in 1994–5. If there is an adult who depends on you for financial support, you can claim extra. Maternity allowance is paid for a maximum of 18 weeks in the same way as SMP – see Chart 1.1.

The allowance is not taxable and, while you are getting the allowance, you can get National Insurance credits to protect your record.

Q *I work part-time in a local supermarket and only earn £50 a week. I gather this is too low for me to get maternity pay. Where's the money to come from while I'm off work having the baby?*

A Your income is too low for you to have to pay National Insurance contributions, so you don't meet the conditions for either SMP or maternity allowance. But, if you would have no money coming in or only a very low income while you're on maternity leave, you might qualify for means-tested state benefits, such as income support (see pages 106–17). Among other factors, whether or not you qualify will depend on your household income, including that of a partner, and any savings that you and your partner have.

Even someone getting SMP or maternity allowance may still be on such a low income that she qualifies for income support.

Q *Is child benefit paid to all parents or only if they are on a low income?*

A Child benefit is a **non-means-tested** benefit, so you get it whatever your level of income or savings. In 1994–5, child benefit is set at £10.20 a week for your oldest or only child and £8.25 a week for each subsequent child. Child benefit is not taxable. To qualify, your child must either live with you or you must be paying at least as much as the amount of benefit towards your child if he or she lives elsewhere. Only one person can claim the benefit for each child and there is a priority for claimants, so that, for example, the mother is given preference over the father. To make a claim, get form CB2 or CB3 from your local Benefits Agency.

Q *I want to give my baby daughter a small nest egg for later years. What's the best investment to choose?*

A As a parent, you must keep an eye on the tax position when you give money or investments to your children. A child, just like anyone else, has a tax allowance (see page 143) and can therefore receive a certain amount of income each year without having to pay tax on it. But if gifts from a parent produce a taxable income of more than £100 a year, this is taxed as the *parent's* income, not the child's. The limit applies to each parent, so a child could have an income of up to £200 a year from this source without it counting as the parents' income. Instead it would be treated as income of the child, who could set his or her personal allowance against it. Bearing this in mind, you should avoid investments which produce a taxable income (such as bank and building society accounts) unless you are giving a relatively small amount – up to £2,000 or so. Choose instead investments which produce tax-free income or capital growth. Two investments which are particularly suitable as gifts from parents to children are National Savings Children's Bonus Bonds and 'baby bonds' offered by friendly societies, both of which offer a tax-free return.

Q *My son Tom, who's seven, has been given £500 by his gran. How should we invest it for him?*

A Unlike the previous questioner, you need not limit your choice to tax-free investments. Where a gift is made to a child by someone other than a parent, any income arising from the gift counts as the child's own. Consider the National Savings Children's Bonus Bond, but look also at National Savings Investment Accounts and at bank and building society accounts – ones geared to children are more likely to pay higher rates on relatively small sums and they often include free gifts. Although income from these investments is potentially taxable, Tom has unused personal allowance and can get the gross (i.e. before tax) rate. An advantage of a building society account for a child around Tom's age is that he can start to learn about handling money by using the account actively to save and make withdrawals. If the money is to be invested over the long term, consider unit or investment trusts too (see pages 217–19).

Because of the Inland Revenue's distinction between gifts from parents and gifts from other people, you should keep any letter or note accompanying the gift or ask gran to provide such a note, so that you can prove to the Revenue, if need be, that the money was not from you.

Q *What is a baby bond?*

A 'Baby bonds' are savings-type insurance plans issued by friendly societies. What makes baby bonds special is that they are the only insurance policies which can be taken out directly by children and the return on them is completely tax-free. Investment in a baby bond is initially for at least ten years, after which your child can either take a

Table 1.2: Selected children's bank and building society accounts

Bank or society and account name	Age range	Before-tax interest on £100 balance[1]	Gifts and incentives
Abbey National Bank Action Saver	Up to 15	2.5%	Membership card and gift pack Magazine and offers
Bank of Scotland Supersaver	Up to 12	2.75%	Backpack, management folder or Squirrel bank, magazine
Bank of Scotland Express	12–17	2.75%	Regular newsletter and audio cassette tape
Barclays Bank Junior Barclays Plus	0–10	1.0%	Account opening pack
Barclays Bank BarclayPlus	11–16	1.0%	Our Price Music Club membership with £10 vouchers
Britannia BS Brighter Savers	Up to 16	3.4%	Piggy bank
Britannia BS LTD	11–17	3.4%	–
Halifax BS Little Xtra Club	Up to 9	3.75%	Money box, bike sticker, badge, magazine, Christmas and birthday cards
Halifax BS Quest Club	10–15	3.75%	Magazine, careers guide
Lloyds Bank Young Saver	Up to 11	2.0%	Stationery pack
Lloyds Bank Headway	12–18	2.0%	Discount vouchers
Midland LIVE!Cash	11 upwards	2.47%	Free/cheap driving lessons, cinema tickets, voucher book
TSB Firstsave	Up to 16	3.25%	Discount vouchers at age 11+
Woolwich BS Woolwich for Kids	Up to 12	1.0%	Money box and wallet, magazine and birthday card

Source: *MoneyFacts*
[1] Interest rates in June 1994

tax-free lump sum or leave the money invested on a tax-free basis. Your savings are invested in shares and other assets either on a **with-profits** or **unit-linked** basis (see page 228).

The government limits the amount anyone can invest tax-free with a friendly society. The maximum for 1994–5 is £200 a year (£18 a month). Societies will sometimes accept smaller investments but rarely less than £100 a year or £9 a month. Most societies let you invest a lump sum which is invested to produce the required sum each year to be paid into the bond. The minimum lump sum investment is around £800. Because the amount invested is fairly small, charges are often high as a proportion of the return.

Q *Which is the best investment for a child: baby bonds or the National Savings Children's Bonus Bond?*

A National Savings Children's Bonus Bonds offer a tax-free, guaranteed return over five years which, at the time of writing, was relatively high at 7.35 per cent a year. They can be bought for children up to the age of 16 and held by them until age 21. The return on baby bonds is not guaranteed and depends on the performance of shares and similar investments. Therefore, which you choose depends to an extent on whether you want the chance to get a higher return with the baby bonds but at the same time run the risk that it will be lower than you could have got with the Children's Bonds.

You can invest from as little as £25 up to £1,000 in Children's Bonds, which makes them more suitable than baby bonds if you have only a small sum to invest, and also a useful option if you want to invest more than £200 year after year.

Q *My teenage son's friends always seem to have masses of money to spend and he complains that we don't give him enough. What is the 'going rate' for pocket money?*

A Table 1.3 shows the results of a pocket-money survey by Consumers' Association's *Check It Out!* in 1993. But this is only a very rough guide to how much teenagers have to spend because, in addition, many parents pay separately for their children's clothes, fares and even nights out at the disco or cinema. For some children, pocket money is a fixed weekly handout, for others it's earned by doing odd jobs – Table 1.4 shows *Check It Out!*'s suggested rate for a variety of jobs around the house.

By the time the child has reached the age of 15 or 16, you might consider switching from pocket money to a monthly allowance – for example, £50 a month or so – out of which your son could pay for, say, entertainment and clothes. This would give him a good introduction to managing a budget.

Table 1.3: Pocket money

Age of child	Average amount of weekly pocket money in 1993 £
11	1.94
12	2.46
13	3.24
14	3.60
15	4.76

Source: *Check It Out!*, September 1993

Table 1.4: Rough guide to odd-job rates

Job	Suggested rate in 1993
Vacuuming	20–50p per room
Dusting	30–50p per room
Washing up after a party	£2–3 for the lot
Washing the car	£2 for the basic wash
Weeding the garden	£1.50 per hour
Walking the dog	from 50p depending on distance

Source: *Check It Out!*, September 1993

Q *We're very unhappy with the local secondary schools in our area and are thinking about sending our two children (aged nine and four) to a public school. Just how expensive is this and what would be the best way to pay?*

A School fees vary greatly but you should expect to pay at least £1,000 per term for each child and, on past experience, expect fees to rise by around 10 per cent a year. This puts a heavy financial burden on any family. There are basically five ways in which the cost can be met:

- invest a lump sum in advance to provide an income when fees start to be paid
- save regularly from income now to build up a fund which will meet the fees when they start to be paid
- pay the fees as they fall due out of available capital (for example, an inheritance)
- pay fees as they fall due out of income (which may mean taking on extra work)
- take out a loan or extend your mortgage to cover the fees when they start to be paid and spread the repayments into the future.

Given the age of your children, you might need to use a combination of these methods. Nearer the time that your children are ready to move on from primary school, find out from the public schools you choose what scholarships, grants or assisted places might be available to help with the fees.

Q *We are putting down our baby son's name for my husband's old public school and want to pay something towards the fees now. What are our options?*

A As you know which school you want to send your son to, find out from the bursar whether the school itself runs a suitable scheme. Many operate **composition fee** schemes, which are a tax-efficient way of providing for future fees. You pay a lump sum to the school, which has charitable status and, therefore, does not have to pay tax on income from investing the money. The school uses the lump sum to buy an annuity (an investment that can be used either to provide an income at some time in the future or straight away) which will meet part of the fees as they become due, leaving you to pay only a reduced amount. Some schools will accept a lump sum as full payment of the future fees.

Before using a composition fee scheme, you should be quite sure about your choice of school. Some schools let you transfer your fee to another school if you change your mind, but many don't.

Given the extreme youth of your son at present, you might prefer to keep the option of which school open for now. With an

educational trust you are not committed to a particular school. Your money is invested in the trust, where it builds up until needed. Then it is used to buy an annuity to meet part or all of the fees. An educational trust has charitable status, so it pays no tax on its income, giving you a tax-efficient return.

Apart from these schemes, a wide range of mainstream investments can be used. You need to consider how long to invest for, the amount you will require to meet the fees and how much risk you are happy to take with your investments. Consider getting advice from an independent financial adviser (see page 236).

MORE INFORMATION ABOUT PRIVATE EDUCATION

The Independent Schools Information Service (ISIS) (see Addresses section) publishes a guide for parents to independent schools and various booklets covering, for example, ways to pay fees and the availability of assisted places, scholarships and grants.

There are six main educational trusts, run by the Allchurches Life, Equitable Life, Royal Life, Save & Prosper, School Fees Insurance Association (SFIA) and Sun Life. You can contact the providers direct (see phone book for local offices) or through an independent financial adviser – see page 236.

Q *Should we be putting money aside now in the hope that our two children go on to university? And, if so, what's the best way to do this?*

A Your position is very similar to that of parents financing school fees. You might be able to support your children out of your income at the time they are at college, but you cannot be sure of that, so establishing savings is sensible. If your eldest child could be going to university within the next five years, you might consider National Savings investments. If you have longer to save, consider investments whose return is related to the return on shares – a unit or investment trust **personal equity plan (PEP)** could be a suitable, tax-efficient option. See pages 217–23.

Protecting your family

Q *A salesman, visiting the college where I'm studying, has suggested I take out an insurance policy as a way of saving and 'giving something back to my parents' if I died. Is this a good idea?*

A If anyone is financially dependent on you – for example, a child, a partner who cares for your children or an elderly relative who lives with you – then it is certainly a good idea to take out insurance which would ensure that he or she would have enough money to live on in the event of your death. In this case, we would recommend you take out 'term insurance', which can provide a lot of cover relatively cheaply. Other types of life insurance (see Box, *Main types of life insurance*) which have an investment element are an expensive way of buying life cover. If no one is financially dependent on you, you do not need life insurance. Furthermore, if your income is currently low and your future earnings uncertain, investment-type life insurance – which commits you to regular, long-term saving – is not a good idea at all. If you stopped the policy in the early years, you would get little or nothing back.

MAIN TYPES OF LIFE INSURANCE

Term insurance: pays out only if you die within a given period – the 'term'.
Family income benefit: type of term insurance which pays out an income rather than a lump sum.
Endowment insurance: pays out if you die within a given period and also pays a lump sum at the end of the period.
Whole-life insurance: pays out whenever you die and gradually builds up an investment value which you can get back by cashing in the policy.

Q *We are expecting our first child and want to sort out some life insurance. What would you suggest?*

A Your greatest need is to ensure that there will be enough income available to provide for the child until he or she becomes independent

– at the age of 18 or 21, say. Therefore, you should choose term insurance to cover that period. You could choose a lump sum policy – the money paid out would then need to be invested to provide a regular income. But a cheaper and perhaps more convenient option would be a family income benefit policy. With this, a regular tax-free income is paid out in the event of death during the term. Choose a policy where both the income which would become payable increases each year and the income, once it starts to be paid, increases each year – this will help to protect your income against inflation. The insurance should cover not just the main breadwinner but also the person caring for the child, since if he or she were to die, you would need to pay for someone to carry out these duties. Therefore you need what is called a **joint life, first death** policy. If you expect to have more children, consider a policy which allows you to revise the amount of cover on the birth of further children.

Q *What is a 'flexible cover plan' and what are the advantages of this type of life insurance?*

A A flexible cover plan is a type of whole-life insurance which combines protection with investment, and you can choose the balance of these two elements. You pay regular premiums which are used to buy **units** in an investment fund. You elect how much life cover you want between a minimum and a maximum level and enough units are cashed in each month to pay for this. The rest of your units are left invested to build up a pool of savings. So, for example, if you first take out the policy when you have a young family, you might choose to have a very high level of life cover, in which case most of your units will be used up paying for this. Later in life, when your need for cover is lower, you might reduce your cover and leave most of the units invested.

Really, the only advantage of these plans is the flexible cover they offer but, if cover is your main need, you could take out a term insurance policy with as much flexibility as you are likely to need. On the minus side, flexible cover plans lock you into long-term payments and long-term investment. If your ability to make the payments or your investment needs change in the future, you could find yourself having to stop the plan and getting very little – if anything – back.

These plans also usually give the insurance company a lot of discretion to increase charges and/or premiums in future. A better idea is to keep your protection and investment needs separate – that way you can maximise your investment flexibility as well.

Q *How do I work out the amount of life cover I need?*

A There is no simple or single correct answer to this. You really need to sit down with pen and paper and work out what capital and income would be available to your family if you were to die and how the family spending would be affected. Factors to take into account include earnings lost, pensions payable from your employer, benefits available from the state (see below), the scope for using any savings to generate income, any existing life insurance, (for example, covering the mortgage), the cost of a funeral, the effect of losing a company car, the cost of child care if needed, and so on. Any shortfall between the income which would be available and the predicted expenditure indicates the amount of life cover you need. Don't forget to go through the calculations for each of you, if you are a couple – even if one of you is not working, it would still cost a lot to pay someone else to perform your duties at home.

Q *My husband is terminally ill. He has no life insurance and, after so long a period of invalidity, we have no savings left. Will I get a widow's pension from the state?*

A There are four benefits paid by the state for which you might qualify:

- **widow's payment** – a single lump sum of £1,000, payable if you are under 60, or if you are older but your husband was not entitled to a state retirement pension
- **widowed mother's allowance** – a regular income if you are caring for children
- **widow's pension** – a regular income if you are aged 45 or more and have no dependent children
- **retirement pension** – if your husband is getting state retirement pension and you are aged 60 or more, you might get retirement

pension instead of widow's pension. Retirement pensions are covered on pages 243–6.

Whether or not you'll qualify for these benefits depends on your husband's National Insurance record (see Box). Table 1.5 shows the amount of widow's allowance and pension payable in the 1994–5 tax year. If you are entitled to the allowance or pension, you may get extra if your husband has belonged to the State Earnings Related Pension Scheme (SERPS) – see page 244.

When your husband passes away, there will be various formalities to complete and you will be given a special certificate with a form on the back. You complete this and send it to your local Benefits Agency, which will send you a claim form, BW1. For more information about widows' benefits, see DSS leaflet NP45, *A Guide to Widows' Benefits,* available from Benefits Agencies and some post offices and public libraries.

Table 1.5: Help from the state for widows

	Amount of allowance or pension in 1994–5 £ per week
Widowed mother's allowance	
Full rate for widow	57.60
Addition for each child	11.00
except addition for only	
or eldest child if also	
receiving child benefit	9.80
Widow's pension	
Full rate payable according to	
age at the time of husband's death:[1]	
45	17.28
46	21.31
47	25.34
48	29.38
49	33.41
50	37.44
51	41.47
52	45.50
53	49.54
54	53.57
55 or more	57.60

[1] For women widowed before 6 April 1988, the relevant ages are five years younger.

HOW TO QUALIFY FOR WIDOWS' BENEFITS

Widow's payment Your husband must either have paid at least 25 Class 1, Class 2 or Class 3 contributions before 6 April 1975 *or*, since then, have paid National Insurance contributions in any one tax year on wages of at least 25 times the lower earnings limit for that year – the limit is £57 a week in 1994–5. If this condition is not met, you get no payment at all.

Widowed mother's allowance and widow's pension Your husband must have paid 50 Class 1, Class 2 or Class 3 National Insurance contributions before 6 April 1975 *or*, between 6 April 1975 and 5 April 1978, have paid contributions on earnings of at least 50 times the lower earnings limit in any one tax year *or*, since 6 April 1978, have paid contributions on earnings of at least 52 times the lower earnings limit in any one tax year *and*, for the allowance or pension to be paid at the full rate, your husband must have paid (or been credited with) contributions for roughly nine-tenths of his working life. If he paid for fewer years, you will get a reduced allowance or pension, provided he had paid for at least a quarter of the years in his working life.

For the purpose of these rules, a Class 2 or Class 3 contribution is equivalent to a Class 1 contribution at the lower earnings level. For more information about National Insurance contributions, see pages 54–7 and 69.

Q *I've had an odd letter from the Department of Social Security inviting me to pay extra National Insurance contributions for the years I was at university. It seems I don't have to pay them, so why should I want to?*

A Your entitlement to certain state benefits depends on your record of paying National Insurance contributions. For some periods in your life when you are not working, you will be credited with contributions to protect your record, but this is not the case while you are at college – these years show up as a gap. You can have some gaps without affecting your claim to benefits, but too many could reduce your eventual state retirement pension and, more importantly if you are a man and married or likely to marry, could mean that your widow would get less help from the state if you were to die – see Box (*How to qualify for widows' benefits*). As you point out, you do not have to make good any gaps in your record, but you can choose to by making voluntary Class 3 National Insurance contributions (which cost £5.55 a week in the 1994–5 tax year). But you cannot usually go back further than six years to make up gaps. For more about paying voluntary contributions, see pages 247 and 55.

Q *Do widowers get any state benefits similar to those available for widows?*

A No, there are no state benefits specifically for widowers. If you are caring for one or more children and you are getting child benefit (see page 23), you may also qualify for **one-parent benefit**. In 1994–5, this is paid at a single rate of £6.15 a week regardless of the number of children you have. The benefit is paid along with your child benefit and is not taxable. To claim one-parent benefit, obtain DSS leaflet CH11, available from Benefits Agencies and some post offices and public libraries.

If your income is low, you may qualify for income support – see pages 106–14.

Q *I'm in my late sixties and, being realistic, I need to think ahead to when I'm gone. I've seen a brochure for a funeral plan which allows me to pay regular sums now to cover the eventual cost of my funeral. Are these schemes sound?*

A The average cost of a funeral is currently about £1,000. Many elderly people do worry about how this will be paid and some are anxious to ensure that their surviving families will not have to pay. For many years, the funeral industry has operated pre-payment plans of the type you describe and, in recent years they have become increasingly popular. Following a scandal in 1993 when 30 people were defrauded of £35,000 paid into pre-payment plans, two industry bodies – the Funeral Planning Council (FPC) and the National Association of Pre-paid Funeral Plans (NAPFP) – have both set up codes of practice which require plan operators to keep your money in a separate trust fund and to ensure that funds are invested suitably. The NAPFP code requires member firms to have proper procedures for handling complaints but the FPC has the edge here because its members belong to the Funeral Ombudsman Scheme (FOS) – see Addresses section – which can deal with complaints and make awards of up to £50,000. It would be sensible to deal only with a funeral plan operator which belongs to either the NAPFP or the FPC.

Separation and divorce

Q *After 15 years of marriage, my husband is leaving. He always handled our financial affairs and I simply don't know where to start. What advice can you offer?*

A Divorce, because you're likely to be unprepared for it, can put a huge strain on your finances. Suddenly, there will be two households to support and you'll have to divide the family assets between you. So the first step is to get a solicitor to draw up a clear and proper agreement between you and your husband. If there are children involved, a legally binding settlement is even more important and, if you and your husband cannot agree, you may have to go to court and/or ask the Child Support Agency (CSA) to work out an amount of child maintenance to be paid by your husband. If there are no children, try to settle matters without using the courts or you'll see a lot of money swallowed up in legal fees.

When splitting your family assets, don't overlook the value of pension rights. Commonly, a wife has forgone a good job and membership of a pension scheme in order to care for the couple's children. If you divorce, you may be giving up a share in your husband's retirement pension as well as your right to a widow's pension in the event of his death. If you are over the age of 40, a court would take these into account in deciding how the family assets should be shared between you – unfairly, younger women usually lose out. You should try to ensure, whatever your age, that any divorce agreement made without a court's intervention does take pension rights into account.

Tell your tax office that you are splitting up and make sure that you claim all the allowances you qualify for – see below. If you have one or more children to care for, you can claim **one-parent benefit** – an addition to the child benefit you get for your first or only child (see page 35). If your income and capital are low, you may be able to claim state benefits – see pages 106–17. If so and you have children, your case will be referred to the CSA to assess and collect child maintenance.

Q *My husband and I have split up. He's buying out my share of our home and, with the proceeds, I'll buy myself a small flat. Will we both be able to get tax relief on our mortgage payments?*

A Yes, you are both eligible for tax relief on interest you pay on the first £30,000 of a mortgage from the date on which you split up. Although your husband is buying out your share of the old home, you might legally still retain some right to the home. To protect your husband against this, your separation agreement should state that you give up this right. Even this is not watertight and your husband might insist on a court order formally dismissing your claim to the property in exchange for the lump sum. To qualify for tax relief on the interest on your new mortgage to buy the flat, you must be paying the interest yourself – although it does not matter if the money you use comes from your husband or the Department of Social Security (as it might if you are on a low income and claim certain state benefits).

Q *My wife has left me, taking the children with her. Do I carry on getting the married couple's allowance or must I let the tax office know that we're no longer a couple?*

A You should let the tax office know that your marital status has changed as it will affect your tax position in future years. But just for the tax year in which you separate or divorce, the tax rules let you carry on getting the married couple's allowance (see page 10). From the next tax year, you and your wife will both be treated as single people for tax purposes. This means you will get the single person's allowance plus any other allowances you qualify for (see page 143). If you pay maintenance to your wife, you may get extra tax relief (see below).

Q *Before we split up this year, I was getting half the married couple's allowance and my husband had the other half. Do I carry on getting my share of the allowance?*

A Yes, just for this tax year, you carry on getting your share of the allowance. And, if you and your husband had children and one or more of them is living with you, you can claim extra tax allowance this tax year to make up the married couple's allowance you are getting to the same amount as the additional personal allowance (see page 11); from the next tax year, claim the additional personal allowance.

Q *Since our separation and (now) divorce, I've made sure that my ex-wife has enough to live on. This has been a private arrangement and I haven't thought to declare it to the tax authorities. Should I have done so?*

A No, there is no need. When you make voluntary maintenance payments – see Box – you cannot claim any tax relief on the amount you hand over and there is no need to inform the Inland Revenue that you are making them. They count as tax-free income for your wife, so she doesn't have to declare them either.

WHICH TYPE OF MAINTENANCE?

There are two types of maintenance payments:

- **voluntary payments** The payer cannot be forced to make them and the recipient has no legal redress if payments are missed or stopped
- **enforceable payments** These are made under a court order or a legally binding agreement, including an assessment by the Child Support Agency (CSA). If the payer does not make the agreed payments, the recipient or the CSA can take the payer to court.

Q *My wife and I are getting divorced. Our solicitors are drawing up a divorce settlement and I have agreed that I will pay my wife maintenance of £230 a month. Can I claim tax relief on the payments?*

A You can claim tax relief on the first £1,720 of such payments. In 1994–5, the relief is given at a rate of 20 per cent; from 6 April 1995, it falls to 15 per cent. There is no tax relief on the excess above £1,720. For example, in 1994–5, you'll pay maintenance of £2,760 and get tax relief of 20% x £1,720 = £344. The net cost to you of the maintenance payments would be £2,760 – £344 = £2,416. The relief is given either through your PAYE code (see page 11) or tax assessment.

Q *I have been paying maintenance of £100 to my ex-wife under a court order made in December 1987. But, having heard about a new and better paid job I started recently, my wife took me back to court and has had the payments increased to £135 a month. What's the tax position regarding the old and new awards?*

A There was a change in the tax rules for maintenance payments a few years ago, and different rules now apply to 'old' enforceable payments and to the increases which have been made since:

- **old enforceable maintenance payments** These are payments made under a court order or legally binding agreement before 15 March 1988. At one time, tax relief was given on the full amount of these payments, but now tax relief is limited to the amount you were paying in the 1988–9 tax year – or the actual amount you pay now, if this is less. In 1994–5, tax relief on the first £1,720 of these payments is given at a rate of 20 per cent – from 6 April 1995, it falls to 15 per cent. If the amount of payments which qualifies for tax relief is greater than £1,720, you get tax relief at your top rate on the excess
- **increases made on or after 15 March 1988** There is no tax relief on these payments.

In your case, you will carry on getting tax relief on the £100 a month which you pay your wife under the old court order – i.e. relief of 20 per cent x £1,200 = £240. But you can't claim any extra relief on the £35 a month increase. This means that the net cost to you of the £1,620 you pay in maintenance is £1,380.

You can, instead, choose to have the full £135 a month payment treated under the rules which apply to enforceable maintenance payments under agreements made on or after 15 March 1988 (see previous question). As your yearly payments of £1,620 are less than the limit for tax relief of £1,720, you would get tax relief on *all* the payments. In 1994–5, the relief would be 20 per cent x £1,620 = £324, bringing the net cost of the maintenance payments to £1,215. Clearly, it would be worth your while switching to the new rules. You can do this at any time during the tax year or within 12 months of the end of the year using form 142, available from your tax office. You'll also have to inform your wife in writing that the payments she receives are now treated under the new tax scheme. Once you've opted for the new rules, you can't switch back.

Q *I pay my ex-wife £2,000 a year under a court order dated 14 October 1986. I've paid the same amount since the order began although the way I get tax relief on them changed a few years back. What I'm wondering is whether I'm better off under the tax rules for 'old' maintenance payments, or whether I should switch to the new system. I pay tax on my income at a top rate of 40 per cent.*

A If you were paying £2,000 in enforceable maintenance payments to your ex-wife in the 1988–9 tax year, you have been able to continue to get tax relief on that amount since then. In 1994–5, relief at 20 per cent on the first £1,720 is £344. You get relief at your top rate of 40 per cent on the remaining £2,000 – £1,720 = £280, which comes to £112. Under the old rules, then, you get tax relief of £456 on maintenance payments of £2,000, bringing their net cost to you to just £1,544.

Under the new rules, you would get tax relief of 20 per cent only on the first £1,720 of the payments – there would be no tax relief on the rest. Therefore, you are better off staying with the old rules.

Q *Under a 1987 court order I pay £50 a month maintenance to my daughter – not to her mother. We arranged it like that at the time so that my daughter could set her personal tax allowance against the amount she received. I, of course, have been getting tax relief on the amount I pay her. Will this be reduced with most maintenance tax relief being restricted to lower rates?*

A Yes, you are affected by changes to maintenance payments which were introduced in the November 1993 Budget. This means that, for 1994–5, you get tax relief on the first £1,720 a year of maintenance payments only at the 20 per cent tax rate (instead of your highest rate as in previous years). In 1995–6, relief on the first £1,720 will be cut further to just 15 per cent.

If the maintenance you pay came to more than £1,720, you would still get tax relief at your highest rate on the excess. However, in your case, the £50-a-month maintenance amounts to £600 a year, which will cost you £480 in 1994–5 after tax relief.

The £600 still counts as income in the hands of your daughter and she can set her personal allowance against it.

Note that if you were making payments to your child under an agreement or court order made on or after 15 March 1988, there would be no tax relief on the payments at all and they would count as tax-free income in the hands of your child.

Q *I've never really understood the tax position regarding the £2,000 a year maintenance which my former husband pays me. The maintenance order was drawn up in October 1986. Can you explain how I'm taxed on the maintenance now?*

A The first £1,720 of maintenance which you receive in 1994–5 is tax-free. Anything above this is taxable at your top rate of tax, with the exception of any increases to the maintenance which have been made on or after 6 April 1989. Any such increases are treated as tax-free income in your hands.

Q *The Child Support Agency has made a maintenance assessment against my ex-husband. Will I have to declare the amount he pays me for tax?*

A No. Maintenance payments you receive under the new rules always count as tax-free income and do not have to be declared for tax. However, if you are receiving a means-tested state benefit, the amount of maintenance you get will usually affect the amount of benefit you can claim – see pages 11 and 115.

Q *My ex refuses to pay any maintenance for the children. I know I could ask a court to make an award, but I don't qualify for legal aid and can't really afford big solicitors' bills. Is there any other way I can make him pay up?*

A If there is no maintenance agreement between you and your ex-husband, you could ask for an assessment from the Child Support

Agency, though there is a fee for this service (£44 for each parent in 1994 unless they are getting certain state benefits, are still at school or are on a very low income). If there is already a maintenance agreement, you cannot ask the CSA to review it until after April 1996. You can also ask the CSA for help in collecting maintenance, if your ex will not pay up in accordance with an agreement – once again, there is a charge for this service. For how to contact the CSA, see Addresses section.

Q *I was divorced ten years ago and now I'm approaching retirement. During the years I was married, I paid the married women's reduced stamp, so it looks as if my state pension is going to be a pittance. Is there anything I can do at this late stage to increase it?*

A You are correct in assuming that the **married women's reduced-rate National Insurance contributions** (see page 57) do not count towards state retirement pension. But special rules apply to divorced women who have not remarried. You may be able to use part or all of your husband's contribution record to help you qualify for a pension. The rules are complicated and you should get advice from your local Benefits Agency (see Addresses section).

MORE INFORMATION FOR SEPARATING COUPLES

See leaflet IR93, *Separation, Divorce and Maintenance Payments,* available from tax offices, also NI95, *National Insurance for Divorced Women,* from Benefits Agencies.

Inheritance

Q *My partner and I are not married but have lived together as common-law husband and wife for many years and have two grown-up children. I'd assumed that, if one of us died, the other would get everything, but now I gather that's not the case. What would happen?*

A If you each have a will, you can specify who will inherit your belongings – your **estate** – when you die. If there's no will, then this is decided according to the **rules of intestacy**. If you are not survived by a husband or wife – and English law does not recognise 'common law' partners – and you have children, the rules specify that your estate is divided equally between your children. 'Children' includes offspring from a current marriage (where applicable) and from any previous marriages, as well as those who are illegitimate or adopted, but does not include step-children. In other words, your partner has no automatic right to a share of the estate, although he or she might be able to go to court and establish a claim under the Inheritance (Provision for Family and Dependants) Act 1975. This could be a costly, time-consuming and upsetting process and might not be successful. You and your partner are strongly advised to make wills.

Q *The intestacy rules are designed to protect your family, aren't they? I would want to leave everything to my wife anyway, so surely there's no point my making a will?*

A It's true that the law aims to protect your family, but that doesn't mean that the rules of intestacy necessarily coincide with your own wishes. The rules would require:

- if you have children, the first £125,000 of your estate (or the whole estate if it's worth less than this) to go to your wife, who would also get a **life interest** in half of the remaining estate. A life interest gives the right to income from or use of the possessions but not any rights to own or sell the possessions themselves. Your children would inherit the other half of the remaining estate and the right to the capital bearing the life interest on the death of your wife
- if you have no children, the first £200,000 of your estate to go to your wife plus half of whatever remains. The other half of the remaining estate would go to your more distant relatives in this order of priority: parents or brothers and sisters. Only if your estate were worth no more than £200,000, or if your parents were dead and you had no surviving brothers and sisters, would your wife inherit the whole estate.

The rules apply equally to a husband whose wife dies without leaving a will.

Q *I have no family. Who would inherit my possessions if I died?*

A If you have no husband or wife or children, the intestacy rules rank your heirs in the order in which they would inherit your estate:

- if you are survived by parents, they share the estate
- if your parents are dead, but you have brother(s) and/or sister(s), they share the estate. If any brother or sister has died but has children, the children would inherit in place of the brother or sister
- if you have no parents, brothers or sisters, your grandparents would share the estate
- if none of the above relatives survives you, the estate would pass to your uncles or aunts to share equally. If any uncle or aunt had died but has children, the children would inherit in place of the uncle or aunt
- if none of these relatives survives you, your estate would pass to the Crown, though someone who felt he or she should have inherited could make a request for a share, but whether or not this person received anything would be at the discretion of the Crown.

However, if you make a will, you can decide who will inherit your possessions – for example, friends or charities.

Q *Isn't making a will expensive?*

A It need not be. If your circumstances are relatively straightforward, a solicitor or franchise will-writing service might charge only in the region of £50, say. But expect to pay more if you want, say, to set up trusts under your will or your affairs are complicated, in which case you are strongly advised to seek advice from a solicitor.

You don't have to use a solicitor at all. It is possible to draw up a do-it-yourself will. But take care: you could cause a lot of problems for your heirs if the wording of your will is ambiguous or unclear. Only make your own will if you understand what you are doing and are aware of the pitfalls. Get a good book or kit to guide you – for example, Consumers' Association publishes *Wills and Probate* and the *Make Your Will* Action Pack (see Addresses section).

Q *Is it better to appoint professional executors under one's will or could I choose a member of my family?*

A An executor is the person or firm which sorts out a deceased person's affairs in accordance with the terms of the will. In 1993, *Which?* reported on serious problems which its members had faced when dealing with a professional executor – e.g. a bank or solicitor – including unreasonably large fees, lack of communication with beneficiaries, long delays and incompetence. Professional executors have considerable power and cannot be dismissed by your beneficiaries if problems do arise. A safer course might be to appoint 'lay' executors from your family or friends. They can always employ professional help, if they need it, and would have the option to switch from one expert to another if they were unhappy with the service provided. But make sure that whoever you appoint is willing to take on the work involved and is capable of doing so. It is also safer to appoint two executors – just in case one dies before the winding up of your affairs is completed.

Q *I'm getting married. For the time being, I'd still like to leave my belongings to my parents if I died, so is there any need to alter my will?*

A Yes, there is. A will is automatically revoked on marriage (unless the will was made specifically in contemplation of marriage). A will is also invalidated by divorce, but not by separation.

Q *In my will, I want my estate to be divided equally between my wife and two daughters. Can I simply say that I leave a third of everything to each of them?*

A You need to word your will very carefully. If the value of your estate is above a given level, there may be **inheritance tax** to pay on part of what you leave. Unless you specify that the gifts you make under your will are to bear their own tax, they will usually be treated as after-tax gifts and the tax on them will come out of the residue of the estate. So, for example, if you said that a third of your estate was to be left to each daughter and that your wife was to get the remainder (the residue), your wife could end up with less than your daughters. Get advice from a solicitor.

Q *I live with my girlfriend and I changed my will so that everything I have would go to her if I died. Could my ex-wife challenge the will?*

A A person who was dependent on you does have the right to make a claim against your estate under the Inheritance (Provision for Family and Dependants) Act 1975. The main people entitled to make such a claim are your husband, wife, former husband or wife (provided he or she has not remarried), an unmarried partner, your child or a child of your family. The claim must be made through a court, which will decide whether or not the person is entitled to financial support from the estate and to what extent.

Q *I'm not a rich woman – including my house, I doubt that everything I own comes to much more than £200,000. But my solicitor says that could be enough to trigger an inheritance tax bill when I die. Is he right?*

A When you die, you are deemed to make a gift of all your possessions just before death. If the value of everything you leave together with the amount of any chargeable gifts and PETs made within the seven years before death comes to more than a given level – £150,000 in 1994–5 – there could be inheritance tax to pay on your estate. In working out the value of your estate, any debts you had at the time of death are deducted, as are reasonable funeral expenses. You can also deduct bequests you make in your will, or transfers made under the intestacy rules, which are tax-free. These include:

- amounts left to your husband or wife
- amounts left to charity
- gifts for the public benefit – e.g. land, buildings or works of art of outstanding national interest which are given to a suitable non-profit-making body
- most gifts to political parties
- gifts of land to a registered housing association.

In 1994–5, if the remaining estate and chargeable gifts and PETs over the last seven years come to more than £150,000, the first £150,000 is tax-free, but tax at 40 per cent is due on the excess.

Q *Inheritance tax is sometimes called a voluntary tax. What legitimate steps can one take to avoid paying it?*

A There are many schemes for avoiding inheritance tax, some extremely complex. If your estate is large, you should get advice from a solicitor and/or accountant who specialises in this area. But here are some basic principles of inheritance tax planning:

- remember some bequests – e.g. to your husband or wife or to charity – are always tax-free
- make use of your tax-free slice (£150,000 in 1994–5). For example, leaving everything to your husband and wife means no tax bill when you die, but could lead to a large bill when they come to die. By leaving up to £150,000 in your will to your children, say, you can reduce the total tax on the estates of both you and your spouse
- make lifetime gifts. See below for the ways in which you can make tax-free gifts during your lifetime. These will reduce the value of your remaining estate. In particular, consider giving away assets – such as shares – the value of which is expected to rise: the increase in value will accrue to the recipient instead of you
- use trusts as a way of giving assets without losing all control over them. This is a complex area, so get professional advice
- make interest-free loans which the borrower can invest, keeping the proceeds of the investment. Again, there are complications you need to be aware of, so get professional advice.

It is important to bear in mind that inheritance tax is a problem for your heirs – not you. So don't give away more in your lifetime than you can afford to.

Q *What gifts can I make during my lifetime without incurring an inheritance tax bill for either myself or the recipient of the gift?*

A The following lifetime gifts are completely free from inheritance tax:

- gifts between husband and wife
- gifts to charities, museums, art galleries and similar bodies
- gifts of land, buildings, works of art, etc. of outstanding national interest to a suitable non-profit-making body
- gifts to political parties provided a party has at least two MPs and polled a minimum of 150,000 votes in the last General Election
- gifts of land to a registered Housing Association
- normal expenditure out of income. Gifts are tax-free provided you can show they form part of a regular pattern of giving and making them doesn't leave you with too little for your ordinary day-to-day expenses. Gifts which would qualify include regular premiums on a life insurance policy taken out to benefit someone else, or payments made under a deed of covenant
- gifts for the maintenance of your family
- small gifts of up to £250 per person to any number of people. This exemption cannot be combined with any other to cover larger gifts
- wedding gifts (see page 13)
- up to £3,000 worth of gifts each tax year which are not covered by any other exemption. If you do not use up the full £3,000 in one tax year, it can be carried forward to the next, but not to any subsequent year.

In addition, most other gifts between people count as **potentially exempt transfers (PETs)**. They are tax-free provided the giver survives for seven years after making the gift. If the giver dies sooner, the PET is reassessed as a chargeable gift – see Box.

GIFTS WHICH ARE TAXABLE

Gifts to some types of trust and company may give rise to an inheritance tax bill at the time they are made. All chargeable gifts during the last seven years are totalled; the first slice of gifts – £150,000 in 1994–5 – is tax-free, but tax at the lifetime rate of 20 per cent is payable on the excess.

If the giver dies within seven years, the gifts are reassessed and taxed at the death rate (40 per cent in 1994–5) and PETs are also reassessed and taxed at death rates. But in both cases, only a proportion of the tax is payable if the giver dies between three and seven years after making the gift.

MORE INFORMATION ON INHERITANCE AND WILLS

See IHT3, *An Introduction to Inheritance Tax*, available from Capital Taxes Offices – see Address list. For a more detailed discussion of wills and inheritance, see *The Which? Guide to Giving and Inheriting*, published by Consumers' Association (see page 273).

CHAPTER 2

YOUR WORK

PAID employment means you cannot avoid getting involved with the complexities of tax and National Insurance. As an employee, you might hope that your employer and the tax office can be relied on to get the sums right, but the Inland Revenue itself has admitted that about 10 per cent of Pay-As-You-Earn tax codings for 1994–5 were incorrect; other experts suggest the figure may have been even higher, at over a third. If you are self-employed, sorting out your tax and keeping the bill to a minimum can be even trickier. But even these problems pale into insignificance against the financial worries of unemployment, so make sure you know what income you are entitled to.

Working for an employer

Q *My new employer has asked me for my P45. I don't remember ever having one. What is it and where do I get it from?*

A When you work for an employer, income tax is deducted direct from your pay under the **Pay-As-You-Earn (PAYE)** scheme – see Box overleaf. In order to start deducting the correct amount of tax, your employer needs to know details of your earnings and tax position during the tax year to date. If you are changing jobs, this information is contained in your form P45, which you will have been given when you left your last job.

But if you have not worked before, you won't have a P45. And if you are coming back to work after a break – e.g. to bring up children or because you have been unemployed – then you may have lost your P45, which, in any case, won't be up to date. Either way, your employer will instead have to complete a form P46, which you must sign, and this is sent to the tax office that deals with your employment. The tax office will contact you and ask you to fill in a coding claim form, P15, which is like a tax return. The details you provide enable the tax office to give your employer the information needed to be able to tax your pay correctly.

PAY-AS-YOU-EARN (PAYE)

The PAYE scheme is used to collect income tax from your pay as you earn it. The scheme can also be used to collect tax due on other items too, such as taxable perks you get through your job and income from certain investments. Under the scheme, you are given a tax code, which tells your employer how much of your pay is free of tax because it is covered by your allowances, outgoings and so on. With the help of tax tables, the employer can then deduct the correct amount of tax from your remaining pay and hand this to the Inland Revenue. The PAYE system is also used to collect your National Insurance contributions.

Q *I've recently started a new job and I'm on 'emergency tax'. How long will I have to wait before I get a tax rebate?*

A If your new employer does not have an up-to-date P45, there will be a delay while the tax office works out your correct tax code. In the meantime, you have been allocated an 'emergency' tax code which tells your employer either:

- to pay you without deducting any tax at all, if your pay is below the PAYE threshold – this is about £66 a week or £287 a month in the 1994–5 tax year, or
- if your pay is above this limit, to assume that your tax-free pay is one-52nd (if you're paid weekly) or one-twelfth (if you are paid monthly) of the single personal allowance (i.e. roughly £66 a week or £287 a month in 1994–5) and to tax all pay in excess of this limit.

If you are entitled to other allowances, or if you have unused tax allowances from the earlier part of the tax year, you will end up paying too much tax under the emergency code. The overpaid tax is usually paid back through your pay packet as soon as your correct tax code is received by your employer. Alternatively, it could be repaid after the end of the tax year.

Q *I've received a Notice of Coding telling me that I have a new tax code of 516H. What does that mean?*

A The code tells your employer how much tax-free pay you are allowed for the whole tax year (unless there is a 'K' in the code – see below). The number in the code is worked out by taking all the allowances you are entitled to and deducting the taxable value of any fringe benefits you get – e.g. a company car. The last digit is then ignored. For example, in your case, for 1994–5 you get the personal allowance of £3,445 plus the married couple's allowance of £1,720, making £5,165 in total. Knocking off the last digit leaves 516 and that's the number in your code. When your employer works out your tax, he has to replace the last digit, but for simplicity this is always assumed to be a '9', so in fact you'll get slightly higher allowances of £5,169. The letter in the code gives information about the type of allowances you're getting and enables your code to be changed automatically when allowances are altered in the Chancellor's annual Budget.

Q *What are the different letters used in tax codes and what do they stand for?*

A The most common letters that you'll find in a tax code are as follows:

L – you get the personal allowance

H – you get the personal allowance plus either the married couple's allowance or the additional personal allowance

P – you get the full age-related personal allowance for people aged 64 to 73 at the start of the tax year

V – you get the full age-related personal allowance plus the married couple's allowance for people aged 64–73 at the start of the tax year

T – you get other allowances

K – the value of your benefits or other income to be taxed exceeds your allowances. The amount shown in the code must be *added* to (not deducted from) your pay before tax is calculated, but your pay cannot be reduced by more than a half as a result

D – all your earnings are taxed at the higher rate of tax (40 per cent in 1994–5).

Q *During the day I work for an insurance company. I'm about to start teaching evening classes two nights a week at the local college, as well. How will the code for my second job be worked out?*

A You will have a separate code for each job. Your allowances will be given against earnings from the job which you regard as your main employment – i.e. with the insurance company. Therefore, the full earnings from the second job will be taxed.

Q *In April 1994, the amount in my pay packet dropped sharply even though my pay hadn't changed and my tax code stayed the same. Why was this?*

A April is when changes announced in the annual November Budget come into effect. In April 1994, although the amount of the main allowances was not changed, the amount of tax relief given by the married couple's allowance and certain related allowances was restricted to 20 per cent. This means that if you were a basic rate taxpayer, the full allowance gave you tax savings of only £344 over the tax year instead of £430 as previously. From April 1995, these allowances are being further restricted to give just 15 per cent relief – i.e. saving tax of just £258 assuming the allowances stay at the 1994–5 level of £1,720. Your April 1994 pay packet was also affected by a 1 per cent increase in the main rates of National Insurance.

Q *National Insurance contributions often seem to be ignored when politicians talk about tax on earnings. But they take quite a chunk out of your pay packet, don't they?*

A National Insurance is a substantial tax which, according to government figures, is expected to raise nearly £43 billion in 1994–5 – about the same as the take from VAT – compared with £64.4 billion from income tax. It is slightly different from other taxes, because most National Insurance contributions help you to qualify for certain state benefits, such as retirement pensions and unemployment benefit – see Table 2.1.

Table 2.1: National Insurance contributions and state benefits

Type of contributions	Who pays them	Which benefits they count towards
Class 1 – full rate	Employees	Unemployment benefit[1] Sickness benefit[2] Invalidity benefit[2] Maternity allowance Widow's payment Widowed mother's allowance Widow's pension Retirement pension
Class 1 – married women's reduced rate	Some married women and widows who are employees	None
Class 2	Self-employed	Sickness benefit[2] Invalidity benefit[2] Maternity allowance Widow's payment Widowed mother's allowance Widow's pension Retirement pension
Class 3	Voluntary – can be paid by anyone	Widow's payment Widowed mother's allowance Widow's pension Retirement pension
Class 4	Self-employed	None

[1] To be replaced by job seeker's allowance from April 1996.
[2] To be replaced by incapacity benefit from April 1995.

Q *How much am I likely to pay in National Insurance contributions this year?*

A Employees pay **Class 1** National Insurance contributions. If your earnings are below a certain level, called the **lower earnings limit** (£57 a week in 1994–5), you pay no contributions at all. If your earnings are at or above this limit, you pay one rate of National Insurance on earnings up to that level and a higher rate on earnings above it. But you don't pay any National Insurance on earnings above the **upper earnings limit** (£430 a week in 1994–5). If you have contracted out of the State Earnings Related Pension Scheme (SERPS) through an employer's pension scheme – see page 245 – you pay National Insurance at a lower rate on your earnings between the lower and upper limits. See Table 2.2. Your employer must also pay National Insurance contributions on your earnings.

If you carry on working after you have reached state pension age, you no longer pay National Insurance on your earnings.

Table 2.2: Standard Class 1 National Insurance contributions in 1993–4

If you earn:	You pay:
Not contracted out of SERPS	
Less than £57 a week	Nothing
£57 a week or more	2% on the first £57 plus 10% on the excess up to £430 a week
Contracted out of SERPS	
Less than £57 a week	Nothing
£57 a week or more	2% on the first £57 plus 8.2% on the excess up to £430 a week
Married women's reduced rate	
Less than £57 a week	Nothing
£57 a week or more	3.85% on earnings up to £430 a week

Q *I pay the 'small stamp' because it's cheaper than paying the full-rate National Insurance. Are there any drawbacks to doing this?*

A Until 1977, married women and widows could opt to pay Class 1 National Insurance at the **married women's reduced rate** – sometimes called the 'small stamp' (see Table 2.2). Since 6 April 1977, it has not been possible to opt for this, but if you were already paying at the reduced rate you have been allowed to continue doing so. The drawback of paying at the reduced rate is that it does not qualify you for any state benefits – the idea was that you would rely on your husband and his contribution record for your pension etc. Also, nowadays, paying at the reduced rate does not necessarily mean that you're paying less National Insurance: because the single 3.85 per cent rate is higher than the standard rate of National Insurance on the earnings up to the lower earnings limit, if your pay is fairly low you could actually be paying more at the reduced rate. In 1994–5, if your earnings are between £57 and £74.15, or £81.24 if you could be contracted out of SERPS, you would pay less by switching to standard Class 1 National Insurance. For more information, see DSS leaflet NI1, *National Insurance for Married Women*, available from Benefits Agencies (see page 273).

Q *What counts as earnings for National Insurance purposes? Can I reduce the amount I pay by giving up part of my earnings and taking it as fringe benefits instead?*

A You pay National Insurance on all wages, salary, overtime pay, bonuses and so on. But you are correct that contributions are not payable on the value of fringe benefits which you get as part of your overall remuneration package. In the past, this has led to all sorts of attempts to evade National Insurance: people were paid, for example, in gold bars or coffee beans. But this loophole was largely closed in the November 1993 Budget, which stipulated that payment in marketable assets – i.e. things which can easily be converted to cash – or assets which the employer arranges to convert into cash are to be subject to National Insurance as if they were normal pay.

Q *Are all perks that come with a job taxable?*

A No, there is no income tax at all on some fringe benefits – see Box overleaf. Some others are always taxable – for example, most vouchers which you can exchange for goods, personal debts which your employer settles and cheap or free accommodation unless there is a special reason for the employee to live in it (see page 63).

Many benefits are taxable only if you earn at a rate of £8,500 a year or more including the value of the benefits. 'At a rate of' means that you will be caught by the rules if you earn, say, £4,500 over six months. You will usually be treated in the same way if you are a company director, whatever the level of your pay. Benefits which are taxable under these rules include company cars, cheap loans and mobile phones.

TAX-FREE FRINGE BENEFITS

You won't normally pay tax on the following perks through your job:
- employer's contributions to an approved pension scheme
- most life and sick pay insurance schemes
- fees and subscriptions paid by your employer to an approved professional body
- the first 15p a day of luncheon vouchers
- workplace nursery provided by your employer
- free or subsidised canteen meals provided for employees generally
- clothes specially needed for your job and paid for by your employer
- reasonable removal and relocation expenses when you have to move to a new job or are transferred and need to move home as a result, up to a maximum of £8,500 per move
- genuine personal gifts – e.g. on your retirement (provided the gift is not money) or marriage
- awards (not money) for long service of 20 years or more, within limits
- gifts of up to £100 from business contacts
- Christmas party or similar annual function open to all staff and costing no more than £50 a head
- business lunches and other entertainment provided by someone other than your employer – e.g. by clients
- shares you get through an approved profit-sharing, SAYE or executive share option scheme
- new shares in your employer's company bought through a preferential scheme, provided certain conditions are met

- prizes of up to £5,000 for ideas put forward through a staff suggestion scheme
- books and fees paid by your employer for some external training courses and, possibly, related extra travelling and living expenses
- redundancy counselling services
- in-house recreational facilities open to employees generally
- retraining courses for employees who are leaving, provided certain conditions are met
- taxis paid for by your employer to take you home if you work until 9 p.m. or later, provided public transport is either not available or it would be unreasonable to expect you to use it
- free car-parking spaces at or near your work.

Q *The company I work for provides me with a car which I use a lot on business, but I don't use it at all privately – we use my wife's car instead. Why should I have to pay extra tax because of the company car?*

A The tax rules assume that, if you have a company car, it is available for your private use (whether or not you choose to use it for this purpose). This counts as a fringe benefit and is taxable, if your pay is over the £8,500 limit (see previous question). And are you sure that you don't use the car privately? Travel between home and work counts as private mileage, not business use.

Q *I've been promoted and, as part of the new package, I'm allowed to choose a company car. How will the car affect the tax I pay? Are some types of car taxed more heavily than others?*

A The taxable value of a company car is assumed to be 35 per cent of its list price at the time it was first registered (including the cost of any 'extras'). However, this can be reduced:

- by one-third, if you drive at least 2,500 business miles a year
- by two-thirds, if you drive 18,000 business miles a year or more
- by a further one-third, if the car will be four or more years old by the end of the tax year
- by £1 for every £1 you yourself pay for private use of the car.

If your employer pays for fuel, this will also count as a taxable benefit (see below).

Q *My company car was bought new in May 1993 for £14,000. I do about 20,000 miles a year in it on business. How much tax will I pay on the car?*

A You can work out the tax you will pay on the car as follows:

- take 35 per cent of the list price, i.e. 35% x £14,000 = £4,900
- reduce this by two-thirds – i.e. 2/3 x £4,900 = £3,267 – because you are over the 18,000 business miles threshold
- this gives a taxable value of the car as £4,900 – £3,267 = £1,633
- if your marginal rate of tax is 25 per cent, you'll pay 25% x £1,633 = £408.33 in tax as a result of having the car.

Q *I run a 1960 Aston Martin DB4 as a company car. Do I still use the original list price to work out its taxable value?*

A Unlikely. For cars over 15 years old and with an open-market value of £15,000 or more, the market value is used when this is greater than the list price.

Q *My company has an account with a nearby petrol station, so I get all my petrol free. Presumably this also counts as a taxable fringe benefit?*

A Yes, if your earnings are above the £8,500 limit, then fuel paid for by your employer is assumed to be partly for private use and is taxed accordingly. The value of this benefit is worked out according to the scale shown in Table 2.3, based on the type of fuel you use and the engine capacity of your car. The scale applies without any reduction, even if you partially reimburse your employer for the private fuel you use. But if you reimburse your employer *in full* there is no tax to pay.

Q *My employer pays for my business – but not private – fuel, and also pays for all the maintenance and insurance on my company car. Do I have to pay tax on these?*

A No, these items do not count as fringe benefits if your employer pays for them. If you paid for them yourself you would be able to claim them as allowable expenses qualifying for tax relief.

Table 2.3: Car fuel scale charges in 1994–5

Engine size	Fuel scale charge £
Petrol	
0–1,400cc	640
1,401–2,000cc	810
2,001cc or more	1,200
Diesel	
0–2,000cc	580
2,001cc or more	750

Q *When I need to go on a business trip, I use a car from the company pool. Usually, I return the car the same day, but occasionally I keep it overnight, if I have to make an early start or get back very late. Will I be taxed on this as if I had a company car?*

A No. Use of a pool car does not count as a fringe benefit, provided the car is available to – and actually used by – more than one employee and is not *normally* kept overnight at or near your home. Any private use of the car must be purely incidental to the business use, e.g. travelling from home to work at the start of a business trip.

Q *I pay for my own fuel at the time I buy it, but then claim a mileage allowance for my business journeys. Does the allowance count as part of my income and do I have to pay tax on it?*

A If an expense for which your employer pays does not count as an **allowable expense** it does indeed count as part of your income and you will be taxed on it. But, provided the expense is allowable (see next question), as is the case with your mileage allowance, you won't have to pay tax on it. How it is dealt with varies:

- if your earnings are below the £8,500 limit, the expense is ignored

- if you earn more than this, you still won't have to declare the expense for tax if your employer has a **dispensation** from the Inland Revenue for the allowance – check with your employer
- if there is no dispensation, you will need to declare the expense as income for tax purposes, but simultaneously claim the same amount as an allowable expense on which you qualify for tax relief.

Q *I'm a carpenter. I work for someone else but I have to provide my own tools. Can I claim tax relief for what I spend on them?*

A If an item counts as an **allowable expense** you can claim tax relief on the amount you spend on it. The general rule is that for an expense to be allowable, it must be incurred *'wholly, exclusively and necessarily in the performance of the duties of your employment'*. In some trades and professions – including carpentry – where it is customary to provide your own tools or special clothing, a fixed allowance has been negotiated with the Inland Revenue. You can claim the full allowance as an allowable expense even if you do not spend that much. But, if you spend more than the allowance, you can claim the excess. For more details about the fixed allowances, see Inland Revenue leaflet IR1, available from tax offices (see Inland Revenue in Addresses section).

Q *My company lets me have an interest-free loan each year to buy my rail season ticket. Do I have to pay tax on the loan?*

A Probably not. Cheap and interest-free loans from your employer can count as a taxable benefit, if your earnings are at or above the £8,500 limit. But small loans – defined as up to £5,000 – are exempt. The exemption is large enough to cover most season ticket loans.

If all your cheap and interest-free loans (excluding any which qualify for tax relief) together exceed £5,000, you are taxed on the difference between the interest you actually pay on the loans and an official interest rate set by the Inland Revenue.

Q *I work for a bank, so now I'm buying my own home I'll do it with a mortgage from the bank. Will this count as a taxable fringe benefit?*

A If the loan is provided on the normal commercial terms offered to the general public, it will not count as a fringe benefit and you won't have to declare it for tax purposes. But, if you get the loan at a special cheap rate, there may be tax to pay on this perk. The taxable value of the loan will be the difference between the interest you pay and the official Inland Revenue rate. If the loan qualifies for tax relief – most loans to buy your own home do – the relief will be worked out as if you had been paying interest at the (higher) official rate – i.e. you get tax relief on both the interest you pay and the interest you save.

Q *Through my job, I get a rent-free home. I'm not clear whether or not I have to pay tax on this perk. If I do, how would the tax be worked out?*

A A low-rent or rent-free home is a tax-free benefit if any of the following apply:

- you have to live in the home to do your job properly – e.g. you are a caretaker
- living in the home enables you to do your job better and is customary – e.g. you are a vicar
- there is a threat to your security and you live in your home as part of special security arrangements.

Otherwise, the benefit is taxable, even if your pay is below the £8,500 threshold. The taxable value of the home is the greater of either the old rateable value of the property or the amount of rent paid by your employer less any rent you pay. And if the cost of providing you with the accommodation is more than £75,000 there may be extra tax to pay.

Q *My employer runs a scheme offering a range of benefits – such as a car, health insurance, extra holiday and so on – and, for a reduction in pay, we can choose which we want to include in our benefit package. I'm thinking about taking up the private medical insurance option. Is this a taxable benefit?*

A The system your employer operates has been called **cafeteria benefits** and is likely to become more widespread. If your earnings are over the £8,500 limit, private medical insurance does count as a taxable benefit. Its value is the cost to your employer of providing the cover – i.e. the cost of premiums less anything you pay towards them yourself.

Q *I have the long-term loan of a computer from work. Presumably there's no tax to pay on this?*

A Not if the computer is solely for business use. But if an item is lent to you for your private use, it does count as a fringe benefit which is taxable if your earnings are above the £8,500 limit. The value for tax purposes is 20 per cent of the market value of the item at the time it was first lent to you less anything which you pay for its use.

Q *In my job, I often have to deal with colleagues from our parent company in Germany. I'd like to learn German so that I can communicate better. Can I claim tax relief on the cost of lessons?*

A It depends whether the cost of the lessons counts as an allowable expense. Fees and the cost of books for a full-time training course in the UK lasting between four weeks and a year are allowable expenses, provided your employer requires or encourages you to go on the course and carries on paying you while you are on it. But fees and books for other courses, such as evening classes, are not allowable and cannot be claimed as deductions when you work out your tax position.

Q *I work for a property company and part of my pay each year is in the form of a bonus linked to the profits the company has made. Do I have to pay tax and National Insurance on the bonus in the same way as the rest of my pay?*

A You will have to pay National Insurance on the bonus, but it might be free from income tax if it is paid under a profit-related pay scheme approved by the Inland Revenue. To qualify, the scheme must:

- be set up by a profit-making private sector employer
- run for at least one year and be open to at least 80 per cent of the workforce or of a section of the workforce – e.g. a department. Part-

timers and people who have been with the company less than three years can be excluded

- be registered with the Inland Revenue before it starts.

Profit-related pay up to £4,000 or 20 per cent of your total pay, whichever is less, is tax-free under such a scheme. The tax relief is given through PAYE.

MORE INFORMATION IF YOU WORK FOR AN EMPLOYER

From tax offices:
IR33 *Income Tax and School Leavers*
IR34 *PAYE Pay As You Earn*
IR95 *Shares for Employees – Profit-sharing Schemes*
IR97 *Shares for Employees – SAYE (Save As You Earn)*
IR99 *Shares for Employees – Executive Share Options*
IR115 *Tax and Childcare*
IR133 *Income Tax & Company Cars: a guide for employees*

From DSS offices:
NI268 *Quick Guide to National Insurance Contributions, Statutory Sick Pay and Statutory Maternity Pay*
NP28 *National Insurance for Employees*

For more information about your tax position, see also *Which? Way to Save Tax*, published by Consumers' Association.

Working for yourself

Q *I'm about to set up my own consultancy business. What are the pros and cons of doing this as a self-employed person or, alternatively, as a company?*

A The main advantage of setting up your business as a company is that you can benefit from **limited liability**. This means that the shareholders (of which there must be at least two) are liable for the debts of the company, but only to the extent of the nominal value of the shares they hold. By contrast, if you are self-employed, you are personally responsible for the debts of your business and so your whole personal wealth is at risk. However, the advantage of the former option is partially lost if your company borrows money and you have to give a personal guarantee for the loan. Other factors to weigh up are:

- a company is more costly to set up and there are more formalities involved, though you can overcome some of these by buying an established company 'off the shelf'. Becoming self-employed is cheaper and more flexible
- a company has a separate legal identity and continues to exist even after you stop working for it, unless the company is wound up
- a company is subject to company law and insolvency law with which you should become familiar. There is less red tape if you are self-employed
- you will almost certainly need to use an accountant if you operate as a company. As a self-employed person, you may be able to handle your accounts and tax affairs yourself
- a company may need to use an auditor, but if your turnover is less than £90,000 this will not be necessary. Self-employed accounts do not need to be audited
- with a company, you will need to file annual accounts and other company details with the Registrar of Companies. There is a fee for this and penalties if you fail to do so. The information is open for inspection by the public – and business rivals
- a company is likely to pay more tax than a self-employed person on any given level of profits
- you may have greater credibility with clients and bankers if you operate as a company
- you will have greater flexibility over your pension arrangements if you operate as a company.

Q *How is a company taxed?*

A Unlike a person, a company does not pay income tax or capital gains tax. Instead, it pays **corporation tax** on its profits from all sources. Taxable profits are worked out in the same way as for a self-employed business – see pages 73–7. Tax on the profits for each financial year – usually a 12–month period – is due nine months after the end of the period, but if the company pays out dividends some tax will be due earlier than this. A company has no tax-free allowances, so the whole profit is taxed. For the financial year 1994, a company with profits below £300,000 pays corporation tax at the **small companies rate** of 25 per cent.

Q *If I run my business as a company, what's the best way to take money out of the company for my personal use?*

A If you run your own company, you will be an employee and also a shareholder. This gives you two routes by which to take money out of the company:

- you can pay yourself a salary, as an employee. This is a fairly expensive route because both you and the company (as employer) will have to pay Class 1 National Insurance contributions on your pay (unless it is less than the lower earnings limit – see page 56). But you may decide it is worth paying yourself a salary at least at the lower earnings limit so that you can protect your right to social security benefits (see page 55)
- you can declare a dividend for the shareholders. There is no National Insurance on dividends. The company has to pay **advance corporation tax** (at 20 per cent in 1994) on the dividends, but the shareholders get a corresponding tax credit (see page 219 for more information about how dividend income is taxed). The dividend must be paid to all shareholders, but you can arrange matters so that you hold all the shares but one, say.

Within limits, the company can make loans to the directors or employees without incurring an immediate tax charge. This enables you to draw living expenses in advance of salary or dividend.

Q *If I pay myself a salary from my company, how do I work out the National Insurance due on the pay?*

A You, as an employee, will pay Class 1 National Insurance in the same way as any other employee, so the rates in Table 2.2 will apply for 1993–4. But the company, as an employer, must pay **secondary Class 1** contributions on your earnings too (see Table 2.4).

Table 2.4: Employer's secondary Class 1 National Insurance contributions in 1993–4

If you earn:	Your employer pays:
Not contracted out of SERPS	
Less than £57 a week	Nothing
£57–99.99	3.6% of all your pay
£100–144.99	5.6% of all your pay
£145–199.99	7.6% of all your pay
£200 or more	10.2% of all your pay
Contracted out of SERPS	
Less than £57 a week	Nothing
£57–99.99	0.6% of your pay[1]
£100–144.99	2.6% of your pay[1]
£145–199.99	4.6% of your pay[1]
£200–430	7.2% of your pay[1]
Over £430	10.2% of your pay[1]

[1] Applies to pay between the upper and lower earnings limits. Not-contracted-out rates apply to the rest.

Q *I'm about to start up in business as a self-employed plumber. Whom do I need to inform?*

A As soon as you have started the business, you should contact the tax office local to the area in which you are trading (see Addresses section). It will send you a form, 41G, to complete. You also need to contact the local Department of Social Security office, which will ask you to fill in form CF11 giving details about the business and your National Insurance number. If you decide to register for VAT (see page 78), you need to contact the local VAT office (see Addresses section) and ask for form VAT1 (if you are working alone) and also VAT2 (if you are working in partnership with others).

Q *Following the birth of my second child, I decided to leave my full-time job with a market research firm, but I've carried on working for the firm on a freelance basis. Do I count as self-employed or will I be taxed as if I'm still an employee?*

A The tax and National Insurance treatment regime applying to the self-employed is more liberal than the regime for employees – you will generally pay less National Insurance and be able to claim a lot more allowable expenses as a self-employed person. Not surprisingly, then, the authorities are on the look-out for any abuse of the system with people being artificially classified as self-employed. Normally, you will count as genuinely self-employed if you can answer 'yes' to all the following questions:

- Do you have the final say about how your business is run – e.g. where you work and when?
- Do you put your own money at risk?
- Do you bear the losses of the business as well as keeping the profits?
- Do you provide the main equipment which you need for your work – e.g. computer, car and so on?
- Are you free to take on employees on terms you choose?
- Do you have to correct unsatisfactory work at your own expense?

If the answer to some of these questions is 'no', you might still count as self-employed but you would be wise to check the position. You can get a formal ruling from either your tax office or the DSS – see joint Inland Revenue/DSS leaflet IR56/NI39, *Employed or Self-employed?*, from tax and DSS offices.

Q *What National Insurance do I pay as a self-employed person and how do I make the payments?*

A You pay flat-rate **Class 2** contributions, which are set at £5.65 a week in the 1994–5 tax year. But if your earnings – basically, your profits from being self-employed – arising in the tax year are under a given limit (£3,200 in 1994–5) you can apply not to pay contributions at all. Obviously, this saves you money but bear in mind that you will not be clocking up any entitlement to National Insurance-related benefits either (see Table 2.2). You can either be billed each quarter for your Class 2 contributions for the previous 13 weeks or you can pay monthly in arrears by direct debit from a bank or building society account.

In addition, if your profits exceed a given limit, you will have to pay **Class 4** contributions. For profits being assessed in 1994–5, the limit is £6,490. If your profits exceed this, you pay Class 4 National

Insurance at 7.3 per cent of profit above £6,490 up to £22,360. There is no National Insurance charge on profits above the upper limit (£22,360). Class 4 contributions are collected by the Inland Revenue along with the income tax due on your profits.

Q *Can I claim any allowances against income tax on my profits from self-employment?*

A Your business does not have a separate legal identity from yourself if you are self-employed. This means that the profits from your business are added to any other income you have – e.g. from investments or a job. Your personal allowance, any other allowances and your outgoings are then deducted, in the normal way, in order to work out your tax bill for the tax year in question (see pages141–3).

Q *When do I pay tax on my profits if I'm self-employed?*

A Until the 1996–7 tax year, you will normally be taxed on your profits on a **preceding-year basis**. This means that, in any tax year, you are taxed on the profits made in the accounting period which ended in the previous tax year. You choose the accounting period for your business and it need not correspond with a tax or calendar year, so there could be a long delay between making the profit and paying tax on it. For example, if your accounting year runs from 1 August to the following 31 July, your profit for the year ending 31 July 1993 (i.e. during the 1993–4 tax year) would not be assessed until the tax year 1994–5. Tax, together with any Class 4 National Insurance, would then usually be payable in two equal instalments on 1 January 1995 and 1 July 1995. Different rules apply in the opening and closing years of a business and, from 6 April 1996, profits from self-employment are to be taxed on a **current-year basis** – see Box on page 72.

Q *Since starting in business, I seem to have been taxed on the same profits for three years running. Why is this?*

A Normally, profits from self-employment are taxed on a preceding-year basis, but special rules are applied when you first start up in business:

- **in the tax year in which you start to trade**, you are taxed on the actual profit which you make during that year. If your accounting period straddles two tax years then you are taxed on a fraction of the profits worked out as

$$\frac{\text{profits for accounting year} \quad \times \quad \begin{array}{c} \text{number of months} \\ \text{of accounting year} \\ \text{falling in the tax year} \end{array}}{\text{total number of months in accounting year}}$$

- **in the second tax year**, you can either be taxed on the profits which you made during your first twelve months of business, or you can be taxed on the profit you actually made during the tax year
- **in the third tax year**, you can either be taxed on the profit you made during the accounting year ending in the preceding tax year or on your profits during the first 12 months of trading, if your accounting period has not yet ended. Alternatively, if you chose to be taxed on the current year's profits during the second year, you will also be taxed in the third year on the actual profits you make during the year.

For example, if you started in business on 1 August 1990 and your first accounting period covered 12 months, your tax bill for the tax year 1990–1 would be based on $\frac{8}{12}$ of the profit you make during your accounting year ending 31 July 1991. In the tax year 1991–2, if you chose the first option, tax would be based on profit made in the 12 months to 31 July 1991. And, in tax year 1992–3, tax would be based on profits for the accounting year ending in 1991–2 – in other words, the accounting year ending 31 July 1991.

As part of the transition to taxing the self-employed on a new basis, any business starting up from 6 April 1994 onwards will be taxed right from the start on a current-year basis – see Box overleaf.

Q *I've been a self-employed electrician all my life but I retired from business earlier this year. How will my tax bill for the final year be worked out?*

A Under the current rules, if you are self-employed, the normal preceding-year basis for taxing profits does not apply when you close down or sell your business. Instead, for the final tax year that you are in business you will be taxed on the actual profits made from 6 April to the date of the closure or sale. You will have to pay this tax on 1 January of the tax year and the following 1 July in the normal way. The Inland Revenue also has the option to re-open the assessments for the previous two tax years and to put those on to a current-year basis too, if this would result in a higher tax bill. You will receive a Notice of Assessment if extra tax is due and you will usually have to pay it within 30 days of receiving the Notice.

Once you are covered by the new rules (see Box), a simpler system will apply. In the final tax year of your business, you will be taxed on your actual profits from the end of the previous accounting year to the date you cease trading. The Inland Revenue will no longer be able to reassess the tax bill for the previous two years.

NEW RULES FOR TAXING PROFITS FROM SELF-EMPLOYMENT

For the 1997–8 tax year onwards, self-employed people will be assessed on the profits for the 12-month accounting period ending in the same tax year – e.g., if your accounting year ends on 31 July, tax for 1998–9 will be based on profits for the 12 months to 31 July 1998. (Tax for the year in which you first start to trade will still, as now, be based on actual profits made during the tax year – see previous page.) Tax will be due in instalments on 1 January of the year of assessment and the following 1 July.

Transitional rules will apply to the 1996–7 tax year, when you will be taxed on the average of profits made in the accounting period ending in 1996–7 and those made in the period ending in 1995–6.

From 1996–7, a new system of self-assessment will also be introduced, under which you can work out your own tax bill if you wish. You'll be expected to send in your tax return and tax calculation by 31 January following the end of the tax year and the Inland Revenue will have broadly a year within which to take up any queries. If you prefer to carry on letting the Revenue work out your tax for you, you will have to send in your tax return by 30 September following the end of the tax year.

Q *How are my profits from self-employment calculated for tax purposes? Is it in the same way that I draw up my business accounts?*

A Your tax accounts are not usually drawn up in quite the same way as your business accounts, because not all the costs of your business are allowable expenses for tax purposes and some items – such as depreciation – are treated in a special way for tax purposes. But the general principle is the same – in other words, to work out your profit, you take turnover less the costs of goods for resale or raw materials less other expenses incurred in the course of business. Normally, you can draw up your business accounts and then make various adjustments to them to arrive at your taxable profit.

Q *What expenses can be deducted when I work out my taxable profits?*

A The general principle is that you can deduct items which are incurred *'wholly and exclusively for the purpose of the business'*. This includes:

- cost of raw materials and goods bought for resale
- accountants' fees
- heating, lighting and business rates for business premises
- repairs to business premises
- phone, post, stationery
- trade or business magazines, some books
- computer software (though this could be treated as capital expenditure, especially if bought at the same time as computing equipment)
- certain costs of using your home for work (see next question)
- costs of employing someone – e.g. their wages, employer's National Insurance, pension payments made on their behalf, employees' life, health and sick pay insurance, redundancy pay
- interest on a business loan or overdraft and any arrangement fees
- subscriptions to certain professional bodies
- costs of entertaining staff. Gifts (other than food or drink) up to £10 a year per person, if the gifts advertise your business
- travel between places of work. Car running costs less a proportion for private use, if any
- reasonable cost of meals on overnight business trips
- legal costs of recovering bad debts. Specific bad debt provisions for specified doubtful debts if your tax office agrees

- legal costs incurred in defending business rights, preparing service agreements, business rate appeals and some lease renewals
- business insurance, advertising costs, reasonable charge for hire of capital goods including cars (subject to some restrictions), fees for registering a trade mark or design or obtaining a patent
- VAT you have paid if you are not registered for VAT.

The Box lists common items of expenditure which do not count as allowable expenses.

EXPENSES WHICH ARE NOT ALLOWABLE FOR TAX

The following expenses cannot normally be deducted when you are working out your profits for tax purposes:
- the cost of capital equipment, cars etc. or depreciation – claim capital allowances instead (see opposite)
- alterations, extensions and improvements to business premises – these count as capital payments
- ordinary clothing which you wear for work (even if you would not choose to wear it outside work)
- your own wages, income tax and National Insurance
- payments to political parties
- entertaining customers or business associates other than staff
- travel between home and your normal place of business
- general reserve for bad or doubtful debts
- legal costs incurred in acquiring land, buildings or leases, legal costs if you break the law, cost of contending tax cases
- life, accident and sickness insurance for yourself
- buying patents.

Q *If I work from home, can I claim some of the costs of running the home as allowable business expenses? And will I have to pay business rates?*

A In working out your taxable profit, if you work from home, you can deduct a proportion of the phone bill and costs of heating, lighting, cleaning and insurance corresponding to your business use. Usually, with the latter items, you will agree with the tax office a reasonable proportion of the bills based on, say, the number of rooms you use for business as a proportion of the total rooms in the home.

Where part of the home is used exclusively for business, business rates are payable in respect of that part of your home. But if you work from a room which is also used for domestic purposes, you should not be charged business rates. For income tax purposes, if you use part of the home exclusively for business, you can also deduct part of the rent, council tax (rates in Northern Ireland) and business rates. However, using part of the home exclusively for business also means you'll be liable for capital gains tax (CGT) on any profit made on that part of the home when you come to sell the home – that could mean a substantial CGT bill (see page149). So you might prefer to retain some private use of the business areas of your home and claim fewer expenses.

Q *I'm planning to buy a new computer for my business. I understand that I can't claim the cost as an allowable expense against my profits. Presumably, I have to claim capital allowances instead. How do I work these out?*

A You are correct in assuming that you cannot offset the full cost of an item which counts as capital equipment – a computer, office furniture, company car and so on – against profits for the year in which you buy the item. This is in line with normal accounting principles, whereby capital equipment would be depreciated over its expected lifetime. But, for your tax accounts, you cannot deduct depreciation either. Instead you claim capital allowances. You do this by recording your capital expenditure in one or more pools and you can deduct a **writing-down allowance** of up to 25 per cent of each pool each tax year. The value of each expenditure pool can change in several ways:

- it is reduced each year by the amount of writing-down allowance which you claim
- if you buy or acquire a new item, its value is added to the pool before you work out the writing-down allowance
- if you sell or otherwise dispose of an an item, its value must be deducted from the pool before the writing-down allowance is calculated. If the amount to be deducted from the pool comes to more than the total value of the expenditure pool, a **balancing charge** equal to the excess is added to your profits

- if you close down your business and the proceeds from selling the capital equipment come to less than the value of the pool, a **balancing allowance** equal to the shortfall is deducted from your profits.

More favourable rules apply to **short-life assets**. These are items which you expect to have a useful life of less than five years, and it would be usual to include computer equipment in this category. Each short-life asset must be put in its own separate pool of expenditure and, if you sell or dispose of it within five years, any shortfall of the disposal value compared with the pool value can immediately be deducted from your profits as a balancing allowance. If you keep the item for five years or more, the separate expenditure pool is discontinued and the value remaining in it is added to your main pool of expenditure.

Q *Does a company car go into my main pool of capital expenditure or can I claim that it is a short-life asset?*

A Neither. Most cars are specifically not allowed to be treated as short-life assets. But cars do not go into your main pool of expenditure, unless they are basically trade vehicles not suitable for carrying passengers. Instead you put them in a separate expenditure pool. And in the case of a car costing £12,000 or more it must have its own expenditure pool – even separate from other cars owned by the business, and the writing-down allowance must not exceed £3,000 in any year.

Q *I've spent a lot on capital equipment this year and the writing-down allowance comes to more than my profit for the year. Can I carry some of the allowance forward to set against future profits?*

A Yes, if the allowance cannot be fully used, it will be carried forward. But you can avoid this situation, because the 25 per cent writing-down allowance is the *maximum* you can claim – you are free to claim less than this or even to claim nothing at all. There is no point claiming more allowance than would be needed to reduce your taxable profits to zero. If you do not claim the full allowance in any year, the value of the expenditure pool does not decrease so rapidly and, consequently, the maximum possible writing-down allowance in future years will be higher. This has the same effect as carrying forward unused allowance.

Q *I'm confused. Do I claim capital allowances for my accounting year (which may not be taxed for some time) or for the tax year for which I'm being assessed?*

A At present you work out your capital allowances on the basis of expenditure during a given accounting year. When you send the Inland Revenue your accounts for that year, you also make your claim for capital allowances. But, for income tax purposes – i.e. if you are self-employed – capital allowances are deducted from your tax assessment rather than subtracted in working out your taxable profit. Therefore, you will see them listed separately in your Notice of Assessment and they may be given in a different tax year from the one in which the related accounts are assessed. If you run your own company, capital allowances are treated as deductions in arriving at the taxable profit. Once new tax rules apply (see Box on page 72), capital allowances for the self-employed will be treated in the same way as for companies.

You do not have to work out your capital allowances yourself. Your accountant will do this, if you use one. Alternatively, you can ask your tax office to work out the allowances for you, provided you send it a list of the items of capital equipment you have bought and sold, giving the price or sale proceeds and the date of purchase or sale.

Q *I'm a consultant electronics engineer and I've worked with a friend on a number of projects recently. We're both self-employed at present. How would our tax position be affected if we went into partnership?*

A A partnership has a separate legal identity, but its taxable profits are worked out in much the same way as those of the business of a self-employed person. To work out the tax, the profits (usually for the preceding tax year) are apportioned between the partners in the same ratio as profits will actually be shared during the current tax year. Each partner's top rate of tax is then applied to his or her notional share of the profits and the total tax arrived at is the bill for the partnership. The partners can sort out between them how they intend to share the tax bill – they do not have to pay the amount corresponding to their share of the taxable profit. But partners are **jointly and severally liable** for the whole tax bill. This means that, if one partner does not pay his or her share, the others have to. Partners pay the same type of National Insurance as self-employed people and have no liability for each other's contributions.

Q *I'm working as a freelance lecturer and expect to have fees of about £30,000 this year. Is it worth my while registering for VAT?*

A Value Added Tax (VAT) is a tax paid by end-consumers on many goods and services. The standard rate of VAT is 17.5 per cent, but some things are zero-rated – e.g. non-luxury foods, children's clothing, public transport, books and newspapers. In 1994–5, the rate on domestic fuel is 8 per cent, but is due to increase to 17.5 per cent from April 1995. Other items – such as postal services and insurance – are exempt from VAT.

If you are not registered for VAT, like any other consumer, you may have to pay VAT on things you buy for your business. If you do register, you can claim back any VAT you pay on business items but you must normally also charge VAT on the goods or services you provide and hand this over to the government. If your turnover – in your case, the fee income – is above a certain limit (£45,000 from 1 December 1993 onwards), you must by law register for VAT. Below this limit, you can choose whether or not to register. Factors you need to consider when making your decision are:

- are your goods and services all exempt from VAT? If so, you cannot register
- will adding VAT to the price of your goods and services make you uncompetitive compared with other suppliers?
- could your clients claim back the VAT you charge? Usually they can if they themselves are registered for VAT, even if their goods or services are zero-rated
- could you claim back a significant amount of VAT, e.g. on your raw materials, machinery, computer equipment, stationery and so on?
- are you prepared to deal with the paperwork which VAT entails, or to employ an accountant to do this for you?

- do you have the discipline not to spend VAT collected and waiting to be paid to the VAT office?

VAT is normally collected on an **accruals basis**: this means that VAT is paid on the basis of invoices you have sent out or received, regardless of whether payment has been made. This could cause a problematic drain on your cashflow if your clients are fairly slow to pay. But if your turnover is below £300,000 a year you can ask instead to pay VAT on a **cash accounting basis** so that you only hand over VAT on money you have actually received.

LEAFLETS AND BOOKLETS ABOUT WORKING FOR YOURSELF

Available from tax offices:
IR24 *Class 4 NI Contributions*
IR26 *Changes of Accounting Date*
IR28 *Starting in Business*
IR53 *Thinking of Taking Someone On?*
IR56 *Employed or Self-employed?*
IR57 *Thinking of Working for Yourself?*
IR64 *Giving to Charity: how businesses can get tax relief*
IR69 *Expenses: form P11D*
IR104 *Simple Tax Accounts*
IR105 *How Your Profits are Taxed*
IR106 *Capital Allowances for Vehicles and Machinery*
IR109 *PAYE Inspections and Negotiations*
IR132 *Taxation of Company Cars: employers' guide*
P7 *Employer's Further Guide to PAYE*

Available from DSS offices:
NI27A *National Insurance for People with Small Earnings from Self-employment*
NI35 *National Insurance for Company Directors*
NI255 *Class 2 and Class 3 National Insurance Contributions: direct debit – the easy way to pay*
NI269 *Employer's Manual 1 on National Insurance Contributions*
NI269A Supplement to NI269
NP18 *Class 2 and Class 4 National Insurance Contributions*
FB30 *Self-employed? A Guide to Your NI Contributions and Social Security Benefits*

Available from VAT offices:
VAT booklet 700 *The VAT Guide*
VAT leaflet 700/1 *Should I Be Registered for VAT?*
VAT leaflet 700/12 *Filling in Your VAT Return*
VAT leaflet 700/15 *The Ins and Outs of VAT*
VAT leaflet 700/21 *Keeping Records and Accounts*

For more about your tax position, see also *Which? Way to Save Tax* and *Starting Your Own Business,* both published by Consumers' Association.

Coping with unemployment

Q *I couldn't stand my job any longer and handed in my notice last Wednesday after a row with the boss. I don't have another job to go to immediately. Can I claim unemployment benefit?*

A Not immediately. If you become unemployed voluntarily (i.e. you choose to leave your job) or you were dismissed for misconduct, you are disqualified from claiming **unemployment benefit** for 26 weeks. If your income and savings are low enough, you may be able to get **income support** instead, but the amount you get will be lower than normal because of your disqualification from unemployment benefit. For more about income support, see pages 106–14.

Q *Having been unemployed, I found a job last month. But my new employer has gone bust and I'm out of work yet again. How soon can I claim unemployment benefit?*

A When you first claim unemployment benefit, you are not paid for the first three days of your period of unemployment: these are called **waiting days**. But you can link periods of unemployment if they are separated by no more than eight weeks. This means that your present benefit claim can start straight away without any further waiting days. You should note that, for the purpose of these rules, what is important is the period of unemployment – rather than periods of claiming unemployment benefit – so you may be able to avoid waiting days if you have previously been off work sick and claiming statutory sick pay or sickness benefit or because you are pregnant.

Q *How much is unemployment benefit and is it affected by my other income or capital?*

A Unemployment benefit is not means-tested – i.e. it does not depend on your income or capital resources – and eligibility depends in part on the National Insurance contributions which you have paid – see Box. If you qualify, benefit is made up of one or more of the following parts (rates are given for 1994–5):

- personal benefit of £45.45 a week if you are under pension age or £57.60 a week if you are over state pension age
- an addition for an adult dependant of £28.05 a week, provided he or she does not earn that amount or more if he/she is under state pension age *or* does not earn £34.50 or more if over state pension age (earnings include pensions from employers' schemes or private plans in excess of £35 a week)
- an addition for each child dependant of £11 a week, reduced to £9.80 a week for the first child if you also get child benefit. You also lose the child addition for the first child if your partner earns £120 a week or more and for each subsequent child for each extra £16 he/she earns.

You might be able to claim income support in addition to unemployment benefit (see pages 106–14).

NATIONAL INSURANCE CONTRIBUTIONS FOR UNEMPLOYMENT BENEFIT

There are two contribution tests which you must satisfy:

- you must have paid Class 1 contributions on earnings of at least 25 times the lower earnings limit (£57 a week or its equivalent in 1994–5) in one of the two last complete tax years before the benefit year in which you claim unemployment benefit
- you must have paid, or been credited with, Class 1 contributions on earnings of at least 50 times the lower earnings limit, or have

paid 50 Class 2 contributions, in each of the last two complete tax years before the benefit year in which you claim.

The benefit year for unemployment benefit starts on the first Sunday of the calendar year.

Q *I'm out of work and getting benefit at present. I can't see myself being able to get another job as an architect, so I've been thinking about doing another degree which would help me switch career. Can I claim unemployment benefit while I take the degree?*

A Not if you study full-time. One of the main conditions for claiming unemployment benefit is that you are available for work and are actively seeking work. As a full-time student, you would not be deemed available for work, even if in practice your course occupied your time for only a few hours a day. There is no precise definition of 'full time' in this context, but a normal degree course would almost certainly be included. You may be able to do a part-time course or evening classes and still claim benefit, provided you can convince the unemployment office that you are still looking for work and that you are willing to give up your course immediately if a reasonable job turns up.

Q *If I were working, I'd at least get some time off for holidays. Can I take a holiday when I'm getting unemployment benefit?*

A You can, but you must continue to be available for work. This means that holidays abroad are not usually allowed if you are to carry on getting benefit. But holidays in Britain are fine, provided you can be contacted – or you make a point of keeping in touch with your benefit office – and you would be prepared to cut the holiday short if a suitable job came up. You are deemed to be actively seeking work while on holiday (even if in practice you are not) and holidays can take up a maximum of two weeks in any 52-week period.

Before you go on holiday, you must let your benefit office know what you are planning and you will have to fill in a special form. The first day after your return on which the benefit office is open, you must go and sign on again (even if it is not your normal day for signing on), otherwise you could lose benefits.

Q *This may sound daft, but can I work while I'm getting unemployment benefit if it's not what I'd consider to be my normal work?*

A You can do various types of work and still qualify for unemployment benefit. These include:

- unpaid voluntary work provided you would be available at short notice to take up an appropriate 'normal' job
- jobs which pay you less than £2 a day. Pay for a longer period is averaged out over a six-day week, so you could earn up to £12 a week
- short-time work if you are claiming only for days when you would otherwise normally be working.

A day of unemployment means a whole 24–hour period, so the £2-a-day restriction applies even if you work only in the evenings or at nights and consider yourself to be available for work during the day.

Q *Wasn't there something in the Budget about cutting the length of time during which the unemployed can get benefit?*

A Under the current rules, you can get unemployment benefit for a maximum of 52 weeks. If you are still unemployed after a year, you may be able to switch to income support instead. But in the November 1993 Budget the government announced its intention to replace the current system with a single benefit called **job seeker's allowance** for unemployed people. This would comprise an equivalent to unemployment benefit for a maximum of six months and a means-tested benefit similar to income support. (You would qualify for a means-tested benefit only if your income and capital are below certain limits.) The rates for the job seeker's allowance are to be aligned with those for income support. There are to be tougher rules to ensure that you are really looking for work and a number of new schemes for helping you – especially if you've been out of work for a long time –

to get back into the labour force. The job seekers' allowance is due to be introduced on 6 April 1996.

Q *How do I go about claiming unemployment benefit?*

A You need to contact your local Unemployment Benefit Office (see Addresses section). Claim as soon as possible and take along the P45 from your last job if you have it. Technically, you claim benefit for each day for which you are unemployed (apart from waiting days) and you could be asked to 'sign on' every day. In practice, you will probably be required to sign on once a fortnight on a specified day. If you live some way from the nearest office – generally more than six miles – you can sign on by post, otherwise you will be expected to make a personal appearance at the office. Payment is by girocheque sent to your home, fortnightly in arrears.

Q *I've been made redundant and was given a redundancy payment of £16,000. Does this stop me from claiming unemployment benefit?*

A Payments received from your previous employer as compensation for losing your job will restrict your entitlement to unemployment benefit. But these do not include:

* redundancy payments
* holiday pay
* refund of contributions to an employer's pension scheme
* pay for any period before you became unemployed.

Q *My firm is asking for voluntary redundancies and, as I've always wanted to set up my own business, I'm tempted. How much redundancy pay can I count on and will it be taxed?*

A You are legally entitled to a redundancy payment if you are under 65 (or the normal retirement age for your job) and you have worked for your employer for at least two years. In the past, the minimum period of employment was five years, if you worked less than 16 hours a week, but following a judgment in the House of Lords in March 1994 people working at least eight hours a week were granted the same rights as full-time employees – this is in line with European Union laws. The amount of redundancy pay to which you are legally entitled increases with your age, years of service and weekly before-tax pay. You get:

- half a week's pay for each year with your employer between your 18th and 22nd birthdays
- one week's pay for each year between ages 21 and 41
- one and a half weeks' pay for each year after you reach age 41.

Only pay up to a maximum level counts – £205 in early 1994 – and statutory redundancy pay is based on a maximum of 20 years' service. Statutory redundancy pay is your minimum legal entitlement; your employer may offer more generous terms, especially if he or she is keen to encourage voluntary redundancies.

The first £30,000 of redundancy pay is normally tax-free provided it was not promised under your contract of employment. Anything in excess of this, and termination payments set out in your contract, are taxable as income for the year in which your employment ends. Pay in lieu of notice generally counts as a genuine redundancy payment unless your contract specifies that you can receive this instead of working your notice.

Q *What should I do about my pension rights in my old employer's scheme now I've been made redundant?*

A You have a number of options. See page 264 for more information.

CHAPTER 3

HEALTH AND WELFARE

ONLY the lucky few sail through life without any medical problems. Even a short spell of illness can seriously disrupt your income, making every bill an added burden. So find out what help you can expect from your employer and from the state. If this will not provide adequate protection, consider taking out your own health insurance. There are different types designed variously to protect your income, provide a lump sum or pay hospital bills.

Of course, illness is not the only threat to your income. The welfare state provides a safety net for those on low incomes, for whatever reason, but social security benefits are not generous and it can be financially difficult to ease back into work. All the more reason, then to know your way around the rules.

Help from the state if you're ill

Q A salesman persuaded me that it was a good idea to take out a sickness and accident policy which will pay me so much for each day I'm off work because I'm ill or have an accident, but a colleague says it's a waste of money because I'm covered by the company sick pay scheme. Who is right?

A In most cases, employers are legally required to pay you **statutory sick pay (SSP)** if you are off work for four or more days in a row. Although it is a statutory payment, your employer will pay it to you at one of two rates depending on your earnings:

- a lower rate of £47.80 a week in 1994–5 if you earn at least the **lower earnings limit** of £57 a week (£247 a month) up to £199.99 a week (£866 a month)

- the standard rate of £52.50 a week in 1994–5 if you earn £200 a week or more.

SSP is the legal minimum and is payable for a maximum of 28 weeks. Many employers run their own schemes which give more generous sick pay – e.g. six months on full pay followed by six months on half pay. The amount you get is not reduced if you also get payments from an insurance policy such as the one you have bought, so there is no problem in having the accident policy too, but it could be an unnecessary luxury if you have a good sick pay scheme at work.

Q *Do I have to pay tax on statutory sick pay?*

A Yes. SSP is taxed in the same way as your normal earnings, so you will usually have to pay both income tax and National Insurance contributions on what you get. But the lower rate of SSP is below the lower earnings limit at which Class 1 National Insurance becomes payable (see page 56): to protect your National Insurance record, you should claim National Insurance credits. To do this, contact your local Benefits Agency (see Addresses section).

YOUR CHANCES OF FALLING ILL

Government figures show that a working person under age 65 is eleven times more likely to suffer an illness or disability for six months or more than he or she is to die. And at any one time there are 1½ million people of working age who have been off sick for more than six months.

Q *Some people at my workplace seem to take masses of days off sick. How can the boss know if they're really ill rather than skiving?*

A The terms and conditions for your job will spell out what proof your employer requires that you are really ill (though there are some legal restrictions to prevent employers making unreasonable demands for proof). There will probably be no formal system for the odd day off sick. For longer periods, the proof required will often be the same as you would have to give if you were claiming **sickness benefit** or **invalidity benefit** (see page 91).

Q *I earn £50 a week helping out in a school secretary's office. I've been off work this week because of back trouble. Can I claim SSP from the school?*

A Unfortunately, no. The main condition for receiving SSP is simply that you are an employee, but there are a few categories of employee which are not covered. These include:

- people who have gross earnings which are lower than the lower earnings limit (which applies in your case)
- usually, people over state pension age who are still working
- anyone on a contract lasting less than three months
- employees working for an overseas employer
- pregnant women entitled to statutory maternity pay and those who are not but are within a few weeks of having, or having had, their baby
- people who are on strike unless they were off sick before the strike started and continue to be ill.

If you do not qualify for SSP, your employer should give you a form, SSP1, which includes an application form for sickness benefit, for which you might qualify instead (see next question). Any sickness benefit would be payable in addition to any sick pay which the school pays under its own non-statutory scheme, if it has one.

Q *I've been employed by a large computer software house but, from next week, I'll be a self-employed consultant. I'm making the switch partly because my health is not so good and I have to cut down stress. The drawback is that, as an employee, I was covered by a good sick pay scheme, but if I have health problems now I will have no cover. Is there any equivalent sick pay I can claim?*

A If you do not qualify for statutory sick pay – e.g. you fall into one of the groups of employee listed in the last question, or you are self-employed – you may be able to get sickness benefit instead. This is a state benefit administered and paid by the Department of Social Security (DSS). To qualify, you must satisfy two National Insurance contribution conditions:

- you must have paid Class 1 contributions on earnings of at least 25 times the lower earnings limit, or 25 Class 2 contributions, in any one tax year. For this condition, contributions must actually have been paid – credits don't count
- you must have paid, or been credited with, Class 1 contributions on earnings of at least 50 times the lower earnings limit, or 50 Class 2 contributions, in both of the last two complete tax years before the year in which you are claiming benefit.

But if your health problem counts as an industrial disease or is due to an industrial accident, you will be treated as satisfying the two contribution conditions above, even if in reality you do not.

Q *Is sickness benefit paid at the same rates as statutory sick pay?*

A No. Sickness benefit is paid at the following rates in 1994–5:

- a personal benefit of £43.45 a week if you are under state pension age, or £55.25 if you are not
- an increase for an adult dependant of £26.90. But this is not paid if the dependant earns £26.90 a week or more
- no increase for child dependants, unless you have reached state pension age, in which case, you can claim a further £11 a week for each child. But, if you personally also claim child benefit, this is reduced to £9.80 a week in respect of your first child. The addition for your first child is also lost if you live with a husband, wife or other partner and he or she earns £120 a week or more; each additional £16 a week which your partner earns loses an addition for a subsequent child.

Sickness benefit is paid for a maximum of 28 weeks. Unlike SSP, sickness benefit is tax-free. While you are receiving benefit, you can claim National Insurance credits to protect your contribution record.

Q *How do I claim sickness benefit?*

A For the first seven days of your illness, you do not have to visit a doctor – you can self-certify yourself as unable to work because of your health. Do this by completing self-certification form SC1, which is available from your Benefits Agency (see page 000), your doctor's surgery and hospitals. Send the completed form to the Benefits Agency. If you are an employee, complete form SSP1, which your employer should have given you (see page 89), and send it to the Benefits Agency.

After the first week, you will need to provide the Agency with certificates from your doctor saying that you are unfit for work – there should be no charge for these if you say they are for the purpose of claiming a social security benefit.

If you have never claimed sickness benefit before, your claim can be backdated for up to a month. But for subsequent claims, you usually have only a few days in which to send in your claim, so do not delay.

Sickness benefit is paid weekly in arrears by girocheque, usually posted to your home.

Q *I've been off work for the last five months and it looks unlikely that I'll get back to work before my sickness benefit runs out. What happens then?*

A If you have received sickness benefit or SSP for the maximum 28 weeks and you are still unable to work because of your health, you will automatically be switched to invalidity benefit. This is more generous than sickness benefit or SSP and is made up of two or more parts (rates given are for 1994–5):

- an **invalidity pension** for yourself of £57.60 a week
- an addition to the pension of £34.50 a week if you have an adult dependant (but this will not be paid if the dependant earns more than £45.45 a week and lives with you, or earns £34.50 a week and lives somewhere else)
- an addition to the pension of £11 a week for each dependent child. This reduces to £9.80 a week for the first child if you also claim child benefit. And the child additions are also affected by the earnings of a partner in the same way as the child additions to sickness benefit (see opposite)
- an extra amount based on your earnings under the **state earnings-related pension scheme (SERPS)** – see page 244
- an **invalidity allowance** paid at a lower rate of £3.80 a week if you were aged 50 to 59 (men) or 50 to 54 (women) at the start of your

illness, a middle rate of £7.60 if you were aged 40 to 49, and a higher rate of £12.15 a week if you were under 40. This is reduced by any SERPS addition you get.

Invalidity benefit (or its replacement – see Box) is payable until you are fit again and able to return to work or until you start to get state retirement pension instead. Invalidity benefit is not taxable.

Q *I've been off work as a builder for the last year because of back problems. Now the DSS is saying that I should take up some other form of work and that I can't get invalidity benefit any more. Do they have the right to decide this?*

A When you first claim sickness benefit, you will usually qualify provided you are not fit enough to carry on your normal work. Similarly, SSP is payable when you are off sick from your job. But after six months or so – about the time you switch to invalidity benefit – your position will be reviewed. If it seems unlikely that you will return in the near future, you will be expected to consider other types of work that you could reasonably do given your state of health, age, skills and education. But, provided that you seem likely to get back to work soon, you will probably still get benefit if you cannot do your normal job. However, tougher rules are due to be introduced from April 1995 (see Box).

If you do not agree that you could manage the type of work the DSS suggests would be suitable, you can appeal – contact your Benefits Agency for guidance on how to do this. If possible, you should get a written statement from your doctor saying why the work would be unreasonable.

Q *Can I carry on getting invalidity benefit if I take on some part-time work?*

A Under the current rules, therapeutic work shouldn't jeopardise your right to sickness or invalidity benefit provided you earn no more than £43 a week in 1994–5, but it could be taken as an indication that you are in fact fit enough to work. If possible, get a letter from your doctor stating why, in his or her opinion, the work would help to improve your state of health or your ability to cope with it. And check with the Benefits Agency that this work would be acceptable, before you take it on. New rules which are due to apply from April 1995 may be more restrictive – see Box.

IMMINENT SICKNESS AND INVALIDITY BENEFIT CHANGES

In November 1993 the government announced its intention to replace the sickness and invalidity benefits with a single new scheme called **incapacity benefit,** due to start in April 1995. There will be three tiers of payment covering the first 28 weeks of illness or disability, the next 24 weeks and over 52 weeks. Incapacity benefit will be taxable for people newly claiming benefit on or after 6 April 1995. There will be tighter medical tests to assess who can receive the benefit after the first 28 weeks – in particular, you will be expected to be incapable of *any* work rather than just your normal job.

Q *Having had a string of low-paid jobs over the years and not earning a lot since I became self-employed, I don't qualify for sickness or invalidity benefit. I've been unable to work since June following a motorbike accident which has left me partially paralysed. I've been told I can claim severe disablement allowance. How much would this give me?*

A If you are not entitled to invalidity benefit, you may indeed be able to get **severe disablement allowance** instead. This is a non-contributory benefit, so you do not have to have paid National Insurance contributions in order to qualify. To be eligible you must:
- count as 80 per cent disabled, or have been entitled to the old non-contributory invalidity benefit which severe disablement allowance replaced, or have become disabled before your 20th birthday, and
- have been unable to work for at least 28 weeks because of your disability.

The allowance can be made up of the following components (rates given are for 1994–5):
- a personal allowance of £34.80 a week

- an addition for an adult dependant of £20.70. This is reduced in the same way as a similar addition to invalidity benefit if your partner has earnings (see page 91)
- an addition for each dependent child of £11, reduced to £9.80 for the first child if you also get child benefit. This is reduced in the same way as similar additions to sickness benefit if your partner has earnings (see page 90)
- an age-related addition of £3.80 if you were aged 50 to 59 when your disability began, £7.60 if you were aged 40 to 49 or £12.15 if you were under 40.

If you need help with your personal care and/or you cannot walk (or can walk only with great difficulty), you may also qualify for **disability living allowance** and various other benefits available to disabled people – ask your local Benefits Agency for advice and help in claiming.

Q *My husband has had several strokes and needs continuous looking after so I've had to give up my job to look after him. Can I claim unemployment benefit?*

A No. To claim unemployment benefit, you would need to be available for work (see page 82). But you may be able to get **invalid care allowance**. You'll qualify if:

- you cannot work full-time because you're looking after a severely disabled person for at least 35 hours a week
- you earn less than £50 a week from any work you do
- the person being cared for gets the care component of disability living allowance or attendance allowance (replaced by disability living allowance except for claimants over state pension age) or certain other benefits
- you are under 65.

The basic allowance is £34.50 a week in 1994–5. You can also get an addition for an adult dependant of £20.65 and additions for dependent children.

Private health insurances

Q *My insurance broker has been trying to convince me that I need permanent health insurance. Do I? Won't I get state sick pay if I'm ill?*

A You may qualify for benefits from the state if you cannot work because you are ill or injured, but these are not very generous, so you could see a big drop in your income. Ideally, you should have some other source of finance to top up your state benefits. This could be savings or, if you work for an employer, you might be covered by an occupational sick pay scheme. And, if you have a wife, husband or other partner who works, you might be able to rely on his or her earnings alone while you are off sick. If you have none of these sources of finance, taking out your own permanent health insurance (PHI) would be a good idea. PHI replaces part of your income if it stops or is reduced because you are unable to work through illness, accident or other disability. The policy continues to pay out either until you are fit again or until you reach retirement.

Q *Can anyone take out PHI?*

A An insurance company will want details about your state of health at the time you apply for a policy and your medical history – and you might be asked to have a medical examination (at the company's expense). If your health or medical history is poor, you will probably have to pay a higher premium than normal and, if it is extremely bad, you may be refused cover altogether. Similarly, if your work or hobbies are particularly dangerous, you will either be refused cover or have to pay extra. Also, PHI is available only up to retirement age (the definition of this varies). Once it is taken out, you can continue to renew your PHI policy each year, regardless of the number of times you claim or for how long.

Q *I work for a dental practice and we have to take special precautions against being infected by the HIV virus. Would a PHI policy cover HIV-related problems?*

A PHI policies do not cover every health problem and a common exception is AIDS/HIV-related illnesses. But some companies do include cover either as a standard term or just for people who are employed in the health sector. Other common exclusions from most PHI policies are:

- some or all pregnancy and childbirth complications
- self-inflicted injuries
- illness related to alcohol or drug abuse
- injuries due to war, riot or revolution.

Q *How much cover is it sensible to choose under a PHI policy?*

A This depends on how much replacement income you would need, what you can afford to pay for PHI and the limitations under the policy. Typically, PHI will replace up to 75 per cent of your gross pay less an amount equal to the single person's state invalidity pension – less if your earnings are higher than, say, £45,000 a year. There may also be a cash limit on the payout – e.g. £750 or £1,000 a week. And payments from the policy will usually be reduced if you qualify for an ill-health or early retirement pension from your employer or another private source.

You need to consider how inflation will affect your cover. Depending on the policy, you can choose a benefit which is either level or increases in line with earnings or price inflation. With some policies, the benefit is increased only while you are claiming. With some others, the cover itself increases each year whether or not you are claiming.

Q *I'm a housewife and don't have a job as such. But if I couldn't look after the house and children we'd have to pay someone else to do it instead. So can I take out permanent health insurance?*

A Yes, you can. Many policies now pay out a limited amount – e.g. £10,000 a year – if you do not work because you are a housewife or househusband or are otherwise unemployed at the time you claim.

Q *The PHI policy I'm considering lets me choose how long after I fall ill the policy starts to pay out. The premiums are lower the longer the delay, but is cost the only factor I should consider?*

A All PHI policies give you this choice. The policy does not start to pay out immediately you are off work ill. As you say, there is a **deferred period** which can usually be anything from four to 104 weeks. You should choose the deferred period which suits your financial position. For example, if you are employed, you will not need PHI payments until your employer's sick pay stops or reduces – and, if you would then qualify for an early pension, PHI might not be worthwhile at all. Or, you might choose the period which matches the length of time you could manage on your savings. If you are self-employed and do not have much in savings, you will probably want a short deferred period.

Q *How are payments from a PHI policy taxed? Are they treated like earnings from a job?*

A In general, benefits being paid from an individual PHI policy are subject to income tax at your highest rate, though, unlike earnings, you do not pay National Insurance on them. But payments for the first 12 months that you make a claim are tax-free, if your claim started on or after 6 April 1994. If your claim started before this, you're covered by old rules which can be more generous, because payments are tax-free until the end of the first complete tax year for which you have claimed benefit: this means that if you started to claim early in a tax year, you could have almost two years' benefits tax-free.

Q *Until April 1994, I received payments under my PHI policy tax-free. But, since then, the insurance company has been deducting tax at the basic rate before handing over the payments. I'm a non-taxpayer and I can't afford to wait until I get a tax rebate. The insurance company says that it can't carry on paying me the gross payments – why not?*

A The November 1993 Budget made a change to the way in which tax on PHI benefits was collected. From 6 April 1994, insurance companies have, by law, had to deduct tax at the basic rate before handing over the payments – and there is no scope, as the law stands, for treating non-taxpayers in a special way. All you can do is to make regular claims to your tax office for rebates. You do not have to wait until the end of the tax year, but any claims under £50 won't be dealt with straight away.

Q *A colleague and I both have PHI policies with the same company, but I seem to be paying a lot more than him. How are the premiums for PHI policies worked out?*

A What you pay for PHI depends on a variety of factors:

- your age when you take out the policy
- your sex – women pay as much as 50 per cent more than men. This is because statistics and insurance companies' experience show that women tend on average to claim more often and for longer
- your state of health when you take out the policy and your medical history
- your work – premiums will be lower for 'safe' office jobs than for more risky manual work
- the deferred period you choose – the longer the period, the lower the premium
- the age at which the policy will stop (e.g. the normal pension age for your job, state pension age or the age at which you plan to start taking a pension from a personal pension plan)
- whether or not you smoke
- whether or not you have any risky hobbies such as flying or rock climbing.

Q *To claim on a PHI policy must I be unable to do any work or just my own job?*

A The majority of PHI policies pay out if you are unable to do your normal work. But a few pay out only if you can't follow *any* occupation. This is such a restricted definition that these policies are best avoided, even though they are likely to be significantly cheaper.

Q *Is critical illness insurance the same as permanent health insurance?*

A No. **Critical illness insurance** – also known as **dead disease insurance** – pays out a tax-free lump sum if you are diagnosed as suffering from any of a range of specified illnesses or have to undergo certain types of surgery for life-threatening conditions. Most policies cover, for example, heart attacks, strokes, cancer, major organ transplant and kidney failure, and these account for about 95 per cent of all claims made against critical illness policies. Many also cover paralysis, multiple sclerosis, paraplegia, loss of limbs, loss of sight and heart surgery. Some also pay out if you are diagnosed as having a terminal illness and you are expected to survive less than a year. Only a handful of policies cover HIV and AIDS-related conditions.

Q *What's the point of taking out critical illness insurance? Aren't permanent health insurance and life cover enough?*

A In the past, life insurance was usually sufficient cover if you fell prey to one of the critical illnesses. But dramatic advances in medical science have enabled many people to survive these conditions – often for years. It may be necessary to make significant changes to your life, though: e.g. you might have to give up your job, switch to less stressful work, adapt your home or rely on help from others. All these things can cost a great deal. So you may need extra financial help. But whether critical illness cover or PHI or both is best is very much a matter of personal choice. Comparing PHI and critical illness insurance is like comparing apples and pears – both can address the same sort of needs but in different ways. Table 3.1 summarises the main differences.

Table 3.1: PHI or critical illness insurance?

Permanent health insurance	Critical illness insurance
Along with state benefits replaces up to three-quarters of your income	Pays out a lump sum
Covers most types of illness or disability – exclusions are specifically listed	Covers only specified conditions
Pays out after you have been ill for a specified time – you choose from 4 to 104 weeks	Pays out on diagnosis or following surgery. Often no waiting period; if there is, commonly 28 days

Q *Is critical illness insurance cheaper than PHI?*

A Surprisingly, critical illness insurance is not necessarily a lot cheaper despite the more restricted range of situations in which it will pay out. For example, in 1994, a man aged 39 in good health and with a low risk of health failure (i.e. in a 'safe' job, without any risky hobbies etc.) might pay, say, £200 to £300 a year for a PHI policy paying out the equivalent of £12,000 a year after 13 weeks of illness. Or, for a policy paying out after only four weeks of illness, he might pay £600 a year. The cheapest form of critical illness policy is taken out for a specified term – for example, as with life cover, you might choose a term corresponding to your mortgage or to the period until your children are expected to be independent. A stand-alone 25-year critical illness policy paying out a £50,000 lump sum might cost the 39-year-old in the example above about £400 a year. Policies designed to pay off a mortgage are often a bit cheaper. The comparison is further complicated because there are many different types of of critical illness plan. Some combine cover with an investment element and/or life cover and therefore cost more than a stand-alone policy.

WHO SUFFERS FROM CRITICAL ILLNESSES?

Government figures show that about a quarter of healthy men and a fifth of healthy women aged 20–40 will suffer a critical illness before they reach age 65. However, critical illnesses are not the most common health problems leading to long spells off work – PHI insurer Permanent Insurance finds that musculoskeletal problems, such as arthritis, and mental disorders are the most common reasons for claims by people off work for 26 weeks or more.

Q *If I was really ill, the NHS would treat me straight away, wouldn't it? So is it worth taking out private medical insurance?*

A In an emergency, you would get immediate treatment through the NHS. But there are many non-urgent conditions which are not pleasant to live with and for which there is often a long waiting list for NHS treatment – these include hip replacement operations, hernia repairs, varicose vein removal and so on. It is in these situations especially that private treatment comes into its own. The advantages can be summarised as:

- avoiding hospital waiting lists
- choosing a convenient time to have treatment
- choosing your hospital and consultant
- enjoying comfortable hotel-style facilities such as a private room, own television and good food.

But private treatment is expensive (see Box), particularly if it turns out that you need a series of treatments. One way to cover the bills is to take out private medical insurance.

Typical cost of private treatment for some common problems	£
Hysterectomy	3,294
Hip replacement	5,265
Cataract removal	2,022
Hernia	1,416

Source: BUPA, 1992

Q *My father has a private medical insurance policy. At the start of his illness, it was very good and paid up for him to see a consultant and have various tests. But now he's been diagnosed as having MS the insurer's refusing to pay for any treatment. What use is insurance which gives out just as you really need it?*

A No policy covers all medical conditions. Common exclusions include long-term illnesses (such as multiple sclerosis), pregnancy, psychiatric problems, cosmetic surgery, AIDS and HIV. And there is no cover for medical problems you already have when you take out the insurance – depending on the policy, these will be excluded altogether or, alternatively, just for the first two years, say, provided the illness does not recur during that time. This exclusion may be interpreted very strictly and you will be expected to keep the insurance company informed of all relevant developments. If you are unsure whether, say, a trip to the doctor might be taken to indicate the recurrence of a 'pre-existing condition', it is better to tell the insurer about it anyway rather than risk having a claim unexpectedly refused later on.

Q *My husband had private medical insurance through his job, but he's just taken early retirement and we want to replace the cover ourselves. There seem to be several types of plans to choose from. Which are the best?*

A This depends on how comprehensive you want the cover to be and how much you are willing to pay. The cost of private medical insurance usually depends on your age and the level of cover you choose. Tax relief is available on premiums for certain plans for people aged 60 or over (see next question).

If you are in your late 50s, top-of-the-range policies could easily cost you over £2,000 a year in 1994, but they should cover virtually all hospitals and meet the costs of treatment and hospital stay in full.

Many standard policies cost less if you restrict your choice of hospitals to those on a selected list – this could halve what you pay, but make sure hospitals near your home are included. Watch out for cash limits on specific areas of cover – for example, surgeons' and anaesthetists' fees. If costs exceeded the limit, you would have to pay the rest out of your own pocket.

Budget policies offer a cheaper option still. Avoid policies where the total pay-out in any year is restricted to a low maximum cash sum – £10,000, say – which could easily be inadequate if you had to claim more than once. Worth considering are budget policies which cover you to 'go private' only if there is an NHS waiting list of six weeks or more for the treatment you need. This type of policy could cost you less than £600 a year in 1994, assuming again that you are in your late 50s. Note that many budget policies exclude out-patient treatment unless it is directly related to a spell as an in-patient.

Ask about the many discounts available when you buy private medical insurance – for example, there may be a 5 per cent saving if you pay by direct debit, 15 per cent if you belong to a particular profession or motoring association, say, or use a certain credit card.

Q *My parents have had private medical insurance for many years. Their company has recently suggested they switch to a special plan for the over-60s. The premiums do look a lot cheaper, but I can't work out why. Is there a catch?*

A Private medical insurance plans for a person aged 60 or over, or a couple where either husband or wife is aged 60 or more, can qualify for tax relief on the premiums. Tax relief at 25 per cent in 1994–5 is given automatically as you pay the premium after deducting tax relief, and you get the relief even if you are a non-taxpayer or 20 per cent taxpayer. This means that, where the full premium is £800, say, you would pay just £600 after tax relief. The relief is given to whoever pays the premiums: often this will be the person or people covered by the policy but it could be someone else (but not an employer). For example, if you paid your parent's premium, you would get the tax relief.

To be eligible for the tax relief scheme, benefits under a plan must meet certain Inland Revenue rules and, for this reason, companies often issue separate plans for the over-60s rather than simply giving relief on the normal policies. The range of plans eligible for tax relief is varied and cover need not be much more restricted than you would get with a normal plan. However, you might need to shop around for the terms and conditions you want.

Q *Now we're approaching middle age and should perhaps be prepared for a few more health problems, we thought it would be sensible to take out private medical insurance. But we were horrified to learn how much these policies cost. Is there any cheaper way of covering the cost of private treatment?*

A As an alternative to private medical insurance, you could take out an **operation cost benefit policy,** which pays out a set cash sum if you need surgery. For example, the policy might pay out, say, £12,000 if you had heart surgery privately, but £2,000 for a minor operation such as prostate surgery. It might also pay a lower cash sum if you have surgery on the NHS. You claim every time you have an operation but there is usually an overall cash limit of, say, £100,000 over any five-year period. The cost of these policies is much less than for standard private medical insurance but similar to the cost of budget policies.

Another option is to take out a **hospital cash plan**. These do not cover the cost of private treatment but simply pay out a relatively small set cash sum for each day you spend in hospital and you could use this to help towards the cost of private treatment.

Q *My mother has Alzheimer's disease and has recently moved into a nursing home. The cost is staggering, which made me wonder how I would cope if I* *needed similar care when I get older. Are there special schemes to help people pay for nursing homes, etc.?*

A In the past, families – women, in particular – often took on an informal role of caring for disabled relatives. Nowadays, with more women working and families often fragmented, many elderly people need professional help in coping with everyday activities and, perhaps, eventually, move to a nursing home. You might assume that, if this happened, you could meet the cost of a nursing home out of savings or the sale of your home. But in 1994 the fees for a nursing home were around £16,000 a year on average, which could quickly use up many people's capital. You might also assume that the state would help, but on current rules it would not unless you had less than £8,000 capital left, including the value of a home you own. To meet the need, a new type of insurance has grown up over the last few years. **Long-term care insurance** aims to provide for:

- the cost of help or nursing in your own home, or
- if you need to move to a nursing home, a cash sum towards the fees, which might be increased periodically to compensate for inflation.

HEALTH PROBLEMS IN LATER LIFE

At age 80, a man can on average expect to survive a further six years, a woman eight. But as you grow older, you become increasingly likely to face some kind of disability. For example, four out of every five men and nine out of every ten women over 85 suffer some kind of mobility problem.

Q *How do long-term care policies work?*

A There are two main types of policy:

- **pre-funded** You save now to cover the cost of care later on. For example, you might start saving in your 40s or 50s (though you could start even earlier). Usually, you pay regular premiums to the plan (but a few accept a single lump sum). These plans tend to work in one of two ways: either you simply buy insurance which will pay out only if you become disabled, or your premiums are invested and part of the investment is cashed in each month to pay for the long-term care insurance. Anything left in your investment fund provides a cash value which you can get back if you decide to stop the plan

- **immediate** You use a lump sum (e.g. from the sale of your home) to guarantee you an income to start immediately which you can use to pay for the help you need or nursing (or residential) home fees. The plans work in various ways. For example, with some your lump sum buys an annuity which will pay out an income for life – unusually for annuities, this may take account of your health, paying out a higher income if your health is poor; this type of plan has no cash-in value. Other lump sum plans rely in part on an investment or investment-type insurance, so you get an income for life, but your plan also has some cash value which is paid out if you stop the plan or die.

Most pre-funded schemes start to pay out if you become sufficiently disabled. For example, depending on the policy, you might have to require help with two out of five **activities of daily living (ADLs),** which might be defined as movement, agility (being able to get from your bed to a chair), dressing, personal hygiene and eating. Some immediate schemes also require proof of disability but others are designed to provide an income regardless of your state of health.

Q *Are long-term care plans expensive?*

A At the time of writing there were only a handful of long-term care plans on the market. They work in a variety of ways and cannot be readily compared. But in general they are not cheap. For example, in 1993 one pre-funded plan, providing a range of home-care benefits and £300 a week if the policy-holder has to move into a nursing home, cost £53 a month if the plan was started at age 50 and £86 a month if it started at age 60. One of the immediate plans was offering a yearly income of just over £8,000 for five years and aimed (though there was no guarantee) to keep your capital intact in return for an initial investment of £100,000 if you were a woman aged 82.

Q *Where can I buy PHI, private medical insurance and similar policies?*

A Most health insurance policies, such as PHI, critical illness insurance, private medical insurance and long-term care plans can be bought through insurance brokers or financial advisers. You can find local firms in *Yellow Pages* or contact the British Insurance and Investment Brokers Association (BIIBA) for a list of its members (see Addresses section).

Coping on a low income

Q *My wife died recently and I've decided to stop working to bring up our daughter, who is now two years old. I'm getting child benefit, of course, and one-parent benefit, but is there any other help I can get from the state?*

A Child benefit and one-parent benefit (see pages 23 and 35) do not amount to much. If these are your only income and you do not have much in the way of savings either, you will probably qualify for some or all of the following state benefits:

- **income support** The main benefit for people on low incomes, this is administered by the Benefits Agency, part of the Department of Social Security (DSS)
- **housing benefit** Administered by your local authority, this benefit helps with paying rent. If you have a mortgage, income support may help with interest payments
- **council tax benefit** Administered by the local authority, this provides relief from council tax
- free NHS services – e.g. free prescriptions, dental treatment and eye tests
- free milk – e.g. for children under 5 if the family is getting income support. Milk tokens can be exchanged for seven pints of milk a week
- education benefits, such as free school meals and a school uniform grant for children at school. These are administered by the local authority
- housing grants from the local authority for home improvements
- loans or grants from the **social fund** administered by the Benefits Agency.

To find out what you are entitled to, make an appointment to talk to someone at your local Benefits Agency (see Addresses section). You can also get advice from your local Citizens Advice Bureau (see Addresses section). Benefits administered by the local authority are claimed through your local government offices.

Q *I'd like to take a year or two off work to take a Master's degree. Can I claim income support during that time?*

A It is unlikely. You cannot usually qualify for income support unless you are available for work and actively seeking employment. Not surprisingly, if you are a full-time student you cannot normally get income support. But some claimants do not have to be available for work – e.g. single parents – and they may be able to study full-time and carry on getting benefit. Pensioners can also claim benefit and study full-time.

If you are a part-time student, you might qualify for income support if the course takes up 21 hours a week or less, you are still actively seeking work and you would be prepared to give up the course immediately if you were offered a job.

Q *All the income I have is my state pension, though I do have about £10,000 in the building society as well. Can I claim income support?*

A Income support is a **means-tested benefit**. This means that you qualify for it only if your income and capital are sufficiently low. In particular, you can get the full benefit only if your capital is less than £3,000. If your capital is in the range £3,001–£8,000, your benefit will be reduced (see page 111). You will not qualify for income support at all if you have capital of more than £8,000. Your building society savings count as capital and so you are not currently eligible for income support. But not all types of capital count – an important exception is your home, if you own it, provided you are living in it. Similar rules apply with housing benefit, except that you do not lose all entitlement to benefit until your capital reaches £16,000.

Q *My boyfriend and I are both out of work and on low incomes. Can we both claim income support?*

A If you live together, you will be treated as one unit for the purpose of claiming income support and the various other means-tested benefits. Only one of you can make the claim, but whichever of you does so will be assessed for a higher level of benefit because you are a couple.

Q *How much can I expect income support to give me to live on?*

A This depends on your individual circumstances. Under the income support rules, the amount that you are deemed to need to live on, called your **applicable amount**, is calculated according to a given scale (see Table 3.2). For example, if you are a single parent over age 18 bringing up one child aged two, your weekly applicable amount in 1994–5 would be:

	£
Personal allowance – lone parent	45.70
Child allowance	15.65
Family premium	10.05
Lone parent	5.10
Total applicable amount	76.50

Your actual income is added up and compared with the applicable amount. If your income is less than the applicable amount, you will get income support to make up the shortfall. If your income equals or exceeds the applicable amount, you do not get any income support.

Q *A neighbour has offered me a part-time job with his electronics business. If I take it will I lose the right to income support?*

A You cannot normally get income support if you – or your partner – have a full-time job. 'Full-time' means working 16 hours a week or more. Provided this job would take up less than 16 hours a week, you can carry on claiming income support – though your after-tax earnings less any allowable deductions will reduce the amount of benefit you get on a £1 for £1 basis. If you will work 16 hours a week or more, you may be able to get **family credit** instead – see page 114.

Table 3.2: Main allowances and premiums through income support for 1994–5[1]

Allowance/premium	Weekly amount £
Personal allowance	
– single under age 18 (usual rate)	27.50
– single aged 18 to 24	36.15
– single aged 25 and over	45.70
– lone parent aged 18 and over	45.70
– couple, one or both aged 18 and over	71.70
plus allowances for each child	
– aged under 11	15.65
– aged 11–15	23.00
– aged 16–17	27.50
– aged 18	36.15
– over 18	no allowance
plus premiums if they apply to you	
– family	10.05
– lone parent	5.10
– single pensioner (main rate)	18.25
– pensioner couple (main rate)	27.55

[1] Amounts which are deemed to be enough to live on.

Q *What's included as income in the calculation for working out how much income support I'll get?*

A Nearly all regular payments received by you – and your partner if you are married or living with someone – count as income. This generally includes other benefits you get, such as unemployment benefit, sickness benefit, child benefit and retirement pensions. But some types of income are partly or wholly ignored and some deductions allowed, including (amounts apply to 1994–5):

- actual interest from any savings or investments. But if you have more than £3,000 of capital, it will be assumed that you are getting a notional income from it (see next question)
- tax and National Insurance you pay on earnings or profits from working
- half the contributions you pay to an employer's pension scheme or personal pension plan

- expenses incurred *'wholly, exclusively and necessarily'* because of your job, e.g. travel while you are at work – but not any other job-related expenses, such as travel to and from work or childcare. Similarly, business expenses can be deducted if you are self-employed
- payments in kind
- redundancy pay and golden handshakes will usually be treated as capital not income. But holiday pay and payment in lieu of notice will count as income
- a job start allowance
- the first £15 a week of your (and your partner's) earnings from work, if you qualify for the lone-parent premium or one of the premiums available to disabled people. If this does not apply, the first £5 of your earnings and the first £5 of your partner's earnings
- most benefits you receive if you are disabled
- £10 Christmas bonus paid to retired pensioners
- payments from the social fund
- regular payments from charities provided they are not meant for buying items which income support is supposed to cover, e.g. food, ordinary clothing and footwear (school uniforms are not 'ordinary'), domestic fuel and any housing costs covered by income support. The first £10 of other regular payments from charities. Lump sums from charities may be treated as capital or ignored
- the first £4 a week that you charge any tenants (plus a further £8.60 a week if you pay for their heating) who share your home
- the first £20 a week you charge boarders and half of the remaining charge
- payments to cover your mortgage interest under a mortgage protection policy to the extent that income support is not paying the interest
- part of the income from a home income plan (see page 138) equal to the amount of interest payable on the associated mortgage
- payments you get from a health authority, local council or voluntary organisation for looking after someone temporarily in your care, e.g. under a formal fostering agreement.

Q *I have £4,760 savings in a National Savings account. I knew I'd lose some income support because of this, but I can't see how the DSS has worked out the deduction. It doesn't seem to match the interest I'm getting.*

A Instead of taking into account the actual interest you get, the DSS assumes you get £1 a week for each £250 or part-£250 of the capital you have over £3,000. This rule often works to your disadvantage. For example, from your £4,760 of savings, you would be assumed to be receiving £8 a week income. This represents an interest rate of over 9 per cent a year, which is probably considerably higher than the return you are actually getting.

Q *I'm a single mum. Do the maintenance payments I get from my ex-husband count as income when my income support is worked out?*

A Most maintenance payments do count as income and will reduce the amount of income support you can get. Regular payments (e.g. monthly) will be treated as an equivalent weekly sum spread evenly throughout the payment period. For example, if you get £200 a month in maintenance, this will be treated as £200 x 12/52 = £46.15 a week. Special rules apply to the spreading of regular payments which have been missed and are then paid in arrears. Lump-sum maintenance payments will usually also be treated as income and will be spread according to a formula in such a way as to disqualify you from income support for as long as possible. But a few types of lump sum can be treated as capital – which is preferable provided they do not take your capital over the £8,000 limit. They include:

- lump sums you get as a result of dividing up your property on separation or divorce. Property includes your home, its contents, your share of joint savings and so on
- gifts up to £250 in a 52-week period unless they are paid regularly
- payments in kind.

Note that the DSS, through the Child Support Agency (CSA), will determine the amount of maintenance that your former husband should be paying for the maintenance of your child or children (but not any amount payable for your own maintenance). With few exceptions, you must help the CSA to contact your former husband and ensure that payments are made, otherwise you could lose some or all of your income support. The amount of child maintenance the CSA collects for you will reduce your income support on a £ for £ basis. If you decided to go back to work and qualify for family credit instead, part of your maintenance payments will be ignored (see page 115).

Q *Can I deduct the cost of providing meals, heating and so on from the amount I earn as a childminder when declaring my earnings for income support?*

A Earnings from childminding are treated in a special way. You are classed as self-employed and your profit is taken to be one-third of your earnings after subtracting income tax, National Insurance contributions and half of any contributions you pay towards a personal pension plan. You cannot make any other deductions but the rest of your earnings are ignored.

Q *I think I qualify for income support. What are the chances of my getting housing benefit to cover the £39 a week rent I pay for my council house?*

A If you qualify for income support, you automatically also qualify for housing benefit (and various other benefits such as free NHS prescriptions and free school meals for your children). If you do not succeed in getting income support, you might still be eligible for housing benefit. Entitlement is worked out in a similar, but not identical, way to that for income support.

Q *Last week I was made redundant. I'm signing on for unemployment benefit but that won't be enough to cover the mortgage on the house. Can I get housing benefit to cover this?*

A Housing benefit does not cover mortgage interest payments, but income support can do. Although you are getting unemployment benefit, you may also be eligible for income support. In working out your applicable amount (see page 108), part or all of your mortgage interest will be added to the other allowances and premiums, i.e. increasing the amount of income you are deemed to need. In working out your actual income, the unemployment benefit you get will be included. As in the normal way, if there is a shortfall between your income and your applicable amount, you will get income support of that amount. For the first 16 weeks of your claim, income support will cover only half of your mortgage interest (unless you or your partner are aged 60 or more). After that time, it will cover the full amount indefinitely. Only the first £150,000 of mortgage is covered. Income support will not cover capital repayments or premiums for a mortgage-related endowment policy. Neither will it cover any subsequent increase in your mortgage, e.g. if you move house or extend the loan.

Q *How is income support paid?*

A It is paid either by a fortnightly girocheque or an order book. In either case, you cash the cheque or order at the post office. If part or all of your mortgage interest is being paid, this will be handed by the DSS direct to your mortgage lender. You can also arrange for fuel bills to be paid direct by the DSS under the **fuel direct scheme**.

Q *Recently, my washing machine broke down. That's no joke as I have six children, one of whom wets the bed regularly. I don't have the money for the repairs, which have been estimated at £100, and I thought that the social fund might pay or, at least, make me a loan. But the Benefits Agency has turned me down saying that a washing machine isn't essential equipment. Should I appeal?*

A The discretionary social fund can make payments or loans to you to meet special needs if you are receiving income support. You have no legal right to any payment which is entirely dependent on the discretion exercised by the social fund officers and the amount of money they have available. Each district is allocated a limited social fund budget for the tax year from which all awards must be made. There are three types of award:

- **community care grants** These, which do not have to be repaid, are to help families under stress or people, especially the elderly and disabled, to live in the community rather than in an institution or residential home. To qualify you must be getting income support and usually have no more than £500 capital. Guidance given to social fund officers specifically refers to washing machines where laundry bills are high as an item which might be considered
- **budgeting loans** A loan is not as good as a grant because it has to be repaid, but social fund loans are interest-free and repayments are usually spread over a maximum of 78 weeks. To qualify, you or your partner must have been getting income support for at least 26 weeks

and you must normally have no more than £500 capital. Loans can cover items such as essential furniture and household equipment and even non-essential items (though these are given lower priority)

- **crisis loans** You do not have to be getting income support to be eligible for this type of loan, but you must have insufficient resources to meet your short-term needs and you must need the loan because of some emergency which is likely otherwise to cause serious damage or risk to health and safety.

On the face of it, you would seem to have a reasonable case for a community care grant or, failing that, a budgeting loan. You can ask for the decision to be reviewed by the social fund officers, provided you do this within 28 days. But if you are still turned down, there is no right of appeal to an outside body.

Q *I've been offered a six-week contract with a local firm. It doesn't pay a lot, but it would get me back into the swing of work and would add to my c.v. But how would I stand with regard to income support if I were to accept the contract?*

A If the work is for 16 hours a week or more, you will not be able to claim income support for the period while you are working. Unless you have a bit of capital to fall back on or can borrow some money, this could cause problems, as you may have no income from the time benefit stops until you are paid under the contract. And because income support is usually paid in arrears you will have to wait two weeks when you claim income support again before you receive the first payment. You might be successful in getting a crisis loan from the social fund to cover these periods, but any award will be made at the discretion of the fund officers. The rules for stopping and starting income support claims make it hard for people on benefit to accept contracts for temporary work.

Q *I've been offered a job in the local supermarket. It means working 20 hours a week, which fits nicely with the children's school hours. The pay is about £60 a week. Can I still get benefits from the DSS if I take the job?*

A Working 16 hours a week or more means that you will not be able to claim income support. But you might be able to get **family credit**

– a state benefit designed to top up the income of families on low earnings. However, deciding whether you would be better off taking the job and making the switch is not easy. The rules for family credit are different from the income support rules in some crucial ways – in particular, you will no longer automatically qualify for full housing and council tax benefits. On the other hand, the first £15 of any maintenance payments is disregarded. And, once you have switched to family credit, it is much easier to take on extra work or temporary jobs when they turn up and you lose benefit more slowly than with income support if your earnings increase.

It can be very hard to work out in advance just how your income will be affected. If you think family credit might suit your circumstances, contact your local Citizens Advice Bureau (see Addresses section) for help in deciding whether you would be better off. If you decide to go ahead, you need to complete form FC1, which you can get from your local Benefits Agency, unemployment office, main post office or advice centre.

Q *Is entitlement to family credit worked out in the same way as entitlement for income support?*

A No, though many of the rules are similar: for example, you cannot get family credit if you have more than £8,000 in capital. The starting point for family credit is the maximum rate of benefit, which is made up of an adult credit – this is the same whether you are a couple or a single parent – plus a credit for each child depending on his/her age (see Table 3.3). Your actual income (taken to be the average received in the eight weeks before the period for which you are claiming) is then compared with an applicable amount which is the same for all families and is set at £71.70 a week in 1994–5. If your income is less than or equal to the applicable amount, you get the maximum family credit. If your income is greater, the family credit is reduced at a rate of 70p for each £1 of income over the limit. (This is less harsh than the £1 for £1 loss of benefit under income support.) For example, suppose your income was £90 a week in 1994–5. This is £18.30 above the applicable amount, so you lose 0.7 x £18.30 = £12.81 of family credit. The amount of family credit for which you qualify is fixed for six months at a time and does not vary during that period even if your earnings or other income change.

Table 3.3: Maximum family credit in 1994–5

	Weekly amount £
Adult credit	44.30
Child credit	
– under 11	11.20
– 11–15	18.55
– 16–17	23.05
– 18	32.20
over 18	no credit

Q *Didn't the government introduce an incentive to get people with children who were claiming benefits back into the workforce?*

A In the November 1993 Budget it was proposed that, from October 1994, people claiming family credit should be able to deduct childcare costs of up to £40 a week from the income which is used to calculate the amount of benefit they will get. This means that a working mother (or, exceptionally, father) will get up to £28 a week more benefit towards the cost of using a registered childminder, day nursery or similar formal arrangement to care for children under the age of 11. The government says that it expects 50,000 more families to take up work as a direct result of the change.

In July 1994 the government said it would be looking at ways of extending 'in-work benefits', like family credit, to more people on low incomes, including single people and couples without children, with a view to encouraging more unemployed people to take up jobs.

Q *Are the benefits available for people on low incomes taxable?*

A Income support is taxable, so if you spend part of a tax year on income support and part in work, you may have to pay some income tax. Other means-tested benefits, such as housing benefit, council tax benefit, education benefits, free National Health services and grants from the Social Fund, are tax-free. Family credit is also tax-free.

LEAFLETS ON BENEFITS

The following are available from Benefits Agencies, advice centres and some public libraries:

FB2 *Which Benefit?*

SB1 *Income Support – Cash Help*

INF3 *Living Together as Husband and Wife*

FB4 *Help While You're Working*

FC1 *Family Credit*

The DSS also operates a free information phone line (see page 273).

Your local council offices will be able to supply information about housing benefit, council tax benefit and other benefits for which you might be eligible.

If you need to know more about the Child Support Agency, see its leaflet *Child Support Maintenance for Parents Who Live Apart* (see page 273 for how to contact the CSA). For advice on its assessments, see *The Which? Guide to Divorce*, published by Consumers' Association.

CHAPTER 4

YOUR HOME

MANY people buy their homes with a mortgage, which for most households is a major monthly expense. Choosing the right mortgage at the outset can save you money and headaches later on. The outlay on house insurance is much smaller but it is still vitally important to get a good policy and to have enough cover. A home need not just be a drain on your finances though: for example, taking in a lodger can earn you a tax-free income and, despite a bad press in recent years, some types of home income plan are a good way of boosting income in your retirement years.

Mortgages

Q *What's the difference between a repayment mortgage and a low-cost endowment mortgage?*

A With a **repayment mortgage** – also called a **capital and interest mortgage** – your monthly payments pay off part of the outstanding loan – the **capital** – as well as interest. In the early years, the amount of capital paid off is very low but, by the end of the mortgage term, you will have repaid the loan in full.

With a **low-cost endowment mortgage**, your monthly payments cover the interest, but not any capital repayments, and also the premiums for a **with-profits endowment policy** (see page 228). This is an investment-type insurance policy which pays out a lump sum at the end of the mortgage term. Provided bonus rates during the lifetime of the policy are as high as predicted, the lump sum will be at least enough to repay the loan.

Q *I paid off my mortgage early, when I sold my flat and moved in with my girlfriend, but I still have to pay for the endowment that went with it. Why can't I stop payments for this too?*

A An **endowment mortgage** is really a package made up of two financial products: an interest-only mortgage and a life insurance policy designed to provide a lump sum after a certain number of years. Although you have paid off the mortgage, the separate endowment policy still keeps going. You have several options: you can carry on paying the premiums and eventually receive the maturity proceeds; you can stop paying the premiums and either cash in the policy or make it paid up – but in the early years, the policy may be worth nothing or very little; or you could try selling the policy in an auction. See pages 230–3 for more about these options. If you keep the policy going, you may be able to combine it with another mortgage at some time in the future.

Q *A radio programme recently said that some types of mortgage are more tax-efficient than others. Can this be right – I thought all mortgages qualified for tax relief?*

A Interest which you pay on the first £30,000 of a loan to buy your only or main home qualifies for tax relief. For 1994–5 this relief is applied at a rate of 20 per cent but is due to fall to 15 per cent from 6 April 1995. For loans taken out after 31 July 1988, you get one lot of relief per home regardless of the number of people paying the loan and, generally, you cannot get tax relief on more than one home at a time. Note that mortgage tax relief is restricted to the interest payments and does not apply to any repayments of capital.

With a repayment mortgage, it is never possible to get tax relief on your capital repayments. But with some types of **interest-only mortgage** it is. An interest-only mortgage is any mortgage for which you do not pay off any capital until the end of the mortgage term – your monthly payments simply cover the interest and, usually, payments towards some form of investment which will eventually pay off the loan. An endowment mortgage is one type of interest-only mortgage, though it does not qualify for any extra tax relief. Both **pension mortgages** and **PEP mortgages** do, so they are relatively tax-efficient types of mortgage.

Q *How does a pension mortgage work?*

A Your monthly payments cover the interest on the mortgage and also contributions towards a personal pension plan. Contributions to the plan qualify for tax relief at your top rate and are invested in a tax-free fund. Once you are old enough (minimum age 50) to start taking the proceeds of the plan it can be used to provide a pension and a tax-free lump sum. The tax-free lump sum is used to pay off the mortgage. Since only part of the plan proceeds can be taken as a lump sum, pension mortgages are not cheap because you will be paying to build up a pension as well.

Similar mortgages can be arranged using other types of pension scheme or plan, but tend to be less flexible – for example, you may need to retire from work before the mortgage loan can be repaid. Before taking out a pension mortgage, you need to be sure that you are eligible for the type of pension scheme or plan you will be using (in particular, see page 254) and expect to be so throughout the planned mortgage term. Do not use a pension plan to pay off a mortgage if it would leave you short of money in retirement.

Q *Is a PEP mortgage similar to a pension mortgage?*

A A PEP mortgage is another type of interest-only mortgage, but with one of these instead of contributing to a pension plan you save regular sums through a personal equity plan (PEP) and this plan is eventually cashed in to repay the mortgage. A PEP mortgage is not as tax-efficient as a pension mortgage because there is no tax relief on the money you pay into a PEP, but the investment does build up tax-free and there is no tax on the proceeds of the plan.

Q *My mortgage lender seems very keen that I take out a low-cost endowment mortgage. But would a repayment mortgage be better?*

A The lender earns commission from the insurance company providing the endowment policy so, arguably, has an incentive to sell you the endowment mortgage. But it could be a good choice anyway – you need to weigh up the features of the different loans:

- **cost** Monthly repayments for a basic repayment mortgage may be slightly lower than for the low-cost endowment option but you should also take account of the cost of life cover if you need it

- **life cover** If you have dependants, make sure you have enough life insurance to repay the loan if you were to die before the end of the term. With a low-cost endowment mortgage, life cover is built in and included in the price. With a repayment mortgage, unless you already have adequate life cover, you will have to take out a separate **mortgage protection policy**, which will cost extra

- **risk** A repayment mortgage will definitely pay off your mortgage by the end of its term. A low-cost endowment mortgage will do this only if investment performance is as good as expected. If not, there could be a shortfall, though this is likely to be small

- **flexibility** Repayment mortgages are the most flexible – you can pay off extra capital as and when you like. And, if you run into financial problems, you can usually arrange to extend the term and even miss payments. With endowment mortgages, it is easy to alter the mortgage part of the arrangement, but the insurance policy is less flexible. You cannot easily extend its term, and you should avoid cashing in or stopping payments to an endowment policy early (see page 231). For an extra premium, you might be able to have a **waiver of premium option**, which would allow you to miss premium payments without penalty for a limited period in the event of illness or unemployment

- **moving home** In the early years of a repayment mortgage, most of your monthly payments are interest, so, if you move often, you will constantly be back at square one and will see very little reduction in the capital you owe. By contrast, you can transfer an endowment policy from one mortgage to another as you move, so you will continuously be building up a lump sum towards the eventual repayment.

Q *Years ago I took out an endowment mortgage and now it's paid off my loan and given me a handsome payout as well. I can't understand why people choose any other type of mortgage.*

A Endowment mortgages have changed a lot over the last decade or so. First, when you took out your mortgage, premiums for the associated insurance policy almost certainly qualified for **life assurance premium relief** – basically, partial tax relief on the premiums (now set at 12½ per cent). This subsidy is not available for insurance policies taken out after 13 March 1984, though it can still be given for policies taken out before that date. Secondly, you probably had a **full-cost endowment** policy which guaranteed to pay off the whole mortgage at the end of its term, with any extra payout providing you with a lump sum. Nowadays, this type of policy would be too expensive to compete with other types of mortgage. Instead, lenders market **low-cost endowment** policies. A low-cost endowment policy does not *guarantee* to pay off the whole mortgage but is expected to do so, provided the value of your policy grows at a given rate. If it grows by more, you will get an extra lump sum at the end of the mortgage term (though less than a full-cost policy would have provided). But if the policy value grows less well, it will not pay off the whole mortgage and you will have to fund the shortfall (usually small) in some other way. And, finally, if you had a mortgage during the high-inflation years of the 1970s, you would have seen the real value of your loan fall whereas the value of your policy (being linked to the stock market) kept pace with inflation: it is unlikely that today's mortgage borrowers will benefit from conditions like those.

Q *Should I choose a variable-rate or fixed-rate mortgage?*

A With a variable-rate mortgage, the interest you are charged goes up and down in line with interest rates in the economy as a whole. With a fixed-rate mortgage, the interest is set at one level at the time you take out the mortgage and stays at that level for a given period – for example, one year, three years, even 20 years. The lowest fixed rates tend to match the shortest periods. Whether or not you 'win' or 'lose' by taking out a fixed-rate mortgage depends on how variable mortgage interest rates move during the fixed period. If they fall below your fixed rate, then you would have done better with a variable rate; if they rise above the fixed rate, you've got a good deal. When, by historical standards, the variable rate is low (see Table 4.1) fixed rates look attractive. But, whatever happens to interest rates, a big advantage of a fixed-rate mortgage is that you can plan ahead with certainty because you know just how much your mortgage will cost during the fixed period. Watch out for arrangement fees, commonly £150 to £250, payable when you apply for a fixed-rate mortgage, and early redemption charges (see next question).

Table 4.1: Standard variable mortgage rate since 1976

Date of change	Rate (%)
1.6.76	10.50
1.11.76	12.25
1.5.77	11.25
1.7.77	10.50
1.10.77	9.50
1.2.78	8.50
1.7.78	9.75
1.12.78	11.75
1.1.80	15.00
1.2.81	14.00
1.5.81	13.00
1.11.81	15.00
1.4.82	13.50
1.9.82	12.00
1.12.82	10.00
1.7.83	11.25
1.4.84	10.25
1.8.84	12.75
1.12.84	11.875
1.2.85	13.00
1.4.85	14.00
1.9.85	12.75
1.4.86	12.00
1.6.86	11.00
1.11.86	12.25
1.5.87	11.25
1.12.87	10.30
1.5.88	9.80
1.8.88	11.50
1.10.88	12.75
1.2.89	13.50
1.11.89	14.50
1.3.90	15.40
1.11.90	14.50
1.4.91	13.75

Date of change	Rate (%)
1.5.91	12.95
1.7.91	12.45
1.8.91	11.95
14.10.91	11.50
1.3.92	10.95
1.6.92	10.65
1.11.92	9.99
1.12.92	9.29
1.1.93	8.55
1.3.93	7.99
1.1.94	7.64

Source: Halifax Building Society

Q *Two years ago, I took out a mortgage with the interest rate fixed at 10 per cent for seven years. This now looks high but when I talked to my building society about switching to a lower rate, they said I'd have to pay a penalty of £1,400. How can they get away with this?*

A You should not take out a fixed-rate mortgage unless you are prepared to commit yourself to the loan for the full fixed period. To offer a fixed-rate mortgage, a lender buys wholesale funds which have broadly the same interest rate and term as the mortgage. If you pull out of the mortgage early, the lender stands to make a loss on the corresponding funds. Therefore, it is normal for the lender to charge a hefty fee if you repay or switch a fixed-rate mortgage early.

Q *Are discounts for first-time buyers worth having or is there a catch?*

A A lot of mortgages offer a lower interest rate (for example, 1 per cent off the standard variable rate if you are a first-time buyer) for the first six months, say, of a mortgage. This is obviously a marketing device to attract your custom, but it can also be a good deal for you, easing the financial burden in the early months when you have solicitors' fees, removal costs and so on to face as well. Make sure, however, that the discounts are genuine – with some mortgages, the amount you save is simply added to the mortgage loan so that, not only do you pay it eventually, but you also pay interest on it. And, with many loans, qualifying for the discount depends on taking out a related insurance policy which you may not want or you could buy more cheaply elsewhere (see page 131).

Q *In 1989 I was advised to take out a low-start mortgage. I was told that the interest rate would go up slightly each year, but I wasn't warned that the capital I owe would also increase. At the start the loan was for £112,500 but now I owe £123,000. I tried to switch to a different mortgage, but the lender says I'll have to pay a £150 administration fee and an early settlement charge of over £5,000. I'm at my wits' end. What can I do to get out of this mess?*

A This is a deferred-interest mortgage. In the early years, payments are low because you are paying only part of the interest – the rest is being added to the outstanding loan. This is set out in the terms and conditions of the loan, but if you feel you were misled by whoever advised you to take out the loan you should complain to him or her or to the company which employs the adviser, saying that you are claiming compensation. If the advice was given by a bank or building society, you can take your case to the appropriate ombudsman (see page 157). If not, you might have to go to court to stand any chance of legal redress. This could be extremely costly and the outcome would be uncertain.

As a priority, you should either increase your payments under the loan to cover the full rate of interest and stop the balance increasing any further. Even with the hefty charges, it may be better in the long run to switch to another mortgage and lender now. If you cannot afford to take these steps, get advice immediately from your local Citizens Advice Bureau (see Addresses section).

Q *Last March our mortgage rate was reduced but I decided to carry on with the old monthly repayments in order to reduce the mortgage balance and, thus, the interest we pay on it. But when I received the annual statement this month, I saw that the interest has only just been reduced. The society says this is standard practice, but how can they take my money and do nothing with it for the best part of a year?*

A This is not an uncommon practice. Many lenders calculate the interest on a mortgage by reference to the capital balance outstanding at the start of each year. Although extra capital repayments made during the year do reduce the balance, this is not reflected in the interest payments until the start of the next year. Check the small print in your mortgage terms and conditions and hang on to any extra repayments until just before the annual interest review date.

Q *I've come across an ad for a company which claims it can cut £1000s off the cost of any mortgage in return for a registration fee of £195 and regular administration fees of £2.50. Is this a genuine offer or a rip-off?*

A The ad you saw probably refers to a system of replacing your monthly mortgage repayments with fortnightly payments instead. The 'early' payments earn interest until they are used to meet the normal monthly repayment and you also end up paying for 13 four-weekly 'months' during the year instead of the normal 12 calendar months. The interest and extra payment each year are used to reduce your mortgage balance. Over a period of years, this can have a significant impact on your mortgage and lead to your paying it off earlier than you would otherwise have done and after paying less interest. It is not a bad system, but there is no reason why you should pay anyone registration and administration fees – you can set up the 'system' yourself for nothing by simply paying an extra sum into your mortgage account once a year.

Q *I'm intending to pay off my mortgage early. The bank has told me that not only will I have to pay a £50 fee but if I don't employ a solicitor a further £50 will be charged. Is the bank entitled to impose these charges?*

A A flat fee of £50 or so is very common when you pay off your mortgage. Sometimes it is called a **sealing charge,** but it is basically an administration fee to cover the paperwork involved in handing the deeds of your property over to you; sometimes it is described as a charge for storage of your deeds during the term of the mortgage. It is also standard practice for the lender to try to insist that you use a solicitor.

These are not the only charges you may have to pay. Most mortgages are designed to run for 25 years or so. If you decide to pay off the mortgage in the early years, you may be charged an early redemption penalty – for example, equivalent to one to three months' interest for a variable-rate mortgage. Higher penalties are imposed for withdrawing early from a fixed-rate mortgage (see page 125).

Q *There are so many different mortgage lenders. How on earth do I set about comparing what's on offer?*

A A good starting point is to look through one of the surveys regularly published by a number of personal finance magazines – check out your local newsagent for these – or get the latest *Which?* report on mortgages (available in most public libraries). Then contact the lenders you are interested in for *full* details of their mortgages. You could get help from a mortgage adviser – bank, building society and specialist mortgage broker (see *Yellow Pages* for your area) – but beware! A survey by *Which?* found that many advisers gave misleading or inaccurate advice. Most advisers recommended endowment mortgages even when a repayment mortgage was at least as suitable, perhaps because endowment mortgages earn them commission. To increase your chance of good advice, *Which?* recommends you visit a minimum of *five* advisers including at least one independent broker.

Q *Is it worth insuring my mortgage payments against the threat of redundancy?*

A For many people, the biggest financial worry following redundancy is how to keep up the mortgage payments. In response to this, lenders sometimes include redundancy insurance in a mortgage package or offer it as an optional extra – usually called **mortgage payment protection insurance**. It pays your mortgage payments for you if you cannot work because of disability or redundancy. It may also cover you if you're self-employed and you go bust. But cover usually starts only after you have been out of work for, say, two months and runs for a limited period – often a year. There is generally an upper limit on the amount it will pay out each month, e.g. £1,000, and payment is in arrears. There are also numerous exclusions with these policies and they are not cheap. Given that you might be able to rely on savings for a while or get help from the state with your mortgage payments (see page 112) or be able to rearrange your mortgage payments, these policies are of doubtful value. If, nevertheless, you are interested, insist on seeing and checking the full policy before you commit yourself.

Insuring your home

Q *My dad manages on his pension and has to be careful with money, so finding cheap house contents insurance is important. Would an indemnity policy be suitable for him? If so, where could he get one?*

A There are two types of house contents insurance:

- **new-for-old** policies are the types most people choose. They cover the cost of replacing lost items with new ones
- **indemnity** policies reduce the amount paid out, when you claim, to take account of wear and tear – i.e. you would get enough to replace your belongings with similar-condition second-hand items but not new ones. Even with new-for-old policies, linen and clothing are usually only covered on an indemnity basis.

Indemnity cover is the cheaper option but only worth choosing if you would be content with not being able to buy brand new replacements for lost possessions. Most insurance companies only offer new-for-old policies, but you could try companies which specialise in deals for mature people – contact SAGA Insurance and Age Concern Insurance (see Addresses section). A number of companies also offer discounts on new-for-old policies for people aged 50, 55 or 60 and more, so it is worth shopping around and asking whether any discount is available.

A number of other companies also offer discounts on new-for-old policies for people aged more than 50 (see Box) so it is worth shopping around and asking whether any discount is available.

Q *If I lost all my belongings in a fire, say, I wouldn't want to replace all of them. Can I just insure those items which I would want to replace?*

A No. Buildings and contents insurance work on the basis that you need to be covered for the total replacement if, respectively, your entire house or all its contents were destroyed. If you are insured for less – called **under-insurance** – your insurer may pay only a proportion of any amount you claim even if the claim is just for a single item.

HOUSE INSURANCE SPECIAL DEALS FOR THE OVER-50S

Over 50
Buildings insurance: Bank of Scotland, Eagle Star
Contents insurance: Swinton, GAN Minster, Royal, Prudential

Over 55
Buildings insurance: Royal
Contents insurance: SAGA

Over 60
Buildings insurance: Prospero
Contents insurance: Provincial
Buildings and contents combined: Age Concern

Source: *Which?*, September 1993
For details, contact your local branch or an insurance broker.

Q *Trying to work out the value of everything we own is a daunting prospect. Is there any easier way of deciding how much to insure for?*

A Traditional house contents policies work on a **sum insured** basis. This means you must work out what your possessions are worth and buy the appropriate amount of cover. But nowadays you can instead buy a **bedroom-rated** policy. With this, the amount of cover and the cost are determined by the number of bedrooms in your home. However, there is a maximum level of cover according to the size and type of home you have (e.g. four-bedroom, detached), so you should make sure that the limit is high enough to provide you with adequate cover. Similarly, you should check that you are not paying for more cover than you need. In other words, there is no escape from making at least a rough estimate of the value of all your possessions.

Q *Is it a good idea to choose a combined house buildings and contents policy or better to go for separate policies?*

A Policies which combine buildings and contents insurance can make claiming easier because there is no dispute over which policy covers a given item. But combined policies may not be the cheapest option, so check out separate policies too before you decide.

Q *I'm just in the process of buying a flat and the building society seems to have arranged insurance for it. Do I have to go along with their choice or can I arrange my own building insurance? (I can get a discounted policy through work.)*

A It is very common for a mortgage lender to arrange buildings insurance for the mortgaged property (and sometimes contents insurance too). The mortgage lender earns commission from the insurance company by doing this and you should not assume that the policy selected is necessarily the best for you. It may be a condition of your mortgage package that you accept the lender's choice of insurer; if not, you can choose your own instead and you may be able to get a better deal elsewhere. But watch out for an 'administration fee' – many lenders charge one if you arrange your own buildings insurance. They say it is to cover the expenses of checking that the policy you choose is adequate. The fee may be a one-off charge or may be made on an annual basis and you will need to take it into account when comparing costs.

Q *My insurer is insisting that I fit locking bolts to all the exterior doors of my house before it will renew my contents insurance. I already have mortise locks and ordinary bolts. Do I have to do what they say?*

A In some parts of Britain (especially in urban areas) insurance companies do insist that you have certain minimum levels of security before they will insure you. They may also do this if you have particularly valuable possessions or equipment for a home-based business. A company is entitled to set these conditions and, if you are not happy with them, you may have little option but to switch to another company. With some insurers, if you improve security above the minimum they specify – e.g. by fitting deadlocks and security bolts, or a burglar alarm, or by becoming a member of a Neighbourhood

Watch scheme – you can earn a discount, usually ranging from 5 to 15 per cent.

Q *With my car insurance, I get a discount by agreeing to pay the first part of any claim myself. Are there similar discounts with house insurance?*

A Yes, some buildings and contents insurers offer a discount for this type of agreement, called a **voluntary excess**. Discounts generally range from 5 to 20 per cent depending on the amount of the excess. But watch out if your policy already has a **compulsory excess**, i.e. an amount of any claim which you yourself *must* pay. The voluntary excess will be *additional* to the compulsory excess.

Q *When we were decorating, my husband knocked a can of paint all over our nearly-new carpet. We tried to claim on our insurance, but the company has refused to pay up. What are our rights?*

A Most contents policies include a basic amount of **accidental damage** cover for certain items such as television sets. But accidental damage cover for all items – or for other specified items – is generally an option for which you pay extra. Unless you have taken up this option, it is unlikely that you are covered for the damage caused by the paint spill.

Q *What is 'all-risks' cover?*

A All-risks cover – sometimes called **personal possessions cover** – is a common extension to a house contents policy. It applies to your belongings while they are outside the home, paying out if they are accidentally lost or damaged. You will usually need to pay extra for all-risks cover for valuable items.

Q *My home was burgled and I claimed on my house insurance, but the company has refused to pay up, saying that I should have told them that I'd made a claim on my previous policy. But it was a genuine mistake – I forgot to tell them. Shouldn't they pay up?*

A Your insurers are within their rights. Any insurance company can refuse a claim if you have not told them all the facts which are relevant to their decision about whether or not to insure you and how much cover they will give you. It is not always easy to know what facts insurers will consider are relevant, so industry rules require them to ask clear questions and they must point out that your policy can be cancelled if you fail to disclose relevant information.

Q *I've had to make ten claims on my house insurance over the last five years. They were all genuine and each time the company paid up very promptly, but now it is refusing to renew my cover because of my poor claims record. I've tried several other companies but they all say the same. How can I find a company which will insure me?*

A Yours is not an isolated case. Insurers are in business to make money and it is up to them whom they choose to insure. But the practice of 'cherry-picking' – choosing the good-risk customers and refusing the bad – means that some people are finding it very hard or even impossible to get cover. To make matters worse, if your insurer refuses to renew your cover, you must declare this on future application forms. All you can do is shop around. The British Insurance and Investment Brokers Association (BIIBA) can give you a list of brokers who might be able to help (see Addresses section). Also, if you are in paid employment, see if your trade union or professional association has any special deals with insurance companies.

Q *Three years ago, I discovered that my terraced house has a subsidence problem. I had to have it underpinned and thankfully insurance covered the £30,000 bill. But, since then, my buildings insurance premiums have soared. I now pay nearly £2,000 a year. I've tried switching insurer but no one else will touch me. What can I do?*

A When insurers first introduced cover for subsidence, it wasn't thought to be a big problem but, in recent years, it's turned out to be a major cause of claims. In response, insurers have raised premiums and imposed heavy excesses on subsidence claims and are increasingly reluctant to insure houses which have suffered from subsidence. *Which?*

has called for insurers to establish a common approach to evaluating subsidence repairs and to treat properties equally, where it can be shown that a repaired house is at no greater risk than a house which has never had subsidence problems. But, until that happens, there's little you can do except to carry on shopping around (see previous Question).

Q *My house is insured for £160,000 but I reckon its market price is only £125,000, judging by similar properties in the road. Why can't I reduce the insured value and save on premiums?*

A The value you need to insure your home for is not based on its market value but on the cost of clearing the site and rebuilding the home using similar materials in the event of its destruction. The Royal Institute of Chartered Surveyors (RICS) produces tables giving a guide to the insurance value for different homes. You can get details from the Association for British Insurers (ABI) (see Addresses section).

Q *According to my broker, house insurance premiums will go up this year because of something called IPT. What is this?*

A 'IPT' stands for **insurance premium tax**. This is a new tax introduced by the government in the November 1993 Budget. It comes into effect from October 1994 and adds 2.5 per cent to the premiums of most non-investment insurance policies, e.g. house insurance and car insurance.

Income from your home

Q *My soon-to-be wife has a two-bedroomed house which we won't need when we're married and we've decided to let it. She wrote to her mortgage company to check that this was o.k. and they've written back demanding £175 to 'administer the letting'. As our solicitor has already drawn up the lease agreement we feel we don't need the company's services. Must we pay?*

A The charge by the mortgage company is to cover the work involved in checking that the lease agreement does not jeopardise its rights and in altering the original mortgage contract, not for drawing up the lease. The lender is within its rights to make such a charge, a common one in this situation. Some lenders make a one-off charge, others increase the rate of interest on the mortgage.

Q *We've moved to another city for work reasons but haven't been able to sell our old flat, so we've decided to let it out instead. We've put it in the hands of a managing agent who'll find tenants and arrange maintenance and so on. How will our income from the letting be taxed?*

A It will be treated as investment income and taxed at your highest rate of income tax. But you can deduct certain allowable expenses, such as the fee charged by the managing agent. Other expenses which can be deducted include:

- cost of repairs, decoration
- water rates, ground rent (or feu duty in Scotland), council tax if you are paying this (normally, the tenants pay the council tax)
- interest on a loan to buy or improve the property
- rent you pay, if the property is sublet
- management expenses
- advertising costs, estate agents' fees
- cost of house insurance
- legal fees for renewing leases
- either the cost of buying equipment for the upkeep of the property as the costs are incurred or capital allowances (see page 75).

If the flat is furnished, you can also claim:

- heating, lighting and tenants' phone bills, if you pay these
- cost of preparing an inventory
- either the cost of replacing furnishings and fixtures as the costs arise or as 10 per cent of the rent (less service charges and water rates) as a depreciation allowance.

You will be taxed on a current-year basis with tax payable on 1 January or, possibly, through PAYE. For example, rental income received in 1994–5 is payable on 1 January 1995. This will usually entail estimating your rental income after expenses for the full tax year.

If you and your wife pay tax at different rates, you might consider changing your shares of ownership in the flat and the income from it (see page 13).

Q *I've bought a bungalow in a holiday village which I'll use several times a year but plan to let during most of the holiday season. When will I have to pay tax on the rents I get?*

A There are three main situations when income from letting a property will be taxed as if it were business earnings, rather than as outlined in the previous question. These are:

- if you run a guest house
- if you run a hotel
- if you let furnished holiday property and the property is available for commercial letting for at least 140 days in any 12 months and it is actually let for 70 or more of those days. There is a further condition that for seven months out of any 12 it must not be let to the same tenant for more than 31 days at a stretch.

See pages 68–77 for information about how businesses are taxed. But note that if you are starting up a new business you will be taxed on a current-year basis (see page 71).

Q *I'm thinking of taking in a lodger as a way of earning some extra cash. How will the rent I get be taxed and can I deduct extra money I spend on heating and lighting because of the lodger?*

A You have a choice. You can opt for the **rent-a-room scheme**. Under this, you can receive up to £3,250 a year (£271 a month) from renting a room in your home without having to pay any tax at all on that income. But you cannot also claim tax relief for expenditure on extra fuel and so on. The scheme is not limited to home-owners – tenants can use it too (though they will need permission from their landlord before they sublet a room). Alternatively, you can choose to have all the rental income taxed, in which case you will be able to deduct expenses.

Q *If I use the rent-a-room scheme, what happens if I provide my lodger with meals?*

A Any payment you receive for meals must be added to the amount you get in rents and counts towards the £3,250 a year limit.

Q *Can I rent out more than one room under the rent-a-room scheme?*

A Yes, but the limit of £3,250 a year applies to the total rents you get from all the lettings.

Q *I had planned to use the rent-a-room scheme, but last year the rents I received came to £5,000 – well above the limit for the scheme. Does this mean I'll have to pay tax on the full £5,000?*

A You have a choice. You can either:

- have the first £3,250 of the rental income under the rent-a-room scheme, i.e. tax-free, but you will have to pay tax at your top rate on the income above this without being able to deduct any expenses. This means you'd be taxed on £5,000 – £3,250 = £1,750; or
- you can have the full amount treated as taxable, in which case you can deduct any allowable expenses (see page 135 for a list of the main ones).

If you have high expenses – in your case, more than £3,250 – it would be worth choosing the second option. But if your expenses are less than this stay with the rent-a-room scheme and pay tax just on the excess. You have up to one year after the end of the tax year in which the rental incomes were due to let the Inland Revenue know which option you have chosen.

Q *If I let out my home, will I have to pay tax when I eventually sell the home?*

A If you take in lodgers who have their own room but otherwise share your home with you and your family, there is no tax problem when you come to sell: the normal exemption from capital gains tax (CGT) for a home still applies. But, in other cases where you let part of your home, or if you let a second or holiday home, there may be CGT to pay when the property is sold.

LETTING PROPERTY OR PART OF YOUR HOME

For more information see the following leaflets:

- IR87 *Rooms to Let: income from letting property*
- CGT4 *Capital Gains Tax – Owner-occupied Houses*
- Department of Environment *Want to Take in a Lodger?*
- Department of Environment *Letting Rooms in Your Home.*

The first two are available from tax offices, the second two from Citizens Advice Bureaux. You may also find all these leaflets in your local public library.

The tax treatment of let property is discussed in greater detail in *Which? Way to Save Tax*, published by Consumers' Association (see Addresses section). See also *The Which? Guide to Renting and Letting* (also from Consumers' Association).

Q *I'm retired and on a very tight income. The only thing of any value which I own is my home. Is there any way that I can increase my income without having to resort to taking in lodgers?*

A Provided you have reached at least 70, say, you could consider a **home income plan**. With these, you take out an interest-only mortgage on your home and use the proceeds to buy an **annuity** (see page 227). The annuity pays you an income for life. Part of each income payment is used to pay the interest on the mortgage, the rest boosts your income. When you die, the mortgage is paid out of your estate – which may mean the house then has to be sold. Interest on a mortgage up to £30,000 used as part of a home income scheme qualifies for tax relief at the basic rate of tax, and provided the mortgage is paid through the Mortgage Interest Relief at Source (MIRAS) scheme – and most are – you will get the tax relief even if you are a non-taxpayer. (Under MIRAS, you pay interest with the tax relief already deducted.) Part of the income from the annuity counts as interest and is taxable at your top rate, the rest is deemed to be return of capital and is not taxable. Usually, the annuity is paid with tax at the basic rate already deducted but, if you are a non-taxpayer, you can arrange to have the annuity income paid gross.

To find out about home income schemes, contact an independent financial adviser (see pages 236–41) and always get a solicitor to check the details before you decide to go ahead.

Q *Aren't home income schemes terribly risky? I remember reading about elderly people who lost their life savings through such schemes.*

A A traditional home income plan combines a fixed-rate mortgage with an annuity producing a fixed income. This is a very sound arrangement because you know precisely how much of the extra income will be used to pay the mortgage interest and this relationship does not vary.

However, there have been a number of variations on this theme, with schemes using:

- variable-rate mortgages, so you cannot be sure how much income will be taken up by interest on the loan
- mortgages for which the interest is not paid, or not paid in full, but 'rolled up' and added to the outstanding loan, the result being that the capital owed increases at an alarming rate
- stock market-linked bonds to produce income rather than annuities: this means that the income you get rises and falls and could fall so far that it is not sufficient to meet the interest on the mortgage.

All these variations add considerable risk to the schemes and are best avoided. Stick to a traditional home income plan.

Q *Why do I need to be at least 70 before I can consider a home income scheme?*

A The income from a lifetime annuity is higher the older you are. Below the age of 70, the income you would get would not usually be high enough to meet the interest on the mortgage and still leave you with a reasonable addition to your income.

Q *What happens if I take out a home income scheme, but then decide to move?*

A If you move home, you will have to repay the mortgage. The annuity will not be affected.

Q *Is a 'home reversion scheme' the same as a home income plan?*

A No. With a **home reversion scheme**, you actually sell part of your home but retain the right to carry on living there until your death (or the death of both you and your husband or wife). You can use the proceeds to buy an annuity, but that is up to you – you can use the money in any way you choose. Note that with a home reversion scheme any increase in the value of that part of the home which you sold accrues to the company to which you sold it rather than to you.

Q *Will taking out a home income plan or home reversion scheme affect my other income?*

A It could do. If you are receiving any means-tested state benefits, such as income support or housing benefit, your benefit will probably be reduced if you start to get income from one of these schemes or if your capital increases to above £3,000. Note that state retirement pension is *not* a means-tested benefit and will not be affected.

The extra income from a home income scheme or home reversion plan could also disproportionately affect the income tax you pay, if you are getting **age allowance** (see page 144).

CHAPTER 5

DAY-TO-DAY FINANCES

WE ARE all expected to have working knowledge of personal finance – coping with tax returns, running a bank account, handling loans, and so on. Although you have no choice about the tax system imposed on you, a knowledge of the rules can save you money. With other aspects of day-to-day finances, it is often tempting to settle for the first current account or plastic card which comes along. But a greater understanding of the range available and a little time spent shopping around can save you a small fortune and ensure that you avoid the pitfalls. And if your day-to-day finances *do* get out of hand, it is essential that you get help quickly.

Tax basics

Q *How can I check that I'm paying the correct amount of income tax?*

A The basic calculation is very straightforward. For a given tax year:

- add up all your before-tax income, e.g. earnings from a job, profits from a business, income from investments. But do not include any tax-free income – see Box
- deduct any **outgoings**: these are payments you make which qualify for tax relief – such as covenant payments to charity. Deduct the **gross** value of the outgoings – i.e. the amount before any tax relief is taken into account. Mortgage interest on a loan up to £30,000 is also an outgoing, but relief is restricted to 20 per cent in 1994–5 and 15 per cent from April 1995
- deduct any **allowances** you qualify for: everyone gets a personal allowance, but there are others you might get too – see Table 5.1.

Note that, with some, the tax relief they give you is limited to 20 per cent in 1994–5 and 15 per cent in 1995–6

- the answer you are left with is your **taxable income**: in 1994–5, the first £3,000 of this is taxed at the lower rate of 20 per cent; the next £20,700 is taxed at the basic rate of 25 per cent; anything over £23,700 is taxed at the higher rate of 40 per cent.

In practice, there are a number of complications which you may need to take into account when calculating your tax bill, so it is a good idea to use a special calculator or a computer program, such as the annual *Which? Tax-saving Guide* (free to *Which?* subscribers) or the *Which? TaxCalc* program, both published by Consumers' Association.

TAX-FREE INCOME

The main types of tax-free income include:
- the first £70 of interest from a National Savings ordinary account
- proceeds from National Savings Certificates
- interest from National Savings Children's Bonus Bonds
- part of the income from most annuities (see page 227)
- proceeds from Save-As-You-Earn contracts
- proceeds from a personal equity plan (PEP)
- proceeds from a tax-exempt special savings account (TESSA)
- proceeds from some friendly society savings schemes
- income from family income benefit life insurance policies (see page 30)
- many social security benefits
- housing benefit and council tax benefit
- a few special state pensions, including the £10 Christmas bonus
- most grants or scholarships for education
- some earnings from working abroad
- some job-related fringe benefits (see page 58)
- usually, up to £30,000 of redundancy pay
- certain profit-related pay
- strike and unemployment pay from a trade union
- interest on a tax rebate.

Table 5.1: Income tax allowances for the 1994–5 tax year

Allowance	Amount £
Personal allowance	3,445
Personal age allowance – 64 to 73[1]	4,200
Personal age allowance – 74 or over[1]	4,370
Married couple's allowance[2]	1,720
Married couple's age allowance – 64 to 73[1,2]	2,665
Married couple's age allowance – 74 or over[1,2]	2,705
Additional personal allowance[2]	1,720
Widow's bereavement allowance[2]	1,720
Blind person's allowance	1,200

[1] Age at the start of the tax year.
[2] Gives tax relief only at 20 per cent.

Q *What's a tax year?*

A A tax year runs from 6 April one year to 5 April the next.

Q *I'm 62 and was widowed last year. While my husband was alive, I'd never been a taxpayer and I've never received a tax return. Is it likely that I'll have to pay tax now?*

A You will need to work through your tax position as set out on page 141 to determine this. For the tax year in which your husband died, and for the following year, you qualify for **widow's bereavement allowance** (see Table 5.1) as well as your normal personal allowance. Together, these may be enough to keep you below the tax threshold. In the following year, you will no longer get the bereavement allowance and possibly some of your income will then become taxable. You should get in touch with your tax office, which will probably send you a tax return to complete. If you have problems doing this, contact a local tax enquiry centre (see Inland Revenue in phone book), which will be able to give you advice and help in completing the form.

Q *I'll reach 60 next year, when I'll get my state pension. Will I also qualify for age allowance to set against my income tax?*

143

A No, not yet. Age allowance is a higher personal allowance which you can get from the start of the tax year in which you reach age 65. There are two rates of age allowance: one for people aged 64–73 at the start of the tax year, and a higher rate for people aged 74 or over at the start of the tax year (see Table 5.1). But, if your **total income** (basically income less outgoings) is more than a given limit – £14,200 in 1994–5 – you will lose £1 of age allowance for every £2 of excess income until the allowance is reduced to the normal personal allowance of £3,445 in 1994–5. This means that you will effectively pay tax at a rate of 37.5 per cent on extra income if your total income lies in the band where age allowance is affected: i.e., for 1994–5, total income of £14,200 to £15,710 if you are aged 64–73 at the start of the tax year, or £14,200 to £16,050 if you are older.

Q *My birthday is on 5 April. When will I start to get age allowance?*

A Age allowance is paid from the *start* of the tax year in which you reach age 65. Even though your birthday is on the very last day of the tax year, you will still get age allowance from the beginning – so, for example, if you will be 65 on 5 April 1995, you will start to receive age allowance from 6 April 1994.

Q *Will our married couple's age allowance also be affected if our income is above a given level?*

A Yes. If either husband or wife is aged 65 or over during the tax year, they qualify for married couple's age allowance (see page 14 and Table 5.1). Unlike the personal age allowance, married couple's age allowance only gives tax relief of 20 per cent in 1994–5 and 15 per cent from 6 April 1995. But, in just the same way as the personal age allowance, the married couple's age allowance is reduced by £1 for every £2 by which the total income of the person receiving the allowance (usually the husband) exceeds a given limit – £14,200 in 1994–5. This goes on until the allowance is reduced to the normal married couple's allowance of £1,720 in 1994–5.

Q *Both my wife and I are in the position of losing part of our age allowance because our incomes are over the limit. Is there any way we can keep up our incomes but still retain the extra allowance?*

A Income which is tax-free does not count towards the limit for age allowance. Therefore, consider investments such as National Savings Certificates or tax-exempt special savings accounts (TESSAs – see page 209). And do watch out if you cash in an investment-type life insurance policy: although there is no basic-rate tax to pay on this, if the policy is a **non-qualifying** one (see page 233 for what this means), the proceeds will count as income towards the age allowance limit.

Another way in which you might be able to reduce your **total income** – this means income less outgoings – is to use covenants or gift aid if you would in any case be making donations to charity. See pages 205–6 for more about these schemes.

Q *I'm about to cash in a life insurance bond. Will there be any tax to pay on the proceeds?*

A Presumably the bond is a non-qualifying policy (see page 233). In this case, while there will be no basic-rate tax to pay on the proceeds, there might be a higher-rate tax bill if adding the proceeds to your other income for the tax year pushes you into the higher-rate tax band. However, you may be able to claim **top-slicing relief**. To do this, divide the proceeds of the policy by the number of complete years for which the policy has run (or sometimes fewer years if, for example, you had cashed in part of the policy earlier). This gives you the annual average gain on the policy. Add it to your other income for the year and, treating it as the top slice of your income, work out how much tax would be due on the average gain. If only basic- or lower-rate tax would be due, there will be no tax at all to pay on the policy proceeds. If part or all of the average gain is liable for higher-rate tax, multiply the tax due by the number of years for which the policy has run. This tells you the total tax due on the policy proceeds. You will need to ask the Inland Revenue to treat your policy proceeds in this way – it will not be done automatically.

Q *Should everyone receive a tax return?*

A No. You will usually be sent a tax return if you are self-employed, have substantial investment income or your tax affairs are complicated in some other way. But if your affairs are reasonably straightforward you will probably not get one.

SELF-ASSESSMENT OF TAX

Following proposals in the November 1993 Budget, it is planned that, from the 1996–7 tax year onwards, you will be able to calculate your own income tax and capital gains tax. You will have to send your tax office the completed tax return and your calculations by 31 January following the end of the relevant tax year. The Inland Revenue will have a year in which to raise any queries. If you do not want to work out your own tax, you will be able to send back your tax return earlier and ask the Revenue to work out the tax for you, as now.

Q *I've been getting an income from some National Savings income bonds but I've never paid tax on them. I pay basic-rate tax on the rest of my income. Should I tell my tax office about the bonds?*

A Yes. You are bound by law to give the tax authorities all relevant information about your tax position, and there are time limits within which you must declare income and gains and claim allowances. If you are sent a tax return, you should give all the details on this. If not, contact your tax office. If you do not know where your office is, ask your employer (if you are in a job), check your records (if you are self-employed) or, failing that, contact your local tax office (see phone book under Inland Revenue). If you are working and you do not owe too much tax, the amount due may be collected through the PAYE system (see page 52). Otherwise, you will be sent a Notice of Assessment demanding payment within 30 days or by a specified date. You may be charged interest on the unpaid tax.

Q *I've been sent a Notice of Assessment but I don't agree with the Revenue's figures. They've over-estimated the income I'll get from my consultancy work this year. Do I have to pay the tax they're asking for even though I know it will turn out to be too much?*

A You should appeal against the assessment. You have 30 days from the date of the Notice within which to do this. You must simultaneously ask to postpone payment of the amount of tax which is in dispute. Do this either on the form provided with the Notice of Assessment or in a letter setting out your reasons for the appeal and postponement and your own estimate of the correct amount of tax. If the Inland Revenue agrees with you, they will send a Notice of Amended Assessment. If they do not agree, you will have to pay the amount of tax originally asked for and wait until after the end of the tax year to claim back any overpaid tax. If you miss the 30-day deadline, go ahead and make the appeal anyway. The Revenue has discretion to accept appeals made late for valid reasons – for example, if you were away from home when the Notice of Assessment arrived.

Q *I've discovered that I could have been claiming the additional personal allowance for the last three years. Can I backdate a claim now?*

A Yes, you can go back up to six tax years and revise the amount of tax if you discover a mistake or an allowance you have failed to claim. For example, if you tell your tax office before 6 April 1995, you can go back to the tax year beginning 6 April 1988. Write to your tax office which will probably send you a form to complete. Send this back and a refund cheque should arrive soon after. If the refund is made more than 12 months after the end of the tax year for which tax was overpaid, you may receive some interest as well.

Q *I'm a non-taxpayer, but I've been paying tax on my building society account and on dividends from a small number of shares which I own. How can I get the tax back?*

A Complete form R40, which you can get from your tax office. Send this to your tax office together with the tax credits you have received with the dividends and a statement of interest paid from the building society. You do not have to wait until the end of the tax year to reclaim tax, but claims for less than £50 worth of tax will not be processed until the end of the year or until your claims exceed £50.

For the future, you can register to receive the building society interest (and any bank interest) **gross** – i.e. without tax having been deducted – provided you expect to be a non-taxpayer throughout the tax year. You do this by filling in form R85, available from banks, building societies and tax offices. Hand the completed form to your building society. If it turns out that you do have to pay tax after all, you will need to declare the gross income you've received.

Q *I know there's no tax to pay on the proceeds of selling my home, but do I still have to tell my tax office about the sale?*

A Capital gains tax (CGT) may be charged when you dispose of something and make a profit on it. But various assets and transactions are exempt from capital gains tax (CGT) – see Box. These include (usually) your only or main home. However, if you receive a tax return, you will be asked to give details about the sale of your home.

TAX-FREE CAPITAL GAINS

Gains on some assets and transactions are free from CGT. This also means that you cannot offset losses on them against gains on other assets. Items on which gains are tax-free include:

- gifts between husband and wife
- your only or main home
- private motor cars
- personal belongings and household goods with a predictable useful life of no more than 50 years
- National Savings Certificates, Yearly Plan, premium bonds, capital bonds and Save-As-You-Earn contracts
- foreign currency for your personal use
- betting winnings
- British Government stocks
- investments held through a PEP

- shares issued under a Business Expansion Scheme and held for at least five years
- damages for a wrong or injury (e.g. for assault or defamation)
- gifts to charities and certain national institutions
- gifts of **heritage property** – e.g. land, buildings, books or works of art judged to be of special interest – to a non-profit-making body approved by the government
- everything you leave on death.

Q *I've just sold some unit trusts at a substantial profit. How can I work out whether there's any tax to pay on the sale?*

A To work out whether there is any CGT to pay on an asset you have disposed of:

- take the **final value** – e.g. the sale proceeds
- deduct the **initial value** – i.e. what you paid for the asset or its market value at the time you acquired it
- deduct any **allowable expenses** – these are costs incurred as a result of acquiring or disposing of the asset, e.g. broker's commission, solicitors' fees, etc.
- deduct **indexation allowance** – profits you make purely because of inflation are not taxed, so you are allowed to increase the initial value and each allowable expense by an indexation factor. Adding the results together gives you the indexation allowance. This allowance can reduce – or even wipe out – your gain for tax purposes. In the past, indexation allowances could also create a loss. But from 6 April 1995 this will not be allowed. From 30 November 1994 until that date, such losses may not exceed £10,000
- deduct any **allowable losses** made on other assets.

The result is your chargeable gain or loss. But there may still be no tax to pay, because, you can make a certain amount of chargeable gains each year – £5,800 in 1994–5 – without having to pay any CGT on them.

Q *If I give my daughter a valuable oil painting, will I have to pay any capital gains tax?*

A Maybe. CGT may be payable whenever you *dispose* of an asset. 'Disposal' doesn't just mean selling an asset, it also includes giving it away or even losing it.

MORE INFORMATION ABOUT TAX

The Inland Revenue publishes a wide range of explanatory leaflets about income tax and CGT which are available from tax offices and also some public libraries. They include:

IR37 *Income Tax and Capital Gains Tax: Appeals*

IR80 *Income Tax and Married Couples*

IR90 *A Guide to Tax Allowances and Reliefs*

IR110 *A Guide for People with Savings*

IR114 *TESSA: Tax-free Interest for Taxpayers*

IR120 *You and the Inland Revenue*

IR121 *Income Tax and Pensioners*

IR127 *Are You Paying Too Much Tax on Your Savings?*

CGT4 *Capital Gains Tax – Owner-occupied Houses*

CGT14 *Capital Gains Tax – an Introduction*

CGT15 *Capital Gains Tax – a Guide for Married Couples*

CGT16 *Capital Gains Tax – Indexation Allowance.*

For a more detailed look at how tax affects you, see *Which? Way to Save Tax*, published by Consumers' Association.

Banking

Q *I've been with the same bank for years, but my wife says I should at least look at what other banks offer. Is there any point – aren't all banks much the same?*

A If your present bank meets your needs and you are happy with the service it offers, then you should probably stay with it. But your wife is right – not only is there a big range of different types of accounts these days, but *Which?* surveys have also found that customers are more satisfied with some banks than others. The other main difference between accounts is the charges made if you go overdrawn. The account you choose should match your needs: for example, if you are frequently slightly overdrawn, choose an account with a free or cheap overdraft facility; if you sometimes need to borrow large sums, choose an account which charges only interest, not fees, on agreed overdrafts.

Q *At one time, most banks paid interest on their current accounts if you were in credit. Do any still do this?*

A Yes, a lot of current accounts still pay interest, but the rate is generally very low, e.g. only a few £ £ a year on an average balance of £500. This is better than nothing, but it is sensible to make sure you that you do not keep any more than you need to in your current account and transfer any excess promptly to a savings account where it can earn a higher return.

Q *I asked at my bank branch for a list of current charges and was told that they don't produce one. I can't believe this. Surely they must tell you the price of what they offer just like any other retailer?*

A The Code of Banking Practice (see Box) says that banks and building societies must provide customers with a tariff of charges at any time on request. It is important to know what charges your bank does make and to check your statement carefully – a *Which?* survey in 1993 found that one in eight of the people surveyed had been incorrectly charged by their bank. In the past very few banks notified you in advance of charges they intended to make in connection with your current account (unless you were a business user), but this is changing slowly. The Code requires *all* banks to give customers at least 14 days' notice of charges by December 1996.

THE CODE OF BANKING PRACTICE

The Code of Banking Practice, introduced on 16 March 1992, sets minimum standards for the way in which banks, building societies and plastic card companies conduct business with their personal customers. The banks and societies had two years in which to implement the Code or adopt higher standards. Unfortunately, there is evidence that banks and societies are still not always offering the standard of service which customers have a right to expect. For a free copy of the Code of Banking Practice, called *Good Banking*, ask at bank* or building society branches* or write to the British Bankers' Association or the Building Societies' Association (see Address section).

* Bank and building society branches may offer you their own version of the Code.

Q *The maintenance cheque from my ex-husband bounced last month and my bank charged me £4. It's bad enough that I have to manage without the maintenance but why should I have to pay for the privilege?*

A Banks often charge for 'extras' which you might consider should be a normal part of the service. But practice does vary from bank to bank. In 1993, common services for which charges might be made were:

- bouncing a cheque you paid in – often nil (but could be £3 or £4)
- cashing a cheque at a branch other than your own – often nil (but could be up to £5)
- list of your direct debits and standing orders – often nil (but could be as much as £8)
- banker's reference – often nil (but could be as much as £20)
- stopping a cheque you wrote – up to £10
- duplicate statement – £3–£5.

Q *What's the difference between a standing order and a direct debit?*

A A **standing order** is an agreement which you have with your bank authorising it to make regular payments from your account to a specified person or organisation. A **direct debit** is an agreement which you have with an organisation authorising it to take regular payments from your account. You do this on a special form called a **direct debit mandate**: the organisation presents this to your bank, which will then honour the demands for payment. With a **variable direct debit** the organisation can alter the amount of money it will take, but must give you six weeks' notice of any change. With both standing orders and direct debits, you are reliant on your bank to administer them efficiently and it is sensible to check that payments have been correctly made each time you receive a statement.

Q *My bank refused to cash me a cheque for £200, but I'd paid £400 in cash into the bank the day before. The bank says the £400 hadn't cleared, but isn't cash credited to an account instantly?*

A With most banks and building societies, cash is credited to your account the same working day, provided you pay it into any branch of your own bank or society. But a few of the major banks only do this if you pay cash into the branch which holds your account. If you use another branch, the money takes up to three working days to clear. When you pay in money by cheque, it usually takes three to four working days to clear.

Q *I had a letter from my bank telling me that I was overdrawn. Yet in the same post I received a bank statement showing that my account was in the black to the tune of £600. Despite my complaints, the bank still insists that I was overdrawn. Why can't they believe their own evidence?*

A The balance which most banks show on statements is the **uncleared** balance. This may include cheques, transfers and cash recently paid in though not yet cleared. But the balance used to decide whether or not you are overdrawn is usually the **cleared** balance, which excludes recent credits.

Q *My husband was out of work for a time. He's got a job again now, but we have a backlog of debts including a £600 overdraft. It's depressing to see £94 (interest of £39, a service charge of £36 and account charges of £19) vanish in quarterly charges on this. Is there any way to reduce the charges?*

A Talk to your bank manager. You may be able to take out a personal loan (see page 163) to cover your debt to the bank. In this way, you would avoid the service and account charges and would only have to pay the interest and loan repayments – but make sure that the bank will not charge you for giving you this advice. You may also find it helpful to get some independent advice about your debts (see page 172). For the future, avoid unauthorised overdrafts – you will pay a lot less if you arrange an overdraft first (see next question) – and consider switching to one of the few remaining accounts which does not charge an overdraft fee (service charge) if you are overdrawn.

Q *A few months ago I arranged an overdraft which I have since repaid. More recently, I went accidentally overdrawn for a week or so and was charged nearly twice as much. Surely bank charges haven't risen that steeply over such a short space of time?*

A If you arrange to have an overdraft, you may have to pay some or all of these charges:

- interest calculated on a daily basis
- possibly, an arrangement fee
- overdraft fees on a monthly or quarterly basis – these can range from nil up to about £30 a quarter
- possibly, transaction charges for some or all of the items credited and paid out of your account, e.g. 10–50p per item. These will be charged for the whole charging period (i.e. a month or a quarter) even if you are in credit for most of that period.

If you take an **unauthorised overdraft** – i.e. you did not arrange it with your bank in advance – you may have to pay these charges:

- interest at a higher rate than that charged on an arranged overdraft
- overdraft fees at a higher level than for an arranged overdraft
- transaction charges as described above
- a fee for any warning letters sent to you by the bank, e.g. £20 a letter
- a fee for each **returned item**, i.e. each cheque or other payment you try to make which the bank refuses to honour. In 1993, this was often as much as £11 to £27.50 an item.

Obviously an unauthorised overdraft will work out a lot more expensive than one you arrange in advance. If you frequently dip into the red, switch to an account which allows you to have a small overdraft either free or at low cost.

Q *I've found a current account which would suit my banking needs better than my present account. How do I go about transferring from one to the other?*

A Follow these steps:

- open the new account (the new bank may ask you to sign an **authority to transfer** which enables it to deal directly with your old bank, but you can keep closer control over the transfer if you *don't* sign)
- choose the date, at least five weeks away, on which you want the transfer to take effect
- switch any regular payments you receive: e.g. write to your employer giving details of the new account and the date from which it is to be used. Keep copies of all correspondence
- get a list of your direct debits and standing orders from your old bank. Send a signed list of the standing orders to your new bank with instructions to pay them from the transfer date onwards. Ask your old bank to cancel all the standing orders from that date
- write to everyone that you pay by direct debit requesting a new direct debit mandate form. Complete and return these stressing the date from which they are to take effect. Write to your old bank confirming that no more direct debits are to be paid from the transfer date onwards.

From the transfer date, use only your new account. Leave enough in the old account to cover any outstanding payments and, once you are sure that there are no more, close the old account.

Q *The National Savings investment account always used to be recommended for children, but it will be ages before my son has the £20 needed as a minimum deposit. Are there any accounts with a lower bottom limit?*

A Yes, many banks and building societies have accounts specifically designed for children and with minimum balances as low as £1 (see page 25). However, the return on bank and building society accounts for children is generally a lot lower than that available on the National Savings investment account, so it could be worth switching to this once your child has built up enough.

Q *Is it illegal to write a post-dated cheque?*

A No, writing a cheque with some future date on it is not illegal, but you will not be popular with your bank if you make a habit of using them. If a post-dated cheque is deposited before the date written on it, the bank may not notice the date, so a post-dated cheque can easily slip through and be paid early. If your bank does pay a post-dated cheque before the due date, it has not carried out your instructions properly and the bank is responsible for any charges that arise as a result of the early payment, so you should complain. But it is better to avoid writing post-dated cheques, or to ask people to whom you give such cheques not to present them until the date on the cheque.

Q *My bank made a mistake and accidentally credited my account with £740 that wasn't mine. I didn't notice at the time and, now the bank is asking me to repay the money, I don't have it. Do I have to pay it back?*

A The bank should not simply recover the money from your account without discussing it with you first. But, unless you can prove that you had good reason to believe that the money paid into the account was yours, you will have to pay it back. Any arrangement for repayment should not entail any expense for you, since it was the bank that was in error. You may be able to arrange to pay back the money in instalments over a period of time

Q *Two crossed cheques were stolen from the back of my cheque book while I was at work. I didn't realise that they had gone until my bank statement showed two withdrawals of £2,000 each which I hadn't made. The cheques carry fraudulent signatures which are very poor copies of mine, but my bank says it acted in good faith and is not responsible for the stolen money. The cheques were paid into an account with a false name and address, so should I try to claim from that bank?*

A Try claiming against both banks saying that you hold them jointly responsible. If they do not accept this, take your case to the Banking Ombudsman – see Box.

DISPUTES WITH BANKS OR BUILDING SOCIETIES

The Code of Banking Practice requires all banks and building societies to have a complaints procedure and to tell customers about it. If you exhaust the bank's or society's procedure and are not satisfied, you can take your case to the appropriate ombudsman (such schemes are free to complainants).

Banks and building societies must provide details of the ombudsman scheme to customers, for example, through leaflets, notices in branches or in appropriate literature. There are separate schemes for banks and for building societies but they work in a similar way. Both will consider the evidence and come to a judgement which is binding on the bank or society, but not you (so you could take the case to court if you are not happy with the ombudsman's decision). Both ombudsmen can make awards for compensation up to £100,000. Note that neither ombudsman can consider disputes relating to a bank's or society's commercial decisions about, for example, interest rates. See Addresses section.

Credit, charge and debit cards

Q *I'm a student and my bank has offered me a credit card. Is a credit card a good idea?*

A You are wise to be wary about taking on debts when you are on a low income. However, you do not have to use a credit card for borrowing and you might find it a useful way of paying for things – though a debit card (see page 161) is just as convenient nowadays.

You can buy goods and obtain cash using a credit card provided you do not exceed your credit limit. Once a month, you will be sent a statement and must pay off at least a minimum sum (usually £5 or 5 per cent of the balance, whichever is the greater). If you pay off the full balance, there will be no interest to pay, but there will be a charge for any cash advances and for many cards there is an annual fee of, say, £10 or £12. Five years ago, annual fees were unknown, but now they are widespread. Exceptions are shown in Table 5.2.

Table 5.2: Credit card issuers which do not charge an annual fee

---

Bank of Cyprus
Bank of Ireland (Northern Ireland)
Barclays (Ford Barclaycard only) – fee waived for first year
Beneficial
Co-operative Bank (Robert Owen card only) – no fee if card used 10 or
    more times a year
First Trust Bank (Northern Ireland)
HFC Bank/Vauxhall (The GM Card)
MBNA International – fee waived for first year, thereafter waived if you
    spend enough
National & Provincial Building Society
Northern Bank (Northern Ireland)
Royal Bank of Scotland (Mastercard only)
Standard Chartered
The Sunday Times
TSB
Ulster Bank (Northern Ireland)
Yorkshire Bank

Source: *MoneyFacts*

Q *Despite having paid off £410 of a £1,410 balance on my credit card account, I was charged £47.94 for the month. How can such high charges be justified?*

A Only part of the £47.94 was interest – £12 was the annual fee which is now charged by your card issuer. The remaining £35.94 is the interest charge. If you do not pay off the whole outstanding balance, you are charged interest on the amount shown on your statement before any part-payment you make is deducted, so in your case the interest was worked out on the full £1,410. And, with your card, interest starts to clock up from the date of each transaction – more expensive than the few credit cards which charge interest only from the statement date, giving you up to 31 days' interest-free credit (see Chart 5.1). If you pay the bill in full, you can get up to 56 days' interest-free credit with most cards.

Chart 5.1: Interest-free credit with credit cards

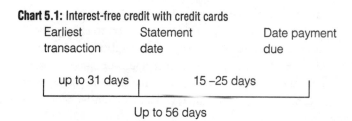

Earliest transaction	Statement date	Date payment due
up to 31 days	15 –25 days	
Up to 56 days		

Q *I'm going touring in the Peak District and want to be able to take out cash as I need it on my credit card. I've heard that there's a way of doing this without having to pay interest. How does it work?*

A Charges for cash advances are made in two ways. With some cards, for example, Barclaycard, you are charged a handling fee which is a percentage of the cash withdrawn. There is no way in which you can avoid this charge.

With some other cards, there is no handling fee but you are charged interest on the cash from the day it is withdrawn. You can avoid this interest, if you pay enough money in advance into your account to cover the intended cash withdrawals, i.e. run a credit balance on your card account.

Q *Three days before the due date, I posted a cheque to pay off part of my credit card account. But the cheque has been credited late and I've been charged a 'late payment fee' of £20. Why should I pay for the company's slow administration?*

A You could try challenging the charge, but the company will probably argue that you should have allowed more time for the cheque to reach it. Most card issuers advise you to allow at least seven working days if you are posting your payment or four working days if you pay it in via a bank. If you pay late, some card issuers levy a penalty charge of up to £20. Others make a charge only if your payment cheque 'bounces' or if you consistently make late payments.

Q *My statement date means that I have to pay off my bill a couple of days before I'm paid, when I never have enough left in my current account. Can I change the date?*

A In the past, statement dates were allocated at random and it was difficult – if not impossible – to persuade card issuers to change them. Nowadays, many card companies let you choose a date to suit you, so ask your card issuer if you can change. If it does not agree, consider changing to another company. This is possible even if you have an outstanding balance, as some companies will let you transfer debts from an existing card.

Q *I cancelled my Access card a couple of months ago, but now I've received an Access bill for renewing my AA membership. I didn't authorise this payment, but Access says I must contact the AA. What's going on?*

A When you joined the AA, you must have paid by credit card and set up a 'continuous authority'. This works like a direct debit arrangement – you instruct the supplier of goods or a service to take payment from your account, and the bank or card issuer will pay the supplier on demand. The continuous authority let the AA bill your initial joining fee to your Access card and also gave it permission to bill the annual renewal fee to your card until further notice. The agreement is between you and the AA – not Access – so, to cancel it, you must tell the AA that the credit card account is now closed and arrange some other means of payment if you want to continue your membership. Until you do this, Access will correctly carry on billing you.

Q *I've been offered free 'purchase protection' with my Visa card. What is it?*

A This is insurance against theft of or accidental damage to purchases you make using your Visa card. The cover is for a limited period only – usually for 90 days after purchase – and may be restricted to items worth more than a given minimum – £50, say. If the cover is free, it may be useful. But, if you had to pay for it, it might not be worthwhile, because the items are likely to be covered anyway under your normal house contents insurance (see page 132).

EXTRA PROTECTION

If you use your *credit* card (but not other types of card) to buy goods or services which turn out to be faulty, the credit card company may be liable as well as the supplier. This means you can claim from the credit card company if the supplier cannot or will not compensate you. See page 176 for more details.

Q *Is a charge card the same as a gold card?*

A Charge cards – the main brands are American Express and Diners Club – work like credit cards except that you must pay off your outstanding balance every month. A penalty charge is levied if you pay the bill late.

Most gold cards are charge cards, but a few work like credit cards (allowing you to pay off only part of your monthly bill). Gold cards often have an overdraft facility that allows you to borrow large sums at lower-than-normal interest rates.

Charge and gold cards have no spending limit but, to qualify, you will usually need to be earning at least £20,000 a year. For most of these cards you pay an annual fee ranging from £25 to £120, depending on the card. But a few either charge no annual fee at all or waive it if certain conditions are met. There is a fee for making cash withdrawals using a charge or gold card, and, usually, for using a charge card to make purchases abroad. Holders may however be entitled to various perks, such as free travel insurance.

With many gold cards, you must agree to pay your monthly bills by direct debit.

Q *What is a debit card?*

A A debit card is essentially a paperless cheque. There are two types in the UK – Visa Delta and Switch. Both work in a similar way. When you pay for something in a shop, the assistant will wipe your debit card through a machine which contacts your bank's computer system to check your current account. Provided there is enough money in the account (including any arranged overdraft limit you have), the bank authorises the transaction and your purchase goes ahead. You can also use a debit card at cash machines or in some shops to withdraw cash from your account. Eventually, the payment or withdrawal may be instantly debited from your account, but at present it takes a few days to be processed.

The main advantage of a debit card over a cheque is that it can be used to pay for items of any value provided the money is in your account, whereas cheques are usually only accepted up to the guarantee limit of £50 or £100.

Q *My new cheque guarantee card is a debit card as well. I don't want a debit card but the bank refuses to send me a simple guarantee card. What can I do?*

A It has become standard practice with most banks to issue customers with one plastic card which has several functions – cheque guarantee, cash and debit card all in one. This is convenient for the banks and they hope it will encourage more customers to switch to using debit cards instead of cheques, which are more costly for the banks to process.

To use the debit card, you must have a personal identification number (PIN). If you do not want the debit facility, then destroy the PIN the bank sends you and tell the bank you do not want the facility – it should ensure that no further PINs are assigned to your account. A few banks, such as Girobank, will still issue a separate cheque guarantee card.

Q *Surely the more functions a plastic card has, the greater the scope for abuse if the card is lost or stolen?*

A Under the Code of Banking Practice the most you can be held liable for, if any plastic card is used to take money without your agreement, is £50. And you are not liable for anything at all if the card is lost or stolen before it ever reaches you. You only lose this protection if the card issuer can prove that you have been 'grossly negligent'.

Q *On my January credit card statement, there was a charge of £50.82 from a shop in Birmingham. I've never even been to Birmingham! After several* *requests, the bank sent me a photocopy of the sales voucher. It had somebody else's number written on it by hand and no name. Every couple of months I get a standard letter saying the bank will contact me when the problem's sorted out. I've refused to pay, but will this affect my credit standing?*

A Quite a lot of people experience these 'phantom debits' – not just with credit cards, but with cash cards too. This is why you should always keep your credit card vouchers or records of cash withdrawals and make sure that you check your statement. If an item on the statement is not yours, query it with the card issuer. Keep copies of all correspondence.

In the case of a credit card, pay only for those items which are correct. Write to the card issuer explaining why you are doing this. The onus is on the card issuer to prove that you authorised the disputed transaction.

If you get nowhere, write to the chief executive of the bank or building society concerned. If that does not succeed, write to the relevant ombudsman (see page 157).

While a charge is in dispute, you will not normally be treated as being in default, so your credit standing should be unaffected. If, however, an adverse entry is made on your file with a credit reference agency, you can correct it (see page 171 for how to do this).

Other types of borrowing

Q *Is it better to use the credit offered by a shop when you buy something or to take out a bank loan to cover the purchase?*

A An advantage of a personal loan from a bank or building society is that you are not tied to a particular retailer and can shop around for the best price. But apart from this consideration you will have to compare the terms of the shop credit with the bank loan. The key points to consider are:

- **repayments** How much do you want, or can you afford, to repay each month? If the interest rate is not fixed, you will need to allow for possible increases in the repayments
- **how long you borrow for** Does one loan let you repay over a longer period than the other? Would this suit you better? Bear in

mind that the longer the term of the loan, the more you will repay in total

- **cost of the loan** This is measured by the **annual percentage rate (APR)**, which takes into account not only the level of interest charged but also when and how frequently repayments fall due. In general the higher the APR, the more costly the loan. But, unfortunately, the APR doesn't necessarily take into account all the costs of a deal (see page 167).

Q *A number of debts have built up over the years and the repayments now take up nearly a third of our income each month. I've been offered a single loan to replace all the others and it will cost a lot less. It seems like a good deal, but is there any catch I should look out for?*

A Given that the interest rate on the new loan offered is so much lower, you should check whether what you are being offered is a **secured loan**. Usually such loans are secured against your home, which means that if you cannot keep up the repayments, the lender has the right to force the sale of your home in order to recover the loan. This makes the loan less risky for the lender, hence the lower interest rate (though you need to watch out for extra charges, such as valuation or arrangement fees). If your finances are fairly sound, a secured loan can be a good idea. But if you are already having problems coping with your debts, don't put your home at risk by taking out this type of loan. Consider getting advice on how to cope with your debts (see page 172).

Q *I want to borrow £2,000 to erect a large workshop in my garden. What's the best loan to go for if I aim to pay it off over, say, two years?*

A If you have a with-profits life insurance policy (see page 228) which has built up a reasonable cash-in value, you may be able to get a loan from the insurance company secured against the policy. The interest rate on an insurance company loan is usually variable but significantly lower than the rate on most other types of loan. This is also a very flexible way of borrowing as you can either repay when the policy finally matures or pay off the loan earlier if you choose.

Failing that, try a personal loan from a bank or building society. This will be for a set period and at a fixed rate of interst. If you want to repay the loan early, expect to pay an **early redemption charge** (see next question).

Q *Six months ago, I took out a £3,000 bank loan. The loan was meant to be for five years, but an aunt has died and left me some money, so I thought I'd pay it off now. What I can't figure out is that I've made payments of £600 and yet the bank says I'll have to pay £3,200 to clear the loan. That's more than I borrowed in the first place – how do they work this out?*

A If you want to repay a fixed-term loan early, the lender is entitled to charge you a certain proportion of the extra interest and charges which it would have received from you had if you kept the loan for its full term. The maximum you will have to pay is worked out according to a formula laid down by law. Generally, the longer the term of the loan and the earlier you settle, the greater the charge will be. To find out how much you must pay, ask the lender for an **early settlement quotation**. If you think the amount asked for is too high, you could try negotiating with the lender. Alternatively, check your loan agreement: it may allow you to make capital repayments. If so, you can pay off all but £1 of what you owe; the redemption charges will then be calculated on the outstanding balance of just £1.

Q *I'm buying a dining-room table and chairs on HP. But I've just had £1,000 win on the premium bonds and would like to pay off the HP debt. Is that possible?*

A No, with **hire purchase (HP)** agreements, it is not possible to repay early and keep the goods.

Q *Earlier this week, I bought a TV in a local shop and agreed to pay using their finance deal, but now my dad has offered to lend me the money. Can I cancel the shop finance?*

A No. With some credit deals, you can cancel the agreement within a few days of taking it out. This right to cancel will be shown on the agreement and lasts for five days from the time you receive a copy of the signed agreement. But the following types of deal *don't* give you this right:

- shop credit
- credit taken out on trade premises, such as offices or exhibition stands
- buying by phone – you can't cancel even if the agreement is sent to you to sign at home
- buying by post.

Q *After four hours' constant sales patter, I stupidly agreed to buy some double glazing from a salesman who called at my home. It means borrowing to pay for it, but the salesman said this was no problem, they could finance it all for me. Now I'm having second thoughts – can I pull out of the deal?*

A This type of credit deal is covered by a right to cancel (see previous question). Moreover, where the credit is tied to specific goods or services – in this case, the double glazing – you have the right to cancel the whole deal, i.e. the agreement to buy the windows as well as the agreement to take out a loan.

Q *I need to borrow £500 for a few months. Is a personal loan a good idea or should I take out an overdraft?*

A Personal loans are not usually available for periods of less than six months. Generally, overdrafts are an expensive way to borrow because of the charges or fees which you may have to pay as well as the interest (see page 154). However, if you have a gold card (see page 161) this may let you take out an overdraft at a very competitive rate of interest. Another option is to use a credit card. Although the annual rate of interest on credit cards is high, there are no extra fees or charges (apart from the annual fee if one is payable on your card and which you will have had to pay in any case). Credit cards also offer a very flexible way to borrow because you choose when and how much to repay subject to the minimum amount. It is also worth checking whether your employer offers cheap loans to staff, though this may affect your tax (see page 62).

Q *I was planning to buy a new cooker on my credit card, but the shop has offered me an 'easy payment' loan. I'm not sure whether this would be better or not. How can I find out more about the loan?*

A Ask for a written **quotation**. Legally, the shop must give you this if you ask. The quotation will provide all the information you need to see whether the loan suits your needs and to compare it with buying on your credit card.

Q *I've got quotations for various different ways of borrowing to buy a caravan. All of them state the 'APR'. Can I rely on this as a measure of the cost of each loan or do I have to look at other details as well?*

A The **annual percentage rate (APR)** is a useful benchmark for comparing the cost of different loans and is a much better guide than the quoted rate of interest. But, unfortunately, the APR doesn't always take into account all the charges you will have to pay. With the following types of loan, you will have to consider extra costs as well:

- **overdrafts** The APR is based only on the interest charges. If you will have to pay fees and/or account charges too, then the APR massively understates the cost of the overdraft
- **personal loans** The APR does not include the cost of credit insurance (see next question), which makes a substantial difference to the overall cost of the loan
- **credit cards** The APR does not reflect whether interest is charged from the transaction or (later) statement date – see page 159. This makes a significant difference to the cost of credit, especially if you pay off most but not all of your monthly bill. If you borrow for a long period, the APR is a good guide to the overall cost.

Q *I'm taking out a personal loan and there's a box on the application form to tick if I don't want credit insurance. Is the insurance worth having?*

A Credit insurance on a personal loan will cover your monthly repayments, including the insurance premiums, for a set period (usually up to a year) if you become unemployed, or until the loan is paid off if you cannot work because of illness or an accident. But this insurance is not cheap – it can increase the overall cost of the loan by anything from a third to more than double. Also the policies are riddled with exclusions (see Box), so insist on seeing the full policy before you decide. If at a pinch you could manage the repayments yourself for a year out of savings or part-time earnings, should you lose your job, then do not take out credit insurance. If you would not be able to manage, then it could be worth having.

By the way, lenders have traditionally used these 'negative tick boxes' to sell credit insurance – a practice frowned upon by the Office of Fair Trading. But the major lenders agreed to stop selling the insurance in this way from 1 January 1994.

Q *Can I take out credit insurance to cover repayments on my credit card?*

A Yes. Usually, the insurance will pay off 10 per cent of your outstanding balance for up to 12 months if you become unemployed. In other respects, the insurance is similar to the policies for personal loans (see previous question).

WHAT CREDIT INSURANCE DOES AND DOES NOT COVER

All policies pay out if you are made redundant or cannot work because of illness or disability. Some policies repay the loan in full if you die. Most do not cover:

- voluntary redundancy
- unemployment if it occurs shortly after you take out the policy – within, say, 30 or 90 days
- the first few weeks of unemployment – often 30 days
- more than a year's unemployment
- frequent unemployment – if you claim once, you may need to be back in work for at least six months before you can claim again.

Q *I applied for a bank loan and to my surprise received a rejection. Despite assurances from my bank, I feel my honesty and integrity have been slighted. Why should I have been turned down?*

A All lenders try to assess whether applicants are likely to make good customers. Usually, they do this by using a technique called 'credit scoring'. Based on its existing and previous customers, a lender will try to identify the features which characterise its good borrowers and its bad borrowers (see Box). The features will be weighted according to how important they are and, from them, the lender will draw up a score-card. When you apply for credit, the lender gets details about you and scores them according to the card. If your score is above a certain level, your application is accepted; if your score is below, your application is automatically rejected. Following recent changes to their code of practice, by 1995 most lenders should broadly indicate why your application has been turned down. Most lenders will take another look at their decision if you can provide additional information which seems relevant.

A lender will have different score-cards for different types of lending; and score-cards differ between lenders, reflecting both their different experiences with customers and their preferences for different types of customer. So even if your bank has refused you it does not mean that other lenders will automatically reject you too.

Q *On my application form for a credit card, it says that my account details will be passed on to a credit reference agency. Why is this and can I refuse?*

A When you apply for a loan or credit, a lender will not just rely on information you give on the application form – after all, a fraudster could simply lie. Credit reference agencies are used to provide:

- so-called 'black information' used by nearly all lenders. It consists of publicly available details about county court judgments and bankruptcy proceedings, together with information about loans on which you are in arrears by, say, four months or more
- 'white information' used by most lenders except most of the big high street banks. It consists of details of your existing and previous loans and credit – including how well you manage them – and gives lenders a much more reliable picture of how creditworthy you are.

To use an agency's 'white information', a lender must reciprocate by supplying similar details. In the past, the big banks have held back from doing this because they viewed information about their own customers to be commercially too valuable to pass on. But some lenders (such as the card company to which you applied, which has been turning down four out of every ten applicants) have decided that to use and supply white information will be worthwhile and will help it to reduce its rejection rate without increasing its bad debtors. It cannot pass on your details without your permission – hence the notice on the application form – but your card company has decided that it will turn away your custom if you do not give your consent. Existing customers are not affected: their account details will not be passed on.

WHAT COUNTS IN CREDIT SCORING?

Lenders treat their score-cards as top secret, but these are the sorts of details that may be taken into account:

- **your income and expenses** – are you already over-committed?
- **employment status** – higher score for employees than for the self-employed. Higher scores for skilled workers compared with unskilled
- **how long you have been in your current job** – less than three years may score less
- **where you live** – score extra if you own your home
- **how long you have lived there** – lose points if less than three years
- **bank account** – lose points if you do not have one
- **credit cards** – you may lose points if you have none
- **age** – both the young and the elderly are deemed more risky
- **marital status** – highest score if you are married
- **number of children and other dependants** – they may reduce your score
- **credit reference agency file** – information from this (see above) may be scored or considered separately.

Q *I applied for a store card in a well-known shop and was refused. I'd like to know why. Can I find this out?*

A Within 28 days of being turned down for a loan or credit, you can ask the lender whether a credit reference agency was used – the lender is obliged by law to tell you and to say which agency was used. There are four main agencies in the UK – CCN Systems, Credit Data and Marketing Services, Equifax Europe and Infolink (see Addresses section). You can get a copy of your credit reference file by writing to the agency enclosing a fee – currently £1, soon likely to double. You will need to give your full name, address and any other address you have lived at during the previous six years, so that your file can be correctly located. If you find an entry in your file which is incorrect, you can ask the agency to remove or amend it. If the agency refuses, or if it fails to respond within 28 days, you can send it a **notice of correction** to be added to your file. This is a statement of up to 200 words giving your side of the story. If the agency will not accept your notice, complain in writing to the Office of Fair Trading (see Addresses section). Once your file is changed, the credit reference agency must send the amended entry or the notice of correction to everyone who has consulted your file within the previous six months.

Coping with debt

Q *I've been having problems paying the bills for some time. Now I'm getting worried about them. What should I do?*

A You have already taken the first step, by being honest with yourself and admitting that you have a problem – simply stuffing the unpaid bills in a drawer doesn't help. Now you can set about putting the problem right. What you do now depends on how big it is. If your finances are not too much out of hand, you may be able to work out a solution for yourself:

- **cut expenses** Can you get back on course quickly through a bit of belt-tightening? Draw up a budget for yourself or your household listing all the income each week or month, all essential expenses – e.g. mortgage or rent, fuel, food – and those expenses which could be trimmed at least for a while, e.g. cigarettes, take-away meals, hairdresser, new clothes
- **boost your income** Are you entitled to any social security or local authority benefits which you have not claimed (see pages 106–17)? Could you take on a job or take in a lodger?

- **let people know** If you cannot see a quick way out of debt, it is essential that you let the people to whom you owe money (your creditors) know that there is a problem and that you are keen to work out a solution. Do this as soon as you can: leaving it not only lets the debts mount up, but you may lose the goodwill of your creditors too. Most creditors will be sympathetic and will see that it is in their interests too to help you find a manageable way to pay off what your owe.

Q *I owe money on my mortgage, my credit card, to the electricity company, my bank and goodness knows how many other people. I simply can't pay them all. What can I do?*

A You need to prioritise your debts and agree with each creditor a system of paying off the debt through regular payments. Some debts are more important than others. Priority debts include:

- paying your rent or mortgage, because otherwise you may lose your home
- paying fuel bills, because you risk being cut off.

You may only be able to afford very small payments to each creditor, but the important thing is that you make them regularly and show that you are committed to clearing the debts. It would be a good idea to get some professional help in prioritising your debts and negotiating with your creditors.

Q *I know my debts have got out of hand, but I just can't see how to sort them out. Where can I get help?*

A Don't be embarrassed if you can't cope alone. There are specialist services which will advise on and help you with debt problems. Remember that their job is not to stand in judgement and, whatever your debts, they will have seen it all before. You could contact:

- **Citizens Advice Bureau (CAB)** Addresses, local opening times and telephone numbers of your local office are in the phone book or can be obtained from your local library. Your local newspaper may also publish details

- **money advice centre** Some local authorities run these advice centres. Look in the phone book under the name of your authority and/or enquire at your town or county hall
- **National Debtline** This is a telephone helpline offering expert advice and a free information pack. See page 276 for telephone number
- **Age Concern** If you are retired, you can contact the advice and information section of your local Age Concern branch. Address in the phone book
- **Benefits Agency** To check what help and benefits you may be entitled to, contact your local agency (address in the phone book under Social Security, Department of)
- **your local library** This may have useful books and leaflets about coping with debt. See, for example, *Debt, a Survival Guide* published by the Office of Fair Trading.

Q *I've got behind with my mortgage payments. I didn't think it would matter for a month or two, but the building society keeps writing to me. What will happen now?*

A You must go and talk to your building society. The solutions offered will depend on your particular circumstances but could include a short payment 'holiday' while you sort out your finances, extending the term of the mortgage, or reduced payments, or interest-only payments, for an agreed period. In the last resort, the society could repossess your home but this would be considered only when all other possible solutions have been exhausted. Larger mortgage lenders may run their own debt counselling services which will look at your whole debt problem and help you to sort out other aspects as well as just coping with the mortgage payments.

Q *I've just discovered that my husband hasn't been paying the rent for the last six months. Can we be evicted?*

A If you fall behind with your rent, try to resume the current payments and pay at least something towards the arrears. If you do this and you are a council tenant, it is unlikely that you will be evicted.

Private landlords may take a tougher line. If you receive an eviction notice, seek help from your CAB or money advice centre immediately.

Q *With VAT now being charged on gas and electricity, I don't seem able to cope with the bills any more. Will I be cut off if I don't pay?*

A If you do not pay your gas or electricity bills, your supply might be cut off, so it is essential that you contact your supplier as soon as you realise you are having problems paying. If everyone in the household is a pensioner, you will not be cut off between 1 October and 31 March provided you genuinely cannot pay. And you will not be cut off if you agree a plan to meet your future bills and to pay off your debt by regular instalments, or agree to have a pre-payment meter installed which will be set to cover the cost of the fuel you use and a payment towards your outstanding debt. The snag with pre-payment meters is that you usually pay more for your fuel (see page 183).

If you are receiving income support, you can join the **fuel direct** scheme, under which some of your benefit is paid directly each week to the gas or electricity supplier to cover the cost of fuel you use and payments towards any oustanding debt.

CHAPTER 6

Your spending

Shopping used to be a pretty straightforward activity. Nowadays, there are several ways to pay, including credit cards, debit cards and store cards, and you do not even have to leave home to do your shopping. But do you know how secure the various methods of payment are and what to do if things go wrong?

When it comes to regular payments, such as household bills, there are yet more options to weigh up. Other key areas of spending are on car insurance and holidays. If you know the ins and outs of these, you are in a better position to save money, get a good deal and guard against possible problems. Finally, you may want to 'spend' some of your money by making gifts – with some, a bit of forward planning can mean that the recipient receives more than you give.

Shopping

Q *It's not surprising that there's so much credit card fraud when you think of the numerous people you give card details to over the phone – you never have to produce the card for theatre tickets, for example.*

A This is not correct. To combat fraud, goods ordered by telephone must usually be delivered to the cardholder's address. There are some exceptions – for example, flowers can be sent elsewhere and theatre tickets can be picked up at the theatre. However, in the latter case, you should be asked to show your card and sign for the tickets when you collect them. You should also make sure that you obtain a copy of the card voucher. If you suspect that your details are known to someone who should not have them, tell the credit card company immediately, cut up and return your card and confirm in writing that you want to cancel your card and be sent a new one.

Q *My wife and I put a £230 deposit on a new three-piece suite a month ago. The store made all sorts of excuses for not delivering by the agreed date and now I've learnt that it's gone bust. Will I be able to get my deposit back?*

A You will count as an **unsecured creditor** of the company which operated the store: that puts you way down in the queue of creditors hoping to be paid or repaid. With the Inland Revenue and the banks ahead of you, it is possible that you may get nothing back at all. Even so, you should contact the firm acting as receiver for the store as soon as possible in order to register your claim.

The picture would rosier if you had paid the deposit by credit card, because the card company would be jointly liable with the store, provided the goods cost at least £100. If you used a credit card to pay the deposit, write to your card company saying that you are claiming from it. This extra protection is given under the Consumer Credit Act 1974 and applies only to payment by credit card, not by debit card, charge card or most types of gold card.

Q *I bought a lighting system from a department store while I was on holiday in Germany. When I got it home, I found that most of the connections were faulty and that the transformer didn't work. I obviously can't take the system back, but I paid by credit card, so can I claim my money back from the card company?*

A This is a grey area. Assuming the goods cost at least £100, the Consumer Credit Act 1974 gives you the right to claim against either the supplier (the department store) or the creditor (your credit card issuer), so there is definitely no requirement to claim *first* against the supplier. But credit card companies generally refuse to accept liability if you have bought goods abroad, claiming that the UK Act does not apply in such cases. The Office of Fair Trading has said that it disagrees and considers that the card companies *are* liable. But until a case is brought in court and an official judgment made, the position is uncertain and your card company is unlikely to pay up.

Q *I bought some tickets for a show and was charged an extra £2.50 per ticket because I paid by credit card. Do customers have a right to know the commission paid by the retailer to a credit card company given that it's the customer who may have to foot the bill?*

A No. There is a contract between the retailer and the card issuer, and customers have no legal right to know the details. But, as you point out, retailers are allowed to charge you more if you pay by credit card rather than cash or some other means. (Alternatively you might be offered a discount if you pay cash.) The extra cost to the retailer of a credit card transaction is significant: for example, one card issuer currently charges retailers 4.15 per cent of the value of each credit card transaction (subject to a minimum charge) and takes three days to credit the retailer with the money if a paper voucher has been used rather than an electronic system. This issuer charges less for debit card (see page 161) transactions, just a flat fee of 40p per transaction, which is one reason, perhaps, why some debit cards are now more widely accepted than credit cards.

Q *On holiday in India, I checked into a hotel and, when I said I would be paying by credit card, they asked me to sign a blank voucher. At first I refused, but in the end I had to sign. What was to stop them charging whatever they liked on my card?*

A Signing blank vouchers is normally to be avoided at all costs – fraudsters could fill in any figure they wanted and you would have trouble proving you had not authorised the amount. But some hotels, and often car hire firms, too, argue that this practice is necessary to take account of any extra costs you incur during your stay which might not be apparent at the time you settle up. Obviously, this system is open to abuse. The hotel or car hire firm must notify you of any extra charges they make and document them clearly. If not, or if you dispute a charge, tell the card issuer. It should take up the matter with the hotel or firm, though disputes abroad may take a long time to sort out.

Q *I tried to use my Switch debit card in the local supermarket, but they wouldn't accept it even though I'd paid £500 into my current account the day before. If that's the way they treat customers, I won't shop there again.*

A Under the Switch system, the shop links into your bank's computer system, through which a check is made on the *cleared* balance (see page 153) in your account overnight on the previous working day. So when you presented your debit card your intended expenditure was compared with your balance on the previous night. The £500 you paid in would have taken three or four working days to clear and therefore would not have shown up in the cleared balance for a least three days, and longer if a weekend intervened. The only information given to the shop by the bank computer is whether or not the particular transaction is authorised. If it is not, the shop has no option but to refuse to accept your card.

Q *My favourite clothes shop makes special offers to customers using its store card. I'm tempted to get a card, but aren't they horribly expensive?*

A There are various types of store card. Some work like charge cards, others like credit cards (see pages 157–63), and yet others are budget accounts for which you pay a regular monthly sum and can borrow a multiple of this (say, 12 times). If you borrow on a store card (by not paying off the full amount each month), the interest rate you are charged will generally be higher than that on a standard credit card and *much* higher if you pay off your bill by any means other than direct debit. However, provided you intend to pay off your monthly bill in full and can take advantage of promotions for cardholders, then a store card may be worth having.

Q *We simply couldn't afford to buy large items if we had to pay all in one go, so I do a lot of my shopping through catalogues. But am I paying extra by buying this way?*

A One of the great attractions of many forms of home shopping is the option to buy now and spread the cost over 20, 38 or 52 weeks, say, without paying more. For example, maybe you want to buy your son a new bike for his birthday but cannot afford £78 in one go: £1.50 a week for the next 52 weeks, however, might be a lot more manageable. And it is not just large items that you can buy in this way: if the children need pyjamas and the kitty won't run to £9.99 this week, a catalogue company might let you pay 45p for the next 20 weeks instead. But remember, if you are trying to manage on a tight budget, that you can sometimes get better prices in the high street. And don't forget to take into account postage and packing costs – large catalogue operations usually deliver free but smaller ones often charge. Comparing prices is not always easy, because you may not be able to get precisely the same items or styles as those offered in a catalogue. But where comparisons can be made, the price differences can be significant. So shop around. Bear in mind, too, that some large high street retailers let you spread the cost of purchases – it is often worth asking in smaller shops, too. Larger stores, particularly electrical retailers, may run '0% finance' deals that let you buy now and pay months later – a good deal, provided you have the self-discipline to set aside the money in the meantime. If you do, then consider getting into the habit of saving a small sum each week, for example, in a bank or building society account (see page 209). That way, you will have the money to hand next time you need to make a large purchase.

Q *I ordered a dress through a catalogue. When it arrived, I found it didn't fit very well. Can I insist on my money back?*

A When you shop by mail order, you have a legal right to your money back if you have been sent the wrong goods or if the goods are not as described in the catalogue or advertisement. If you simply don't like the goods you have ordered (e.g. because they do not fit well), you do not have this right. However, because you are usually buying 'blind', most mail order sellers guarantee to refund your money if you return the goods within a set period whatever the reason for sending them back. The period specified varies, but is usually at least seven days. You may have to pay the postage for returning goods, but larger catalogue companies often provide pre-paid labels or will arrange for unwanted goods to be picked up.

Q *I had to wait two months for a compact disc that I ordered through an ad in a magazine. Isn't it illegal for the company to take so long? I thought mail-order goods had to arrive within 28 days.*

A It is not illegal for a company to take over 28 days to deliver mail-order goods, but it is against the British Code of Advertising Practice, which covers all newspaper and magazine advertisements. The Code requires that these should state what the delivery time will be and that this should be no longer than 28 days. If you think an ad breaches these rules, complain to the Advertising Standards Authority (ASA) (see Addresses section).

Q *I bought some items by mail order two Christmases ago and, ever since, I've been plagued by catalogues – not just from that firm but from several others as well. Is there any way I can stop all this junk mail?*

A Mail-order companies often sell lists of their customers to other firms selling similar or related products. The British Code of Advertising Practice requires all mail-order advertisements appearing in newspapers and magazines to tell you if your name might be passed on in this way and to give you the chance to refuse your permission. If you are being plagued by unwanted mail shots, write to or phone the companies concerned saying that you do not want to receive their literature in future and ask them not to pass your name on to any other companies. You can also register with the Mailing Preference Service (MPS) (see Addresses section). Any company using direct mail marketing should check the MPS register and exclude people who are listed on it from their mailing lists.

Q *How much money actually goes to the charity when I buy charity Christmas cards?*

A From Christmas 1994 you will know precisely how much, because card packs will by law have to tell you this. If present trends continue, *where* you buy will make a big difference. A charity receives most if you buy your cards through its mail-order catalogue or its own high street shops. For example, in 1993 Oxfam received 61 per cent of the price of its cards if you bought that way, compared with 45 per cent if you bought through other shops. (It may cost you extra, though, if you buy mail order, because you will be paying for postage and packing.) Another good way to buy is through temporary shops set up by groups such as Card Aid, Cards for Good Causes and the Charity Christmas Card Council. These groups are owned or controlled by other charities and, in 1993, over 80 per cent of the price of the cards was shared between the participating charities and sometimes other 'guest' charities too. Choose charities' own cards, if you can, rather than the charity cards of manufacturers or retailers: for the latter, in 1993, charities typically received 5–17p in the £.

Q *I'm about to buy a new car. The manufacturer's guarantee covers everything for the first year, but only the bodywork for a longer period. Is it worth paying extra for an extended warranty?*

A The terms **extended warranty** and **extended guarantee** are used freely by car makers and dealers to mean many things. Most often, they are used incorrectly to describe extra-cost **mechanical breakdown insurance (MBI)** that you can take out at the time you buy a car or before the original warranty expires. A genuine warranty is a very broad statement from the car maker accepting responsibility for almost any fault or defect. By contrast, MBI covers specific faults and problems and often includes separate breakdown recovery and cover for hiring a replacement car if yours is off the road. The cover is precisely detailed in the policy document. Research by *Which?* suggests that on average you will pay out more in premiums for MBI than you will make in claims. But, of course, not everyone has average experience and if something serious went wrong with your car you could be very relieved to have an MBI policy. If you attach a high priority to peace of mind, the expense will be justified.

Q *Is it worth buying an extended guarantee for my new washing machine?*

A Extended guarantees offered by retailers are a type of insurance which pays out for the cost of repairs. According to research by *Which?* in 1993, the average cost of four years' insurance to top up the manufacturer's one-year guarantee would be about £140. Even in the fifth year, the chance of a washing machine breaking down is only about one in four. In the worst situation, even if you had to replace the machine at a cost of, say, £400, you might be able to bear the outlay yourself. On the whole, the extended guarantee is probably not worth having.

Paying the bills

Q *Is it better to have a water meter than to pay in the old way?*

A Generally, what you pay for water and sewerage is based on the old rateable value of your property. This means that you pay a fixed amount however much water you use. You can instead switch to a meter, in which case you will be billed according to water use. Making the switch voluntarily will be worthwhile only if you are a low water user (for example, you live alone). Water companies have until the year 2000 to find ways of charging which do not rely on the rateable value (which will not be updated now that we pay council tax instead of rates), so it is likely that there will be a big increase in the use of meters. Other options for the future include linking water bills to council tax.

Q *I moved into a new flat last year and until now all the electricity bills have been estimated. When the meter was read this time, the bill was a staggering £795. I asked for the meter to be read again and it showed that we'd used 670 units in the space of a month. But we were on holiday for two weeks and couldn't possibly have used that much. How can we convince the electricity company that they're wrong?*

A Ask for your meter to be checked. Either another meter will be put alongside yours or your meter will be taken away for testing. If you are still not happy after the tests, you can ask the electricity regulator, the Office of Electricity Regulation (OFFER) (see Addresses section), to investigate. Be warned, though, that if it turns out that the meter is not faulty, you may have to pay a charge of about £20.

FAULTY METERS

See above for what to do if you suspect that your electricity meter is faulty. The Department of Trade and Industry (DTI) tests gas meters for faults. There is no charge if the meter is faulty, but a £30 fee if it is not. Water meters are tested by your water company, or sometimes by a local trading standards officer. Once again, there is no charge if the meter is faulty; if it is not, there is a £20 charge if the meter was tested on site but £70 if it has to be removed.

Q *It's hard to find enough money each quarter to meet the electricity bill. The company we use runs various 'easy payment schemes'. Are there any drawbacks to using these?*

A For gas and electricity you are normally billed once every three months (two months with Scottish Power) in arrears and you will be expected to pay off the whole bill immediately. Otherwise, there are various 'easy payment schemes' including:

- a **monthly budget scheme**, which spreads your payments evenly throughout the year. Typically, your likely bills for the coming year are estimated based on how much you used over the last 12 months. You then pay one-twelfth of the estimated total each month
- buying **savings stamps** from the post office or gas or electricity offices to use in full or part-payment of the bill when it arrives
- a **pre-payment meter** which you feed with coins or, more commonly with new meters, plastic cash cards bought at fuel showrooms, some newsagents or the post office.

A steady stream of smaller payments may be more manageable, but usually you pay for this convenience, because, with all the schemes, you will be paying at least part of your bill earlier than would otherwise have been necessary. And, with pre-payment meters, there is generally an extra standing charge or rental for the meter hire – typically £4–7 more each quarter – on top of the normal standing charge. If you can, it would be better to set aside a little each month in a building society account, which would give you the benefit of any interest earned.

Q *I pay for our gas using a monthly budget plan. The amount I pay has been set at £79 a month, but by the end of last year I was in credit for £191. I've asked for a refund or a cut in my monthly payment, but British Gas has not replied. Can I get a refund?*

A If you use a budget account for paying your gas or electricity bills, expect a surplus to build up during the summer months: this will be used up by the higher bills in the winter. If there is a persistent under-payment or over-payment, this will normally be corrected at the end of the year when the payment for the following year is reviewed and, if necessary, adjusted. But, if you think too high a surplus has built up, you should ask for a rebate from the gas board or electricity company concerned. If you are not happy with the way they deal with your request, the following organisations may be able to help: the Gas Consumer Council, the Office of Gas Supply (OFGAS) or OFFER (see Addresses section).

Q *Each week I buy savings stamps to put towards my electricity bill and TV licence. I must have dropped the ones I got this week while I was out. Will the post office replace them?*

A Various bills – including those for gas, electricity, car tax, TV licences, BT telephone charges and some water company charges – can be paid using savings stamps, which you can buy in small amounts. They help you to spread the cost of the bills, but these stamps are no more secure than cash. If you lose them, there is no way they can be traced and cancelled, and you cannot get a refund or replacements.

Q *Our electricity bills are very high. Can you suggest any way we could try to cut them?*

A Some electricity companies offer a small discount if you agree to pay your bills by direct debit from a bank or building society account, but to benefit from this you will probably have to agree to pay using a budget plan (see previous page).

If you rely largely on electricity for your heating, you may be able to cut your bills by making use of an off-peak electricity scheme – for example, by choosing Economy 7 or the Scottish White Meter system. To benefit, you need a special meter, for which there is a higher standing charge, but you get considerably cheaper electricity for, say, seven or eight hours during the night. On the other hand, you will usually pay more than normal for your daytime electricity. Making the switch is worth doing if, at night, you can charge up storage heaters and heat water but limit more expensive daytime electricity to running cheaper appliances such as your fridge and freezer.

You might be able to make savings by using fuel more efficiently – perhaps changing your heating appliances, insulating your home better and so on. Electricity companies and regional gas boards operate free services to advise on fuel efficiency and publish a variety of useful leaflets. If you are retired, disabled or getting income support or another means-tested benefit, you may qualify for a government grant under the Home Energy Efficiency Scheme (HEES) to cover most of the cost of insulating a loft, pipes or water tanks or installing draughtproofing. HEES (see Addresses section) also offers energy advice.

Q *I'd like my elderly mother to have a phone so that she can at least get in touch in emergencies. But she's worried about the cost. Are there any cheap deals for pensioners?*

A There are no deals for pensioners as such, but BT runs a scheme called Supportline which cuts the cost of BT's standard charges if you use 125 units or less a quarter. A number of cable TV operators also operate their own regional phone services which may work out cheaper than BT for local calls – see your phone book for cable operators in your area.

Q *I'm interested in switching to the Mercury phone system instead of using BT, but I gather I'll still need to rent a line from BT. Is this correct?*

A You will usually link into the Mercury network using your existing BT phone line, though you may be able to use the lines of a local cable TV company instead. Using BT lines means that you will continue to get a bill from BT for your line rental and you can still use BT, e.g. for local calls which would be cheaper than through Mercury. In addition, you will get a bill from Mercury for the calls you make using its service.

Q *We've just bought a house on a road which has been newly designated as part of a ring road round the town. It's made the road much busier and noisier,* *which is why we could buy so cheaply. But the house is in council tax band F, which seems too high now. Can we get the band reduced?*

A You have six months from the date of your move in which to appeal against the council tax band. Your appeal will be dealt with initially by a local **listing officer** (called an **assessor** in Scotland). If it is not resolved within six months, your appeal will be automatically referred to a **valuation tribunal** (called a **valuation appeal committee** in Scotland). The case can be dealt with in writing if everyone agrees, otherwise there will be a formal hearing. You'll get at least four weeks' notice of the hearing. Hearings are very straightforward and it is not worth going to the expense of being legally represented.

Q *Having separated from my husband, I've just bought my own flat. A neighbour has suggested that I shouldn't be paying full council tax. Can I get a reduction?*

A If you live alone, your council tax bill should be reduced by a quarter. If this discount is not shown on your bill, write to your local authority claiming the discount. If there's no reply within two months, appeal to a valuation tribunal.

Q *I've changed jobs and am living in a friend's flat near my work. My own home is empty. Do I still have to pay council tax for it?*

A You can get your council tax bill halved if a property is empty. Different local authorities may interpret the rules differently, but most would probably say that your friend's flat is now your main residence (unless your move there is purely temporary) so you should qualify for the discount on your empty house. If your local authority maintains that the house is still your main residence, you could appeal. The authority might review its decision in six months' or a year's time, say, to assess whether your move is permanent.

Q *I work in London and have a very basic flat there for use during the week. At weekends, I return home to my wife and children. Do I have to pay full council tax on the London flat?*

A No, you should qualify for the 50 per cent discount which is available on second homes. Your family home should count as your main residence.

Q *Because I have severe arthritis and can't climb stairs any more, we have added an extension to our home to provide me with a downstairs bathroom and bedroom. Can we pay less council tax under the disability reduction scheme?*

A The **disability reduction scheme** is designed to ensure that people who need extra room because of their disability do not pay more council tax as a result. The extra room does not have to be specially adapted. If you qualify, you are charged tax for the valuation band below the one your home would otherwise be in. (But if your home is in the lowest band, Band A, already, there will be no reduction.)

It seems likely that you will qualify, but some local authorities have interpreted the rules of this scheme very narrowly. If you are turned down, you should appeal.

Car insurance

Q *I'm about to trade up to a smarter car. Comprehensive insurance will cost me more than double third party, fire and theft cover. Is it worth paying the extra for a comprehensive policy?*

A There are two main types of car insurance:

- **third party, fire and theft** This covers you and your passengers for personal liability for injury to someone else or damage to their property plus cover for any damage to or loss of your car caused by fire, lightning, explosion, theft or attempted theft. Commonly, you will have to meet the first £100, say, of any theft claim yourself
- **comprehensive insurance** This gives you all the cover mentioned above, but also covers accidental damage to your car. There are often other added extras, such as cover for theft of car stereo equipment and personal belongings from your car, hire of a replacement car if yours is off the road or stolen, and so on.

Not surprisingly, comprehensive cover is a lot more expensive than third party, fire and theft. Whether or not you think it is worth paying the extra will depend largely on the value of your car. If you are buying a new car, or a second-hand car which is only a few years old, choose comprehensive insurance. If you drive an old banger, go for the cheaper option.

Q *Do brokers really find the cheapest car insurance quotes?*

A In a *Which?* research exercise brokers did not find the cheapest quotes for two applicants and the range of quotes from different brokers was wide. It is worth checking the most recent *Which?* report on car insurance (available in many public libraries) and ringing round for quotes yourself. There are also a number of direct-only companies, which do not operate through brokers and are generally cheaper provided you are not a high-risk driver (e.g. young or with a record of claims). But if you cannot spare time for your own research, contact two or three brokers rather than relying on just one.

Q *As I hurriedly backed my car out of the gate, the metal bolt-stop in the centre of the gateway caught on the exhaust pipe and tore it away, damaging the rear underside of the car in the process. Repairing the bodywork will cost £114. Is it worth claiming this on my insurance?*

A If you have comprehensive insurance, you may be able to claim on it for this repair but you may find you will lose more in no-claims discount than you would gain through claiming. Most car insurance policies reduce your premium at renewal if you do not make any claims. The size of the discount depends on the number of years without claim – see Table 6.1. If you *do* make a claim, you usually move back two steps on the scale. For example, if you currently have a 60 per cent discount and claim for the bodywork repair, your discount at renewal will drop to 40 per cent. To work out the size of claim below which you would lose more in discount than you could claim:

- deduct your percentage discount at the next renewal from the discount you would have had if you had not claimed. Do the same for the following year, and for each subsequent year in which your discount will still be affected

- add together all the reductions in discount to give a grand total of the discount lost
- multiply the total discount lost by your current premium to tell you how much discount you would lose in £££s (this ignores any future premium increases)
- add to this any amount which you would have to pay yourself if you made a claim – for example, your policy might say that you have to meet the first £50 of any theft claim or the first £100 of any claim if a young person was driving.

The answer tells you the amount below which it would not be worth making a claim.

Q *Will my no-claims discount be affected every time I make a claim?*

A Not all claims affect your discount. Common exceptions are claims for a shattered windscreen or other glass repairs and for emergency treatment for people involved in an accident. With some policies, provided you qualify for the maximum no-claims discount, you can pay extra to protect it. For example, you might pay an extra 15 per cent of the net premium and then be allowed to make, say, one claim a year or up to two claims in any five-year period, without losing discount. Some policies allow an unlimited number of claims (expect to pay about 20 per cent extra for this); but if you make a lot of claims your insurance company might increase your basic premium (because you seem a high risk) while leaving your discount unchanged.

Q *With the edge of my bumper I clipped a parked car the other day, denting its front offside wing. I offered the owner my details but he said it didn't matter (his car was pretty shabby anyway). Do I need to tell my insurance company about the incident, even though no claim is being made?*

A A condition of your insurance is that you tell the company about any event which might result in a claim. You would be wise to let it know about this incident just in case the owner of the parked car decides to claim against you after all. Make it clear in your letter to the insurers that you are telling them 'for information purposes only' and not making any claim yourself.

Q *I can get a reduction in my premium if I agree to a 'voluntary excess'. What does this mean?*

A Some insurers offer a premium reduction if you choose to meet the first part of any claim yourself – this is called a **voluntary excess**. The larger the voluntary excess, the greater the reduction in your premium. It is usually worth opting for an excess which at least matches the amount you would not in any case claim because of the impact on your no-claims discount (see page 188). But bear in mind that you still have to pay the excess yourself even if it is the first part of a much larger claim.

Table 6.1: What you lose if you claim on car insurance

	Year 1	Year 2	Year 3	Year 4	Year 5	Year 6
Typical discount scale[1] Discount each year if you make no claims	30%	40%	50%	60%	60%	60%
Discount at renewal if you have a 60% discount and make a claim	40%	50%	60%	60%	60%	60%
Discount at renewal if you have a 50% discount and make a claim	30%	40%	50%	60%	60%	60%
Discount at renewal if you have a 40% discount and make a claim	0%	30%	40%	50%	60%	60%
Discount at renewal if you have a 30% discount and make a claim	0%	0%	30%	40%	50%	60%

[1] Some companies' scales go up to 65 per cent after five or six years without a claim. One company offers 70 per cent maximum discount to policyholders aged 50 or more.

Q *As I rounded a bend in a narrow country lane, I met an articulated lorry with a tractor on its trailer. I braked hard and stopped at the side of the road, but the lorry was going too fast to stop and its trailer swung into the front of my car, writing it off. The driver was quite reasonable, but when I contacted his* *employer the next day, the firm denied all liability for the accident and said it would fight any claim I make. I'm sure the lorry driver was to blame, but I can't afford to go to court. My own insurance is only third party, fire and theft, so it won't pay up for the car. What can I do?*

A If you are involved in an accident which was someone else's fault, you can try to get compensation from that person – or, if he or she was working at the time, from his or her employer. (A common misconception is that you claim against the other person's insurance, but this is not so. Your claim is against the *person*, although often his or her insurance company will handle the matter and, if your claim is successful, it is that insurance company which will usually pay up.) Proving the other person was to blame may be difficult, time-consuming and costly, especially if it comes to a court battle. But check whether you have any **uninsured loss recovery insurance**. This will:

- provide the help of professionals in contacting the person responsible, setting out your claim and negotiating a settlement
- pay the cost of hiring a solicitor and going to court if this turns out to be necessary. Usually legal costs are covered only up to a given limit – for example, to £10,000 per claim.

Many people do not realise that they have this cover, which is often either included automatically with car insurance or as an optional extra costing about £10 a year; some breakdown recovery services also include it. Check whether you do. If not, certainly consider taking it out in future – it is not expensive and can usually be arranged by your car insurer or broker.

Q *Is there any point taking out uninsured loss recovery insurance if you already have comprehensive car insurance?*

A Even a comprehensive car insurance policy does not cover everything. Examples of uninsured losses are:

- a policy excess: you may be required (compulsory excess) or have opted (voluntary excess) to pay the first part of any claim or certain types of claim
- losses above any limits applying to your policy, for example, your policy might cover car stereo equipment only up to £250

- the cost of hiring a replacement car while yours is off the road. This is covered by some comprehensive policies but by no means all
- compensation for consequential loss, for example, earnings lost while you are off work due to crash injuries
- compensation for pain, suffering or inconvenience.

Even if you have comprehensive insurance, you might want to avoid claiming against it in order to retain your no-claims discount. And if you have lost your discount, but subsequently successfully claim uninsured losses from the other person, you may be able to get your no-claims discount reinstated.

INSURANCE PREMIUM TAX

From October 1994, a new tax must be paid on premiums for most insurance policies other than investment-type policies, such as savings contracts and endowment mortgages. The tax, which affects, for example, car insurance and house buildings and contents insurance, is set at 2.5 per cent of the premiums you pay.

Holidays

Q *I've booked a two-week holiday in Austria, but the tour operator has gone bust. What are my rights?*

A Under regulations which came into effect at the start of 1993 all tour operators must be able to give you a refund, or bring you home from your holiday destination, if they cease trading. They might do this through insurance or through a bonding scheme. As an added protection, it is safest to book a holiday which is already covered by an established bond, such as that of the Association of British Travel Agents (ABTA) or the Association of Independent Tour Operators (AITO) – see Box. If the cost of the holiday per person is over £100 and you paid by credit card, you have the added protection of being able to claim from the card company (see page 161).

PACKAGE HOLIDAY PROTECTION SCHEMES

The major holiday bonding schemes, which guarantee that your money is refunded or that you are brought home if your holiday organiser goes bust, are:

- **ABTA,** which covers holiday operators and travel agents (but check that the particular holiday you are sold is covered)
- **AITO,** which covers holiday operators
- **Air Travel Organiser's Licence (ATOL),** which covers all charter flights, but only some scheduled flights
- **The Confederation of Passenger Transport UK** (which covers bus and coach operators) has a bonding scheme for those members who have chosen to be covered by it
- **The Passenger Shipping Association** also has a bonding scheme which only covers members who have chosen to belong to it.

See Addresses section for how to contact the above.

Q *A few weeks before I was due to go on my holiday, the tour operator demanded an extra £100. I paid up, because I didn't want to risk losing the holiday, but was I legally bound to do so?*

A Check the tour operator's booking conditions to see if they allow surcharges. Some brochures promise 'no surcharge guarantees', which they must honour. Otherwise, surcharges are allowed, but the operator must explain what they are for (typically they cover exchange rate changes or fuel price rises) and cannot impose them less than 30 days before your departure. The operator should absorb up to 2 per cent of any increase in the cost of your holiday but can pass on anything in excess of this. If the increase changes the price by a 'significant' amount (defined by ABTA to mean more than 10 per cent), you are entitled to cancel the holiday and get a full refund.

Q *I'm about to book a villa holiday in France. The package includes holiday insurance. Do I have to rely on this, or can I use my own policy?*

A You should always carefully check insurance included in a holiday package – *Which?* surveys of tour operators' policies have found that some simply do not provide the minimum cover you need. Usually, there should be no problem taking out your own cover instead, but you will need to do this *before* you book the holiday. You will not necessarily get a reduction in the cost of the package if you arrange your own insurance, but try asking anyway.

Q *The holiday brochure I'm looking at just gives a summary of the insurance cover included in the deal. I'd like to see more details before I commit myself. Can I insist on this?*

A Yes, you can and you should. It is essential that you read the full policy, particularly so that you can check the exclusions which are often not spelt out in the summary. However, you may have to be persistent – travel agents sometimes do not have a copy of the policy to hand, despite the usual statement in the brochure that full policy details are available on request. You may have to wait a few days while they obtain a copy or you could ask for the insurance company's phone number and ask for a copy to be sent directly to you.

Q *What does a good holiday insurance policy include?*

A The main features that you should be looking for are:

- **medical expenses**: cover of at least £250,000 for Europe and £1 million for the USA and the rest of the world. There should also be cover for additional accommodation and travel costs if someone has to stay behind and look after the sick person
- **cancellation**: this should cover the full cost of the holiday and any additional charges which have to be paid in advance. It is essential that you have the cover from the time you first book the holiday
- **baggage cover**: how much is reasonable depends on your needs and what cover you have under any other insurance. Check that any limit on individual items is enough – for example, you will need to extend the cover if there is a £250 per item limit and you have a £400 video camera

- **personal liability**: ideally up to £2 million cover for the USA and £1 million for the rest of the world. This covers you for claims made by someone you injure or whose property you damage.

Q *My house contents insurance covers personal belongings I take with me while I'm away from home. Can I delete the baggage cover from my holiday insurance and get a discount for this?*

A You may be able to – check with the agent or company selling you the holiday insurance. But first make absolutely sure that your house contents policy will cover the items you will be taking, your holiday destination and the length of time you intend to be away.

Q *I'm travelling by coach to stay with a family in Germany for a week. Given that I'll be among friends, do I really need holiday insurance?*

A The majority of claims on holiday insurance are for cancellation or curtailment of the holiday; most of the rest are for medical bills and loss or theft of baggage.

If you have to cancel or cut short your holiday or if you lose your luggage, the maximum cost to you is reasonably predictable and you may feel that you can bear this loss yourself, if things go wrong. But the cost of medical treatment is less predictable and can, in the worst event, turn out to be very high. Germany – and both France and Holland, one of which you will probably be travelling through – have reciprocal health agreements with the UK (for which you need a form E111 – see Box). These will cover emergency medical treatment, but that is all. Another risk to consider is what happens if you injure someone or damage someone's property while on holiday – though, if you have house contents insurance, this may cover you. All in all, you can get by without holiday insurance, but you would be much wiser to have its protection.

EMERGENCY MEDICAL TREATMENT ABROAD

If you are taken ill on holiday in a member country of the European Union (EU), you may qualify for free treatment under whatever public health scheme operates there, provided:

- you have a form E111
- you need *emergency* treatment – non-urgent treatment is not covered
- the doctor, dentist or hospital you attend provides treatment under the scheme – private treatment is not covered, nor is the cost of getting you back home for treatment in the UK.

An E111 is a certificate showing you are eligible for free treatment in an EU country. You can get it by asking for Department of Health leaflet T4, *Health Advice for Travellers*, free from the post office or phone 0800 555777. Fill in the forms in the leaflet and take them to a post office, which will validate the E111 for you. If you are travelling as a family, you need only one E111 for all of you. Your E111 is valid indefinitely.

You need to have your E111 with you on holiday, together with at least one photocopy (in case you have to hand in this or the original form when you make a claim) and some proof that you are a UK national – for example, a driving licence or medical card.

Q *My video camera was stolen from my hotel room while I was on holiday in Tenerife. I tried to report it to the police but they were very off-hand and insinuated that I'd 'stolen' it myself so that I could claim on the insurance. In the end, they refused to give me a proper acknowledgement that I'd made the report. Will my insurance company pay up?*

A In general, an insurance policy will not cover you for the loss or theft of an item if you fail to report it to the police within 24 hours and you will need a report from the police as proof that you have done this. However, the circumstances are exceptional in your case, so explain them to the insurance company. Get any supporting statements you can – for example, from hotel staff to whom you may have complained about the theft. If your insurer will not pay up, consider taking your case to the Insurance Ombudsman or the Personal Insurance Arbitration Service (PIAS) – see Box – if the company is a member.

INSURANCE DISPUTES

If you are not happy with the way your insurance company handles your claim, complain first to the company, taking the matter if necessary to the senior management. If you are still not satisfied, take your case to the Insurance Ombudsman Bureau or the Personal Insurance Arbitration Scheme (PIAS), if the insurance company is a member. Both schemes will consider the evidence on both sides and make a judgment. The Insurance Ombudsman's decisions are binding on the insurance company but you can still go to court if you are not happy with his findings. Decisions of the PIAS are binding on both you and the insurance company. See Addresses section.

Q *My insurance policy specifically says that it won't cover items locked in a car boot overnight. My wife and I are about to drive to Southern Italy and intend to spend three or four days stopping in a different hotel each night. It will be impossible to take everything out of the car every time we stop. What can we do?*

A Shop around – not all policies have this exclusion. Consider getting help from an insurance broker if you cannot find a suitable policy. Whatever policy you get, it would make sense to protect yourself as far as possible from theft while you are travelling – for example, choose hotels with secure, off-road parking and take all valuable items out of the car, depositing them, if you can, in the hotel safe for the night.

Q *I've had a couple of minor heart attacks over the last three years. Will I still be able to get holiday insurance for a forthcoming trip to America?*

A As long as you are not travelling against your doctor's advice, there should be no problem getting holiday cover. But note that you must tell the insurance company about the heart attacks even if its policy says that pre-existing medical conditions are accepted. If you do not disclose this information in advance, the company could refuse to pay up in the event of a claim.

Q *While we were on holiday in the Caribbean, a thief stole cash and some jewellery from our apartment. I reported this to the local police and claimed £720 from our holiday insurance on our return. Three months later, I've just received a cheque for £400. Why hasn't the company paid in full?*

A The policy document you have included with your letter shows a limit on the cover for valuable items of £300 per insured person, so £270 of your wife's £570 claim for jewellery is not covered. In addition, there is a policy excess, i.e. an amount of each claim which you yourself must pay, of £25 per person. Therefore, the insurance company has paid you the correct sum in line with the terms and conditions of the policy.

COMMON HOLIDAY INSURANCE EXCLUSIONS

Most policies do not cover you for:
- any loss if you fail to report to the police within 24 hours
- any loss if you have withheld relevant information, e.g. about recent medical treatment, even if the policy does not specifically request it
- any loss if you are travelling against medical advice
- any loss if you have not taken reasonable care
- any loss if you were under the influence of drink or drugs
- damage to fragile objects
- in case of war, riots, nuclear radiation and industrial action
- claims arising from AIDS or HIV
- medical claims made by women over 32 weeks pregnant
- the first part of any claim – commonly £25 – called an **excess**.

Q *During our holiday on the Spanish coast, we were taken to a posh reception in a gorgeous apartment and invited to buy a timeshare in it. The organiser became very pushy and in the end we paid a deposit. But now we're home, we're having second thoughts. Can we pull out of the deal?*

A A timeshare deal gives you, along with lots of other people, a 'slice' of an apartment or villa. Your slice gives you the right to stay in the property for a set one-week period or longer each year either for a given number of years or in perpetuity. Whatever the offer, you need to take as much care over a timeshare purchase as you do over any other decision to buy property.

You should be especially wary of signing up for deals on the spur of the moment – the Canary Islands and Spanish resorts are especially renowned for their timeshare sharks. As you have discovered, typically you will be invited to attend a reception in a luxurious apartment where hard-sell flows alongside the wine and you will be persuaded to sign up and part with credit card deposits. The law offers little protection in this situation. The Timeshare Act 1992 introduced a minimum 14–day cooling-off period for timeshare agreements covered by UK law, during which you can change your mind and get any deposit back, but that excludes the majority of deals signed abroad. An EC directive to give wider protection is still only in the discussion stages. You can certainly pull out of the deal, but in all probability your deposit will be lost.

Q *Seeing an ad for a company reselling timeshare apartments, I phoned up and arranged for them to find a buyer for mine. I had to send in a registration fee of £100 but was told that it would be refunded if there was no sale within six months. But when I phoned the company last week, I couldn't get through and now I've had a letter returned marked 'this company is no longer trading'. How can I get my money back?*

A You probably can't. It sounds as if you have been a victim of a timeshare resale fraud – sadly, a fairly common problem. With so many new timeshares available and aggressively marketed, the resale market is relatively small. Your best bet is to try to sell privately through friends or relatives or by advertising in a specialist timeshare publication. Try also asking the people who own the timeshare weeks just before and after yours whether they would like to buy yours. If you have no luck, see if the developer which originally sold you the timeshare would be willing to buy it back; failing that, try to sell through an agency. The Timeshare Council (see Box) produces a set of guidelines on reselling timeshare as well as a list of members which act as resale agencies.

Q *Are timeshare deals always suspect and best avoided?*

A The timeshare industry has acquired a bad name as a result of various sharp sales practices and you should certainly consider any deal very carefully before committing yourself to it. But the basic idea is a good one and many timeshare owners are very happy with their purchase. Things to think about before you buy a timeshare are:

- do you really want to come back to the same holiday spot time after time? (You may be able to resell or swap a timeshare, but don't bank on this)
- don't treat a timeshare as an investment – you may not be able to resell, or you may have to accept a low price if new units are still available
- don't count on income from renting out the timeshare to help you pay for it
- does the operator seem reputable? Members of the Timeshare Council (see Box) are bound by a code of practice
- find out all you can about the property – for example, has proper planning permission been granted, is it connected to water, gas and electricity services, what are the maintenance arrangements and fees?
- get all the relevant documents and read them thoroughly. If they are in a foreign language, get them translated
- don't be tempted by 'special' deals or 'discounts' into signing anything on the spot. Wait until you get home before making a decision
- don't hand over any money until you are absolutely certain that you want to buy. Unless the deal is covered by the Timeshare Act, a deposit paid by credit card cannot be cancelled
- consider getting advice from a solicitor. Find solicitors in Britain to act for you – they can arrange for legal advice to be provided locally if you are buying abroad.

INFORMATION ABOUT TIMESHARE OWNERSHIP

- **Your local library** Ask what books it has about timeshare or buying property abroad.
- **Government leaflet** *Your Place in the Sun: the timeshare buyers' checklist* Free from local Citizens Advice Bureaux or the

Department of Trade and Industry, Consumer Affairs Division (see Addresses section).
- **The Timeshare Council** This is an industry trade body offering an information pack, help line and conciliation service. Its members are bound by a code of practice. See Addresses section.
- **Your Citizens Advice Bureau, local Trading Standards Office, or a solicitor** For advice and if things go wrong. See phone book for addresses.

Q *What's the best way to take spending money abroad?*

A Don't carry too much in cash – this is easily stolen and usually not replaced while you are abroad (though it might be possible to claim it later on holiday insurance). There are four main options for the bulk of your spending money:

- **travellers' cheques** are reasonably safe and easy to use. You pay commission when you buy them. If they are denominated in £sterling, there will also be commission when you use them abroad, but none if you cash them in on your return. For foreign currency cheques, there is no commission when you use them in the appropriate country, but there is if you cash them in on your return
- **Eurocheques** are relatively safe, widely accepted throughout Europe and the Mediterranean and used just like normal cheques either to pay for goods or to exchange for cash. You need to apply for a Eurocheque guarantee card, for which there is a fee. Once you have, Eurocheques are reasonably cheap: there is just a commission charge when your account is debited. There *shouldn't* be any charge when you use a cheque abroad – if there is, claim it back from your local bank on your return. You can use the Eurocheque card in some cash dispensers abroad
- **Postcheques** are similar to Eurocheques but can be cashed at post offices in many countries. The guarantee card is free, but there is a fee for each book of cheques and commission when each cheque is used
- **credit and charge cards** are widely accepted around the world and essential in North America. They are convenient and fairly cheap – the exchange rate may be better than normal tourist rates. If you use them to get cash there will usually be a fee or interest to pay,

otherwise you can avoid interest by paying off your account in full at the next payment date (see pages 157–9).

If you have a Visa Delta debit card you can use it abroad at any retailing or cash outlet that accepts Visa credit cards. Some Switch debit cards can also be used abroad.

Q *Can I use my normal bank cash card to get money out of cash machines abroad?*

A This is possible with some cards. Check with your local bank or building society and ask them to give you a guide to the location of cash dispensers in the countries you will be visiting.

Q *Is it better to buy foreign currency in the UK before I travel or to wait until I am abroad?*

A There is no hard and fast rule. With some countries, for example, Germany, it makes little difference. With others, you will do better to buy your currency before you go. But whichever you do, be careful when changing money at airports and railway stations – commissions are often high. (However, British Airports Authority has negotiated a competitive deal with bureaux de change operating at its airports.) Generally, beware of 'no commission' deals – you will probably get a worse exchange rate instead.

Q *My son is travelling in Eastern Europe and has phoned asking me to send him some extra money. What's the fastest way to get this to him?*

A There are four main ways in which you can send money to someone abroad:

- ask your bank to telex money to a bank abroad. The transfer is made electronically, which is very safe. In theory, the money can arrive at the foreign bank within 24 hours, but the whole process usually takes longer, so allow three to four days. This method is expensive for small sums (under £500, say)

- ask your bank to post funds to a bank abroad. This costs less than telexing for smaller sums but takes longer – for example, about a week if you are sending money to Europe and two weeks or longer for more remote parts of the world. Again, this method is very safe
- a cheaper option is to buy a banker's draft (a cheque drawn directly on the bank and payable to a named person) and post it yourself. At most banks, you should be able to buy the draft over the counter, but how long it will take to reach its destination depends on the post and how long the foreign bank takes to clear the draft. If a draft is stolen, you can ask your bank to stop its payment. But, as you may not be aware of the theft, consider insuring it by using International Registered post, which provides cover up to £1,000 – but not to all destinations
- (Europe only) send a Eurocheque, provided you already have a Eurocheque card which guarantees cheques up to the equivalent of about £100 (if not, it will take about two weeks to get one). You simply write the cheque and mail it. How long it takes to get to the addressee will depend on the post and time taken to clear the cheque. This is a relatively cheap method of sending small sums abroad.

With all these methods, your son may be charged when he collects the payment or cashes the draft or cheque. With payments sent direct to a foreign bank, you can arrange to pay the foreign bank's charges on your son's behalf.

None of these methods will do if you need to get money to someone really quickly. In that case, your best bet may be to send a banker's draft or Eurocheque by a courier service (see *Yellow Pages*), which would enable delivery to a major European city to be made overnight; remoter destinations could take a day or so longer.

Q *Last year, my wallet was stolen while I was on holiday in Màlaga. It was a nightmare which I certainly don't want to repeat. What's the best way to cope with this sort of situation?*

A The most immediate problems are protecting yourself against fraud and getting replacement cash. Make sure you have any emergency phone numbers for plastic cards, travellers' cheques and so on with you, but keep them in a separate place from your money and valuables. If you use credit or charge cards, it is well worth joining a **card protection scheme**. These allow you easily and quickly to cancel all your cards if they are lost or stolen, and also include other help, such as lending you £750 cash in an emergency abroad. If you lose travellers' cheques, or they are stolen, the issuer may run a scheme to make an immediate refund to you in an emergency. Another option for getting cash is to phone your bank from abroad and ask it to telex funds to a nearby bank. The money will be paid to you only if you collect it in person and you will need to have some proof of your identity. Alternatively, you could phone a relative or friend and ask him or her to send money using one of the methods listed on pages 202–3.

If you have lost everything – money, passport, all means of identification – contact the nearest British Consulate. It can issue you with an emergency passport and, as a very last resort, it *may* lend you the money to get home, but only if there is no other help open to you.

Making gifts

Q *What's the best way to send money as a birthday present to my niece?*

A If you send money through the ordinary letter post and it goes missing, you might qualify for limited compensation if the post office was at fault. But do not be tempted just to slip a fiver inside a card. Lost or stolen cash is impossible to trace and you will have no proof that you ever posted it. A safer option is to send a cheque and check, after a few days, that it arrived safely; if not, contact your bank to cancel it. Cheques are not suitable if you want to send money to someone who does not have a bank account. Instead, you could send a postal order (available from post offices). Unlike cash, these are traceable because you keep a numbered counterfoil, which also provides proof of your purchase. Postal orders come in values up to £20 and you will need to buy two or more if you want to send larger sums. There is a fee for each order. To make a postal order more secure, you can specify that it be cashed at a particular post office, otherwise it can be presented at any office. And, if you know that the recipient has a bank account, you can cross the order like a cheque, so that it can only be paid into a bank account. Once again, it is a good idea to check with the recipient that the gift has arrived.

If you are sending money or similar items through the post it is safer to use registered post, which guarantees next-working-day delivery and compensation for loss or damage up to several hundred ££s.

Q *Can I give my grandchild some premium bonds or will I have to send his mother the money and ask her to buy them?*

A Parents, guardians, grandparents and great-grandparents – but not other relatives or unrelated adults – can buy bonds for children under age 16. The minimum investment is £100. Details and application forms are available from post offices. For more about premium bonds, see page 212.

Q *I'm on the mailing list for Help the Aged, which sends me requests for donations several times a year. I usually give something and I'd like to arrange to donate a regular sum each year. What's the best way of doing this?*

A There are two tax-efficient ways in which you can give regular small sums to charity:

- by using a **deed of covenant** This is a legally binding written promise that you will pay a given sum on a regular basis. It can be used for gifts of any size. Provided you are a taxpayer, you get tax relief at your highest rate of income tax on money you give to charity in this way. (Note that the 20 per cent rate of tax is ignored for this purpose, so you will get relief at the basic rate if you are a 20 per cent taxpayer)
- through a **payroll giving scheme**, often called **Give As You Earn** These are schemes, run by many employers, which let you specify that part of each pay packet be given to one or more charities of your choice. You can give any amount up to £900 a year (£75 a month) and, once again, you get tax relief on the payments at your highest rate.

To make gifts by deed of covenant, ask the charity to send you the appropriate form. If you are interested in payroll giving, check whether your employer runs such a scheme or would be willing to start one up.

Q *After speaking at a conference, I unexpectedly received a £300 fee. To me, the speech was just part and parcel of my normal work and I'd rather give the fee to charity. Is there a set procedure for doing this?*

A There is no special procedure. The fee is legally yours, and you will need to declare it for income tax purposes. You are free to use it in whatever way you choose, including donating it to charity. For sums of £250 or more, you can use the **gift aid scheme**. This gives you tax relief at your highest rate on the gift (though the 20 per cent rate is ignored, so you will get relief at the basic rate if you are a 20 per cent taxpayer). Contact the charity concerned for the appropriate form.

CHAPTER 7

SAVINGS AND INVESTMENTS

IT IS not possible in the space of a few pages to cover all you need to know about saving and investing, but some of the main issues, common problems and most interesting tips are looked at here. These range from homes for small savings to finding a cheap stockbroker, from investing for income to using investment-type life insurance. If you have substantial sums to invest, you should consider getting professional advice. Investment advisers have had a lot of bad publicity lately, and it pays to know what sort of advice is on offer and how to avoid incompetent advisers and rogues.

Choosing investments

Q *There seem to be so many different types of investment nowadays. How can I decide which would suit me?*

A As a first step, your choice of savings and investments should always reflect the amount you can save or invest; your tax position; how long you can invest for; whether you need ready access to your savings; your attitude towards risk; and whether you need an income either now or later. If you already have some investments, you need also to think about how well these will be complemented by any new ones, especially how the overall risk of your **portfolio** (i.e. your collection of investments) will be affected.

Q *I'm looking for an investment which will give me a high income and my capital back in full on demand. What would you recommend?*

A The late 1980s and early 1990s spoiled investors, who could get returns of 15 per cent a year from relatively safe building society accounts. But those were exceptional years. Usually, you can only get higher returns if you are prepared to take extra risks. Expect modest interest rates from deposit accounts; expect some risk to your capital in return for extra income or the prospect of higher gains. Do not take at face value any offers of investments which promise staggering riches for minimal risk — it is just not possible, as many who invested in companies like Barlow Clowes have found to their cost.

Q *I've just inherited £50,000. I don't really know where to start when it comes to investing it. Do you have any ideas?*

A If you have a reasonably large sum to invest — for example, an inheritance, a lump sum on retirement or redundancy, or simply savings you have built up over the years — it is sensible to seek advice from an independent financial adviser. You can get a list of advisers in your area by contacting IFAP, a body which promotes independent financial advice (see Addresses section). For more about getting financial advice, see pages 236–41.

Low-risk investments

Q *Are there particular types of investments which women should consider?*

A Since April 1990, when independent taxation put women on an equal footing with men for tax purposes, there has been little reason for women to take a special view of saving and investing. If you are married or live with a partner, though, you should arrange your investments between you in a way which makes full use of the tax allowances available to both of you (see page 13). If you have a family and have to gear the work you do to fit in with the demands of young children and school holidays, you could be on fairly low earnings, which will tend to restrict the scope of savings and investments available to you.

Q *I'm a part-time lecturer earning about £3,000 a year. I want to save a small sum — say, £10 or £20 a month. What investments would be suitable?*

A For small sums, National Savings, building society accounts and bank accounts may offer the best bet, especially if – as in your case – your income is too low to attract tax, because you can get interest credited to your account without any tax having been deducted. For competitive returns, look in particular at the National Savings Investment Account and building society regular savings accounts – see Table 7.1.

Once you have built up a few hundred pounds, or if you can invest at least £25 a month, say, you could consider unit trusts or investment trusts to give you the prospect of a higher, albeit riskier, return linked to shares (see page 218).

Q *What's a TESSA?*

A The Tax Exempt Special Savings Account (TESSA) is a very tax-efficient investment with a bank or building society. You invest in a deposit account which earns interest at a rate which is usually variable, although some TESSAs have fixed rates. Interest on the account builds up tax-free as long as you leave your money invested for five years. You can withdraw part of the interest without tax penalty at any time, but if you withdraw the rest of your investment before the five years are up you will lose the tax relief on the whole TESSA. You can, in theory, switch from one TESSA to another without losing tax relief, but in practice there are often penalty charges or bonuses to be lost, which make switching expensive.

If you are a taxpayer – and especially if you pay tax at the higher rate – TESSAs can be very attractive investments.

Q *What's the maximum I can invest in a TESSA?*

A Under the tax rules, the most you can invest in the first year is £3,000, followed by up to £1,800 in each of the next four years. But, over the five years, you must not invest more than £9,000 in total. Within these limits, the different TESSA providers set their own rules.

Q *I'd like to invest in a TESSA but I'm not absolutely sure that I can leave my money invested for five years. Would it be better to go for a normal building society account instead?*

Table 7.1: Homes for small savings

Investment	Minimum	Fixed or variable return	Tax treatment	Retrieving money
National Savings Investment Accounts	£20	Variable	Interest is taxable but paid without any tax deducted, which is especially convenient for non-taxpayers	One month's notice
Building society accounts	£1 with many accounts	Variable	Interest taxable and usually paid with basic rate tax already deducted but non-taxpayers can arrange to receive interest in full	Instant access with many accounts
Bank accounts	£1 with many accounts	Variable	Interest taxable and usually paid with basic rate tax already deducted but non-taxpayers can arrange to receive interest in full	Instant access with many accounts
National Savings Yearly Plans	£20 a month for one year	Fixed	Tax-free	Five-year scheme. No interest paid if you cash in during the first year; reduced interest if you cash in during years 2 to 4
Building society regular savings accounts	£1–20 a month	Variable	Interest taxable and usually paid with basic rate tax already deducted but non-taxpayers can arrange to receive interest in full	Withdrawals limited to, say, one to three each year. May be a bonus if you make none.

| Save-As-You-Earn (from some building societies and a few banks) | £1 a month | Fixed in relation to amount you save | Tax-free | Five-year scheme. Bonus if left for further two years. No interest paid if you withdraw during first year. Lower interest paid if you cash in during years 2 to 4 |
| Tax Exempt Special Savings Accounts (TESSAs) (from banks and building societies) | £1–25 with many schemes | Usually variable but fixed with some schemes | Tax-free | Five-year scheme. Interest becomes taxable if you withdraw capital before then but you can withdraw part of the interest. Some schemes pay lower interest if you withdraw early or switch to another TESSA. Some pay a bonus if you invest for the full five years |

Source: MoneyFacts

211

A Not necessarily. TESSAs are a good idea not just because of the tax relief but also because the interest rates they offer tend to match the best available on normal accounts. If you choose your TESSA carefully, you could put yourself in the position where:

- if you keep the TESSA for five years, you get an excellent tax-free return, and
- if you cash in early, you at least do no worse than you would have done by choosing a normal account instead.

Look for TESSAs which either do not have any penalties (other than loss of tax relief) on early withdrawal, or where the only 'penalty' is that you must give notice and you are confident that you could do that.

Q *Are premium bonds just a gamble or do they make good investment sense?*

A Premium bonds do not give you an investment return as such: you buy the bonds which take part in a draw for cash prizes each month (see Table 7.2). Whether you win or not is, of course, a matter of luck, but with a reasonable holding and *average* luck you could get a steady return from these bonds. And there is always the chance of a really big win – up to £1,000,000. What makes premium bonds different from other forms of gambling is that you do not lose your stake money – you can get it back, at any time, by cashing in the bonds. The main risk you take is giving up the return you could have got by investing the money elsewhere. For further information about premium bonds and an application form, ask at your local post office.

Q *Will the new National Lottery be like an investment?*

A No. The government's proposed National Lottery (set to launch in November 1994) will be a form of gambling – you will buy a ticket which will take part in a draw for prizes but you will not get your stake money back. Lotteries cannot be viewed as a form of investment. They are simply entertainment on a par with backing a horse in the Grand National.

Table 7.2: Premium bond prizes

Number of prizes every month	Amount of prize £
Big prizes each month	
1	1,000,000
2	100,000
3	50,000
4	25,000
10	10,000
25	5,000
Rest of fund split depending upon the amount invested – e.g. in May 1994 the smaller prizes were:	
465	1,000
1,395	500
14,335	100
214,356	50
230,596 TOTALS	14,988,800

Source: Department for National Savings

Stock market investments

Q *I have a few thousand pounds saved up and would like to invest it for a better return than the building society gives me. Would shares be a good idea?*

A If you are investing for the long term, then you really cannot afford to ignore the stock markets because over long periods the return on deposits, such as building society accounts, has been consistently much lower than the return on shares and has often failed even to keep pace with inflation. But unless you have very large sums to invest buying shares direct is not a good idea. With a small sum, it would be difficult and expensive to hold a reasonable spread of different shares. Instead, choose unit and investment trusts, which give you a stake in a ready-made portfolio (see page 217 onwards).

Q *How do shares work and who should invest in them?*

A Shares give you a stake in the ownership of a company. Many shares pay a regular income – called **dividends** – but usually investors hope the main part of the return will be a capital gain from being able to sell the shares at a higher price than that at which they were bought. But the price of shares can fall as well as rise, so they are not the home for money which you may need back at short notice (when prices may be low). And you should be prepared to invest long enough to ride out any dips in the market. To reduce risk, it is important to spread your money across a range of companies and industries. As a minimum, you should be investing in, say, seven or eight different companies and, because charges are relatively high for small deals, you will need to invest at least £1,000 in each.

Q *What charges do you have to pay when you buy and sell shares?*

A If you buy shares when they are newly issued – for example, government privatisation issues – there are no dealing charges. But, when you come to sell, or if you are buying shares already traded on the stock market, you will need to buy through a share dealer, e.g. a stockbroker or the broking department of a bank or building society, which will charge you for this service. In addition, there is stamp duty of 0.5 per cent of the amount purchased (rounded up to the nearest £50) when you buy existing shares. And on all sales and purchases over £10,000, there is a Stock Exchange levy of £2. You should also be aware that there are two prices for any share at any one time – a higher price at which you can buy and a lower price at which you can sell. The difference between them is called the **spread** and gives the market maker (whom you can think of as the shopkeeper who stocks the shares) his earnings.

Q *How much do stockbrokers and other share dealers charge?*

A Charges (called **commission**) are often made according to a scale which divides your transaction into slices with different rates applying to each slice. For example, for traditional stockbroking a typical scale might be:

- subject to a minimum charge – say, £20 – 1.5 per cent of the amount of the deal up to £7,000, e.g. 1.5% x £5,000 = £75 on a deal of £5,000

- if you are buying or selling more than £7,000 worth of shares, 1.5 per cent on the first £7,000 and 0.55 per cent on anything above that up to £15,000, e.g. (1.5% x £7,000) + (0.55% x £3,000) = £121.50 on a deal of £10,000
- if you are buying or selling more than £15,000 worth of shares, 1.5 per cent of the first £7,000, 0.55 per cent of anything above that up to £15,000 and 0.5 per cent of any amount above £15,000, e.g. (1.5% x £7,000) + (0.55% x £8,000) + (0.5% x £5,000) = £174 on a deal of £20,000.

Instead, some dealers charge a flat fee, the level of which depends on the size of the deal.

Q *Do all share dealers charge roughly the same?*

A No, this is a competitive sector and there is a lot of variation in charges between different firms. In addition, there are different types of dealing services:

- **execution-only service** The firm simply carries out your instructions to buy or sell shares and does not offer any advice. This is the cheapest service and will be the best choice if you have only a small holding of shares (e.g. you want to sell some privatisation shares) or you have both the time and inclination to do your own research
- **execution and advice service** This generally costs more than an execution-only service. When you first make contact, the dealer discusses with you your personal details and investment aims and will then be available to give you advice when you request it. The firm may also take the initiative in contacting you with suggestions and, possibly, published information. The type of service provided varies from firm to firm
- **portfolio management service** For this, the most expensive option, the firm takes over all the administration of your portfolio, either on an **advisory basis** similar to the execution and advice service already described, or on a **discretionary basis** whereby the firm makes all the investment decisions on your behalf. Many firms offer this service only if you have something in the region of £50,000–£100,000 to invest.

Q *Some execution-only services look incredibly cheap. I've come across one which charges only £5 whatever the value of the shares you're buying or selling. This looks too good to be true What's the catch?*

A Execution-only services are often operated by post, which has the advantage of cheapness and simplicity, but you lose control over the timing and price of your deal. The cheapest services may also be available only for a restricted range of shares, for example, privatisation issues or a selection of **blue chip** shares (i.e. those of large, well-known companies, such as Marks & Spencer and ICI).

Q *I have a financial adviser who usually arranges my life insurance and other investments. Can I buy shares through him rather than going to a stockbroker?*

A Yes, you can, but you may have to pay more. Most financial advisers cannot buy and sell stock market investments directly but will, themselves, have to deal through a stockbroker. The broker will often have a higher scale of charges for such deals and will share the commission with your adviser.

MORE INFORMATION ABOUT SHARE-DEALING SERVICES

The major banks and some building societies operate share-dealing services through their branch networks (or you can get details of their share services from branches). For details of stockbrokers and the services they offer, contact the Association of Private Client Investment Managers and Stockbrokers (APCIMS) (see Addresses section).

Q *I'm sure I've seen advertisements for an investment in shares on which you can't lose your money. How does that work?*

A Not everyone is comfortable taking the risks with their capital which are inherent in shares, so investment firms have launched a variety of guaranteed stock market investments. These work in a variety of ways, but all have the same aim: to give you a return based on increasing share prices but with a guarantee that you will not lose your original capital. Most of the schemes are offered by insurance companies and have names like 'guaranteed bond' or 'capital protector bond'. There are many variations on the theme but, for example, you might invest £5,000 in an investment-type insurance policy with a lifetime of five years (avoid taking your money out early, as there will be surrender penalties). When the policy matures, you get back the higher of the amount you invested or, depending on how the scheme works:

- your investment increased in line with the performance of a fund invested in shares; or
- your investment increased in line with the increase in the FT-SE 100 index, or some percentage of that increase.

Guaranteed bonds based on a fund usually give you the benefit of income from the shares as well as capital growth. This is not so with bonds which link your return to the FT-SE index – you lose out on the dividend income, which would typically be another 3–5 per cent a year (before tax). With both types, but especially bonds using a fund, watch out for charges. If you are not happy with stock market risks, you could also look at with-profits insurance (see page 228).

Q *What's the difference between a unit trust and an investment trust?*

A A unit trust is a ready-made portfolio of a large number of shares and other investments run by professional managers on behalf of lots of investors who buy **units** in the portfolio. Like shares, the value of your units can go up and down reflecting the performance of the underlying investments. You pay a percentage of your original capital – typically 5 per cent – to the trust manager, and there is a further yearly fee of, say, 1.5 per cent of the fund.

An investment trust is similar to a unit trust but is itself a company quoted on the Stock Exchange. You buy its shares to give you a stake in its investment portfolio. The price of the shares will tend to rise and fall with the value of these underlying investments, but can be affected by other factors. Investment trusts can choose a wider spread of underlying investments than unit trusts and, unlike unit trusts, can also borrow money to invest, which increases both risk and potential return.

Q *I gather that unit and investment trusts give you a stake in a portfolio of underlying investments. What sorts of investment are these?*

A There are many different types of unit and investment trust: some aim to provide capital growth, others income; some specialise in small companies or recovery stocks, UK, Japanese or US shares, government stocks, and so on; others invest in all of these, varying the proportions of each investment as market conditions change. You choose the trusts which suit your investment aims. If you want to avoid taking too much risk, consider choosing:

- a **balanced unit trust** which has a very broad spread of investments and aims to produce a mix of income and capital growth
- a **general international investment trust** investing in a broad spread of investments across a range of different countries
- a **UK general unit or investment trust** investing in a wide range of UK-based investments.

More specialist funds, which, for example, invest in a single foreign country, in commodities such as gold or in new ventures, are more risky. The performance of trusts even of one type is very varied (see Table 7.3) so it makes sense to spread your money across more than one trust, rather than pinning all your hopes on just one.

Q *What's the minimum amount I can invest in a unit or investment trust?*

A To invest in an investment trust, you could go to a share-dealing service, such as a stockbroker, in which case charges will tend to make lump sums much below £1,000 uneconomic. But many investment trust companies run savings schemes which let you invest small sums either on a regular basis – minimum about £25–30 a month – or as *ad hoc* lump sums – minimum is commonly £250. To use these schemes you either contact the company direct or through a financial adviser (see page 236).

Unit trusts have similar minimum investments of, say, £250 for lump sums or £25 a month for regular sums. Once again, you can invest either by going to the unit trust management company direct or through a financial adviser.

Table 7.3: How the performance of unit trusts can vary

UK general unit trusts: percentage growth during the year ending 31 December			
Year	Worst-performing trust %	Best-performing trust %	Average trust %
1988	−5.7	21.2	1.9
1989	1.2	34.6	19.8
1990	−39.5	−3.0	−17.1
1991	−1.7	20.8	7.9
1992	1.6	19.0	11.2
1993	8.9	39.8	19.2

Source: *Money Management*

Q *Are shares and unit and investment trusts all taxed in the same way?*

A Yes. The income from shares (including those of investment trusts) and unit trusts is taxable and paid with tax of 20 per cent already deducted. You also receive a tax credit for the amount deducted and, if you are a non-taxpayer, you can use this to claim tax back. If you are a 20 per cent or basic-rate taxpayer, you have no further tax to pay, but a higher-rate taxpayer must pay a further 20 per cent tax on the amount of the income received plus tax credit.

Gains on shares and investment or unit trusts may be liable for capital gains tax (CGT) but only gains in excess of inflation count and you can make up to £5,800 of gains tax-free in the 1994–5 tax year.

Q *Isn't it possible to invest in shares and trusts without having to pay any tax by using a PEP? Are there any drawbacks to doing this?*

A You can invest up to £6,000 a year in shares, investment trusts and unit trusts through a **personal equity plan (PEP)** – and a further £3,000 a year in a PEP investing in the shares of just one company. Provided the rules are kept, all income and gains earned by the PEP are tax-free. Tax-free income can either be paid out to you or re-invested in your plan. PEPs will usually be a good idea for higher-rate taxpayers, but some experts suggest that people who pay tax at the lower rates are unlikely to benefit because:

* only very large investors are likely to pay CGT on gains anyway

- PEP charges may swallow up the tax relief on income. Watch out, in particular, for extra charges levied for sending you a copy of the annual report and accounts or fees charged when you cash in or transfer a PEP or make withdrawals from it.

But the charges made on PEPs have been falling over recent years and the return from a unit or investment trust sheltered in a PEP is now likely to be better than the return from investing directly in the trust, even for a basic-rate taxpayer. The difference will tend to be greater the longer the investment period and the higher the income produced by the underlying investments.

Q *Are there any penalties for withdrawing money from a PEP?*

A You can make withdrawals at any time without losing the tax advantages on the money which remains invested. But some PEP managers levy a charge on withdrawals, which may be higher in the early years of the plan.

Q *I have some unit trust holdings. Can I tell the taxman that I want them to be given PEP status?*

A No, you cannot set up your own PEP. You must use a professional PEP manager. These include, for example, some unit trust management companies, investment trust companies, banks and stockbrokers.

Q *Can I use a PEP whatever the unit trust or investment trust I choose?*

A No. If you invest through a PEP, you can put the full £6,000 every tax year in **qualifying trusts**. A qualifying trust is one that invests at least 50 per cent of its value in UK or European shares. Within the £6,000 limit, you can invest up to £1,500 in **non-qualifying trusts** – these are trusts which do not meet the 50 per cent rule (for example, many international growth or income trusts and funds investing in, say, Japan or North America). A non-qualifying trust must hold at least half of its assets as ordinary shares, which means that funds investing largely in government stocks or bonds are not eligible for PEPs.

MORE INFORMATION ABOUT UNIT AND INVESTMENT TRUSTS

The Association of Investment Trust Companies (AITC) issues free factsheets about investment trusts and a variety of other publications. You can get information about particular investment trust companies by contacting them direct.

The Association of Unit Trusts and Investment Funds (AUTIF) runs a unit trust information service and can provide a free starter pack to those interested. For information about particular unit trusts, contact the management company direct.

See Addresses section for AITC and AUTIF.

Several newspapers list unit and investment trust prices and popular personal finance magazines, available through newsagents, often run surveys. The *Unit Trust Year Book* (published by FTBI) gives a lot of information about each trust and its managers – try your public reference library.

Q *My husband and I retired five years ago. We've topped up a modest pension with income from two building society accounts. But the interest from these is now so low that we are looking for a better way to invest. What do you recommend?*

A Table 7.4 lists some of the investments you might consider as an alternative to the building society. There are three broad factors to weigh up when choosing between them:

- **the effect of inflation** Building society and other deposit-type investments may seem 'safe', but the amount of your capital does not grow and its value is eaten away by inflation. Even with just 2 per cent a year inflation, £1,000 now would be worth only £750 in 15 years' time in terms of what it could buy. To protect the real value of your capital and the income it provides, you need to consider investments which give you capital growth as well as income, or index-linked investments, for at least part of your savings

Table 7.4: Investing for income

Investment	Income	Capital	Comment
Building society income accounts	Variable	Fixed	—
National Savings Pensioner's Guaranteed Income Bond	Fixed for five years	Fixed	A best buy deposit investment for those aged 65 or over
National Savings Income Bonds	Variable	Fixed	—
Guaranteed income bonds (from life insurance companies)	Fixed	Fixed	—
British Government stocks (invest through post offices or stockbrokers)	Fixed	Fixed if held for full term; variable if sold earlier	Buying through the post office is cheapest. Consult a stockbroker if you need advice about which stocks to choose. To invest in a portfolio of stocks, consider investing through a unit or investment trust
Index-linked British Government stocks (invest through post offices or stockbrokers)	Increases in line with price inflation	Linked to inflation if held for full term; variable if sold earlier	
Permanent interest-bearing shares (PIBS) (invest through stockbrokers)	Fixed	Variable – depends on prices at which bought and sold	Minimum investment £1,000 or more

Lifetime annuities (from life insurance companies)	Fixed or increasing – you choose at time you invest	Capital not retrievable as a lump sum	Higher rates the older you are. Men get higher rates than women. More suitable for those aged at least 65
Temporary annuities (from life insurance companies)	Fixed	Capital not retrievable as a lump sum	—
Shares (through stockbrokers)	Usually variable, but some types of shares give fixed income	Variable – depends on prices at which bought and sold	Suitable if you can invest reasonably large sums. If not, choose investment trusts or unit trusts
Guaranteed equity bonds (from a few life insurance companies, banks and building societies)	Fixed	Variable – depends on performance of stock market	Guaranteed 'income' will, in effect, be funded from your capital, if stock market returns lower than expected
Unit and investment trusts (from trust companies direct or through stockbrokers and other financial advisers)	Usually variable	Variable – depends on prices at which bought and sold	Popular way of protecting capital and income against inflation over the long term

- **fixed or variable income** An income which can vary is vulnerable to falls in interest rates. On the other hand, if you lock yourself into a fixed rate of interest, you will miss out if other interest rates rise
- **the risk to your capital** With the main investments which give you a chance of beating inflation – shares and unit trusts, for example – there is a risk that prices will fall and you would lose some of your capital if you had to sell. But, if you are investing for the long term, you should aim to hold on to your investments until prices pick up again.

To achieve a balance between these risks, you should probably choose a mix of different investments, for example, British Government stocks or even a temporary annuity to provide income plus share-based investments to provide capital growth (see Table 7.4).

Q *I've spotted an investment offering guaranteed income of 10 per cent a year. That's way above most other interest rates. Is it a con?*

A There are a number of high-income investments, often called **guaranteed equity bonds**, which 'guarantee' a relatively high income, usually for a set period of time. They also aim to pay back your original capital at the end of that time *provided* that the stock market has performed well enough – if not, you get back less than your original investment. In that case, your high 'income' would, in effect, have been financed partly by payments out of your capital. Similarly, some unit trusts also offer very high levels of income but, once again, there is a higher-than-normal risk that you will not get all your capital back if you cash in your units.

These investments can be very useful provided you realise that your capital may be at risk.

Q *Do British Government stocks guarantee to give you back your original investment?*

A Not necessarily, but they can give you a return which is known and guaranteed at the time you invest. Conventional British

Government stocks – also called **gilts** – give you a return comprising two elements:

- **interest** Every stock offers a fixed rate of interest (the **coupon**). Interest is usually paid twice a year
- **capital gain or loss** If you sell on the stock market, this will depend on prices at the time you sell compared with the price you originally paid. But most gilts have a fixed lifetime, at the end of which the government buys back (**redeems**) the stock at a known and fixed price – the stock's **nominal value** or **par value**. If you paid less than the nominal value and hold the stock until redemption, you will make a capital gain; if you paid more, you will make a capital loss.

Q *In what situations would British Government stocks be a good investment?*

A Gilts are very versatile. It is better to think of them as a whole family of investments which can be used for all sorts of reasons. Here are a few:

- **high-coupon stocks** offering a fixed rate of interest of, for example, 10 per cent or even 15.5 per cent are useful if you need income, e.g. in retirement or to pay school fees. But you may have to pay more than the nominal value for them, so your high income may be at the expense of capital
- **low-income stocks** offering fixed interest of only 2.5–4 per cent, say, can be very tax-efficient investments for higher-rate taxpayers if they can be bought at a good price. This is because although interest from gilts is taxable at your highest rate, capital gains are tax-free
- **guaranteed return** If you know you will need a lump sum at a set time, you can choose a gilt due to be redeemed then and hold it until redemption
- **speculation** The gilts market is influenced by government policies and economic factors. You can speculate on the market in the same ways that you can 'play the stock market' – though this is a fairly risky strategy.

Q *How safe are British Government stocks?*

A You can choose how you use gilts – either as low-risk, guaranteed return investments or as a higher-risk gamble on the way market prices will move. But you may be sure that it is *very* unlikely that the government would not be able to pay back gilts at redemption. Unlike shares in a company, gilts are loans to the government, which has billions of ££ of taxpayers' money to back up its ability to pay. The stocks' nickname 'gilts' is short for **gilt-edged stock**, reflecting how secure they are.

Q *How can I buy and sell British Government stocks?*

A You can buy and sell through a stockbroker (or other dealer – see page 214). You will have to pay dealing charges, though these are usually lower than for shares. But, unless you are buying and selling very large amounts, a cheaper way to buy and sell is through post offices. There are some important differences between the two methods of trading:

- if you buy through the post office, you must also sell through the post office. Similarly, if you buy through a stockbroker etc. you cannot sell through the post office
- if you use the post office you will be dealing by post so you cannot be certain of the timing and price of your deal
- interest from gilts bought through the post office is paid without any tax deducted. Interest on gilts bought through other routes is paid with tax at the basic rate already deducted.

Q *I'm attracted to gilts as a way of boosting my income but I'm confused about which stocks to buy. Would it be better to invest in a gilt unit trust?*

A A gilt or fixed-interest unit trust invests at least 80 per cent of its fund in government stocks and other bonds or shares offering a fixed interest. The fund is professionally managed, usually aiming to combine income with some capital growth, so you are relieved of the worry of selecting the stocks and deciding when to buy and sell. But there are two drawbacks to investing through a trust:

- trust charges – typically 5 per cent of the amount you invest plus an annual management charge of, say, 0.75 to 1 per cent of the fund – are higher than the dealing costs you will incur when making your own investments
- although, with both trusts and direct investment in gilts, income is taxable, the capital gains tax position is different. Gains on direct holdings of gilts are tax-free, but gains from unit trusts are potentially taxable. (Whether or not you do pay capital gains tax depends on what allowances you can claim: see page 149.)

Rather than investing in a trust, you might do better to get advice from a stockbroker.

Insurance-based investments

Q *What exactly is an annuity?*

A This is an investment, offered by insurance companies, which swaps a lump sum for a regular income either for the rest of your life – called a **permanent** or **lifetime annuity** – or for a set period of time – a **temporary annuity**. You cannot get your original investment back as a lump sum. Instead, your 'income' is made up partly of interest and partly return of capital. Only the interest part is taxable.

The interest on annuities closely follows the interest available on gilts, so when interest rates generally are low, the income available from annuities will tend to be poor. The capital element of each payment depends on how long the annuity is to last. In the case of a lifetime annuity, this is not known at the outset, but it is assumed that the annuity will carry on paying out for the lifetime of the *average* person of your age and sex. For this reason, the income from an annuity is higher the older you are, and is higher for men (who have a lower average life expectancy) than for women.

Q *What sort of life insurance policies can be used as an investment?*

A There are two broad types of policy which are used in this way:

- **endowment policy**, which builds up an investment value over a set period of time (the **term** or **endowment period**), often 10 or

25 years. At the end of that time, the policy **matures** and the proceeds are paid out. If you die during the term, the policy also pays out – in this case, either a minimum guaranteed sum or the value of the investment built up so far. Premiums for an endowment policy can either be regular payments or a single lump sum

- **whole-life policy**, designed to run for your whole life rather than for a set term. When you die, it pays out either a minimum guaranteed sum or the investment value which has accumulated up to then. But once the policy has built up a value, you can cash it in at any time to provide you with an investment return. Premiums for a whole-life policy are usually regular payments.

Q *I've been sold a ten-year life insurance savings plan. The booklet which came with it is very confusing. In particular, I don't understand what 'unit-linked' means. Can you explain?*

A If you invest through a life insurance policy or a pension plan, you face a fundamental choice of investment basis: unit-linked or with profits. With a unit-linked plan, you buy units which give you a stake in a fund of investments – usually shares, but possibly bonds, property and so on. The price of your units rises and falls with the value of the underlying fund. So if share prices fall you lose money. But provided you can sit through troughs in the stock market, you should see your investment grow, because the long-term trend is for the market steadily to rise.

Q *What's the difference between a with-profits policy and a unitised with-profits policy?*

A When you invest on a with-profits basis, the return you get depends on the overall performance of the life insurer's with-profits business. A key factor will be investment performance, but other factors, such as business expenses, claims on death, dividends to shareholders (if the insurer operates as a company) and so on, will be important too.

A traditional with-profits policy guarantees you a minimum payout on death or maturity. But at regular intervals the insurance company reviews the performance of its with-profits business, and, on the basis of this, declares **reversionary** bonuses which are added to the minimum sum. Once added, the bonuses cannot be taken away, so – unlike the unit-linked option – the value of your policy cannot fall. When your policy or plan reaches maturity, a further **terminal** bonus is added. The terminal bonus often accounts for as much as half of the total return.

Traditional with-profits policies are giving way – especially in the case of pension plans – to **unitised with-profits** versions. Although these work in a slightly different way, with your premiums buying units to which reversionary and terminal bonuses are added, the bonuses still cannot be taken away once they have been added. The main differences between traditional and unitised with-profits policies are:

- the charges for a unitised with-profits plan are explicit and similar to the charges for a unit-linked plan. By contrast, traditional with-profits expenses are hidden in the bonus calculation
- it may be possible to switch a company's unitised with-profits fund to its unit-linked funds. This is not possible with a conventional policy
- with unitised policies, the company may reserve the right to reduce the value of units on early surrender if investment conditions are exceptionally bad. There is no similar provision with conventional policies.

Both types of with-profits policies aim to smooth out variations in the stock market and provide a way of getting some of the benefits of stock market growth without the risk of losing your capital.

Q *Which is best: a unit-linked policy or a with-profits policy?*

A The standard advice used to be: choose with-profits if you do not like risk; choose unit-linked for the chance of a higher, but riskier, return. Such advice was soundly based. For example, in 1980 the best maturing 10-year with-profits policy would have given you a return equivalent to some 11 per cent a year compared with an impressive 18 per cent from the best unit-linked plan. However, the worst with-profits policy would have given you about 7 per cent a year – a big improvement on the miserly 3 per cent from the worst unit-linked plan.

But the early 1990s broke this pattern. Despite cuts in bonus rates, with-profits policies consistently outperformed unit-linked plans – see

Table 7.5. In part, this reflects the impact of strong bonuses credited during the 1980s when competition forced many insurers to maintain high bonuses by dipping into reserves. Some experts predict that continuing bonus cuts will bring with-profits returns back below the returns on unit-linked policies. If they are right, then a policy linked to a broadly invested managed fund may have the edge over with-profits for new investors, provided they do not mind the extra risk.

Table 7.5: With-profits and unit-linked compared

Maturity values for 10-year endowment policies*		
	With-profits £	Unit-linked £
Policies maturing in early 1990 (£30 a month invested)		
Best	8,958	8,679
Average	7,286	6,766
Worst	6,022	5,507
Policies maturing in early 1991 (£30 a month invested)		
Best	8,475	6,694
Average	7,367	5,307
Worst	5,887	3,897
Policies maturing in early 1992 (£50 a month invested)		
Best	13,693	10,174
Average	11,942	8,895
Worst	9,208	7,335
Policies maturing in early 1993 (£50 a month invested)		
Best	12,300	10,367
Average	11,152	9,128
Worst	9,164	7,850

* For a man aged 30 next birthday.
Source: *Money Management*

Q *I took out an insurance plan three years ago, saving £50 a month. The plan was supposed to run for ten years but I've unexpectedly had to cash it in. I couldn't believe it when the insurance company told me the plan was worth only £1,200. That's less than the £1,800 I've paid in premiums. Surely the company has got its sums wrong?*

A Most investment-type life insurance is designed to run for at least ten years, often much longer. If you can commit yourself to saving for the full term, you can expect a reasonable return. But if you need to cash in early be prepared for a nasty shock: you may get back far less than you have invested – see Table 7.6. Cash-in values are low in the early years because a large chunk of the costs occurs in the first year or so of a policy – for example, an insurance company may pay an immediate lump sum commission of, say, £275 to a person or firm which sells you a £50-a-month, ten-year policy. Moreover, with a with-profits policy, up to half the return is paid as a terminal bonus when the policy matures. If you cash in early, you miss out on this bonus.

Table 7.6: Surrender values for policies requiring £50–per-month premiums[1]

| | Surrender value after this number of years | | | | |
| | 3 | 7 | 10 | 15 | 20 |
	£	£	£	£	£
10-year endowment policy					
Highest surrender value	1,983	6,446			
Average surrender value	1,513	5,263			
Lowest surrender value	1,041	4,553			
Premiums paid	1,800	4,200			
25-year endowment policy					
Highest surrender value	1,796	6,038	11,819	27,820	51,928
Average surrender value	1,190	4,258	7,914	18,785	40,045
Lowest surrender value	497	3,131	5,799	12,210	24,567
Premiums paid	1,800	4,200	6,000	9,000	12,000

[1] For man aged 30.
Source: *Money Management*, May 1993. Surrender values at 1 February 1993.

Q *Having been made redundant, I can't keep up the payments on a 25-year endowment policy which I took out seven years ago. The cash value of the policy just about matches the amount I've paid in over the years – not much of a return on my money. Are there any alternatives to simply surrendering the policy?*

A If you need to raise cash now, but can still afford to carry on paying the premiums in future, you could ask your insurance company if it will let you make a **partial surrender**. This is suitable if your policy has been going for some time and means cashing in part of the investment growth to date, but not all companies allow this.

If you have a with-profits policy which has been running for some years, you may be able to borrow from the insurance company. The maximum loan will be a proportion of the surrender value and you will be charged interest, usually at a favourable rate. You still keep paying the premiums (but you could use part of the loan to do this). You can repay the loan out of the eventual policy proceeds.

If you cannot afford the premiums any more, but do not need cash immediately, you could make your policy 'paid up', leaving the premiums to date invested. How much of the policy's value this will salvage varies with the policy-type and insurance company.

If you have a with-profits policy, particularly an endowment (i.e. a policy with a fixed lifetime), a further option is to sell it. The new owner pays the future premiums and collects the policy proceeds on maturity (or if you die). You receive a lump sum from the sale which is higher than the surrender value offered by the insurance company. Usually you will need to have held your policy for at least five years or a quarter of its term.

Q *How do I set about selling a life insurance policy?*

A There are specialist companies which arrange the sale of policies. For example, Beale Dobie (call the telephone operator and ask for 'Freephone Surrender') is a market maker which buys and sells policies on its own account, making its money through the difference between the buying and selling prices. H. E. Foster & Cranfield (tel: 071–608 1941) is unique in the UK as a financial auctioneer and has been auctioning life policies for 150 years. It takes a charge of one-third of the excess you make over the surrender value, but gains can be high – on average, a policy can be expected to make a gain of 30–40 per cent at auction. Other companies operate mainly by matching buyers and sellers (similar to an estate agent). You can also get in touch with specialist companies like these through a financial adviser. For a list of independent financial advisers in your area, phone IFAP (see Addresses section).

Q *How are the investment returns from a life insurance policy taxed?*

A If you pay income tax at the basic rate or less, you will not have to pay tax on the return from any life insurance policy, but there could be extra tax to pay if you are getting **age allowance** (see page 144) and you cash in a **non-qualifying policy** (see next question). You should be aware, however, that the life insurance company has already paid its own tax on the investment return you get. The Inland Revenue deems this to be equivalent to income tax at the basic rate, but you cannot reclaim any of it if you are a 20 per cent taxpayer or a non-taxpayer.

Q *I'm a higher-rate taxpayer. Will I have to pay tax when my life insurance plan matures or I cash it in?*

A This depends on whether it is a **qualifying policy** or a **non-qualifying policy**.

A qualifying policy is one designed to last for at least ten years and held for a minimum of either ten years or three-quarters of its term, whichever is less. There is no tax for you to pay on the return you get from this type of policy.

All other policies are non-qualifying and there is no basic-rate tax to pay on their proceeds (because the company has already accounted for this). But, for a higher-rate taxpayer like yourself, there could be an extra 15 per cent tax to pay, though you may be able to claim **top-slicing relief** (see page 145).

Q *Do investment-type insurance policies always produce a lump sum or can they be used to provide an income too?*

A There are two ways in which insurance plans can provide an income:

- **partial surrender** You can cash in part of your policy on a regular basis
- **cluster policies** Instead of paying a premium and getting just one policy, you get a number of smaller policies which you can cash in at different times to produce an income.

Whichever method you use, with a qualifying policy there is no tax to pay on the amount you receive. With a non-qualifying policy, there may be tax to pay if you are a higher-rate taxpayer, but special tax rules let you take a limited income from a policy and put off paying any tax on the income until you eventually cash in the whole policy.

Q *Unit trusts and unit-linked life insurance seem very similar. Should I choose one rather than the other?*

A You are right that the basis on which your money is invested is very similar. But there are some important differences between the two investments:

- charges will generally be much higher with a life policy (mainly because of higher marketing costs)
- the structure of life company charges means that you may get a poor return if you cash in during the early years. Unit trusts are more flexible in this respect
- both life companies and unit trusts must pay tax on income from the underlying investments. If you are a non-taxpayer, you can reclaim the tax already paid by a unit trust, but you cannot reclaim tax paid by a life company. On the other hand, if you are a higher-rate taxpayer, you will have to pay extra tax on income from a unit trust, whereas you often will not have to pay extra on the proceeds from a life policy (see page 145)
- unlike a unit trust, a life company must account for tax on gains as well and you cannot reclaim this even if you personally would not have incurred any capital gains tax
- you can take an income from a life insurance policy and put off paying any tax on it. This is a useful facility for a higher-rate taxpayer or someone who would have to pay capital gains tax on cashing in unit trusts
- you can often switch from one investment fund to another much more cheaply with a unit-linked insurance policy than with unit trusts.

Similar arguments apply if you compare investing in an investment trust with taking out a unit-linked insurance policy. Unless you are a higher-rate taxpayer, you will generally do better to choose a unit or investment trust rather than unit-linked life insurance unless you are an active investor who wants to switch frequently from fund to fund.

Q *Are friendly societies the same as insurance companies?*

A Not exactly. Friendly societies grew up mainly in the nineteenth century as self-help groups to give financial help to their members during life's crises – death, ill health and old age. Basically insurance groups, they now have a curious special status which allows them (*inter alia*) to offer highly tax-efficient investments but only for very small sums. The mainstay of many friendly societies' business is the sale of tax-exempt plans. With these, you save up to £18 a month or £200 a year for a minimum of ten years and your money is invested by the society on either a with-profits or a unit-linked basis. What makes these plans special is that the society – unlike a normal insurance company – pays no income or capital gains tax on the returns from investing your savings, so at maturity you get a completely tax-free lump sum. Many societies let you deposit a lump sum (maximum about £1,700 for a ten-year plan), which is invested to provide regular payments into the plan each year.

Q *Will an investment with a friendly society always give a better return than a similar investment with an ordinary insurance company?*

A Not necessarily. The maximum savings limit for a friendly society investment applies per person. With such a low investment, the society's charges for running the plan make a relatively large dent in your savings and will swallow up the tax advantage to some extent. The other factor deciding whether or not the friendly society beats less tax-efficient investments will be how well your money grows. On investment performance alone, one or two friendly societies have a very good track record for with-profits plans compared with normal insurance companies, but other friendly societies have been less impressive and, on a unit-linked basis, ordinary insurance companies have tended to perform better.

Q *Who should consider taking out a friendly society tax-free investment?*

A Provided investment performance is reasonable and charges do not swallow up the tax perk, a friendly society tax-exempt plan can be a worthwhile, though small, investment for any taxpayer but especially those who pay tax at the higher rate. Tax-exempt plans can also be useful for parents wanting to invest money for their children (see page 24).

Financial advice

Q *Isn't financial advice just for people with a lot of money? What help is there for people like me who don't have much but are still confused by all the different investments and the sales hype?*

A Some advisers specialise in the wealthy end of the market, but most are open to all. The majority of advisers do not charge fees, so you do not need to worry about not being able to afford the advice. But that is not to say that the advice is free. Most financial advisers receive commission from the companies whose products they sell to you. And ultimately, of course, that means you are paying through higher product charges. Not all products carry commission – in particular, most deposits (e.g. building society accounts and National Savings investments) do not – so do not expect an adviser to spend a lot of time with you if you have only very small sums available.

Q *I've seen the sign 'independent financial adviser' on a couple of doors in the high street. What precisely does it mean? Aren't these people simply insurance salesmen?*

A No, an independent financial adviser is more than just a salesperson. A good adviser can assess your complete financial situation now and work out the resources which would be available to you and/or your family in possible future circumstances. On the basis of this analysis, he or she can recommend financial products to strengthen your financial position. If the adviser is independent, these will be taken from the full range of products and companies available – deposits, unit trusts, health insurance, life insurance, and so on.

Q *My bank has a life insurance and pensions consultant visiting every Wednesday afternoon. Is he an independent adviser?*

A It is unlikely. The public is often confused about the status of all the various 'advisers', 'consultants' and so on. But, really, it is very simple. For life insurance, pensions and unit trusts, there are just two types of financial intermediary:

- **those who sell the products of just one company** This includes company reps, of course, but also other tied sales outlets. These come in a variety of forms from the one-man-band to huge high street banks and building societies, even to football clubs selling life insurance to their fans
- **independent advisers** These can sell you the products of *any* company. Once again, they come in a variety of forms, and you should be aware that solicitors and accountants who give some financial advice are required to be independent.

A few banks and building societies have decided to offer independent financial advice through their branch networks. But the vast majority are tied outlets selling either the products of their own life insurance company or those of a separate company with whom they have an agreement.

Q *Is independent advice always preferable?*

A You need to weigh the following factors:

- it is unlikely that the products which a tied outlet or company rep can sell you will always be the best for you. So you may get higher-quality products overall from an independent adviser who can match your needs with the products of any company
- a company rep or tied outlet might not have *any* products which are suitable for you. An independent adviser can select from the full range of products available
- you might be very happy with a particular company's products and service – perhaps you are already a customer or you have done your own research. In this case, there is little point going to an independent adviser
- you may find it more convenient to buy through a tied sales outlet or company rep than to seek out independent advice.

Q *If most advisers are paid by commission, how can I be sure that they aren't just suggesting I invest in something simply so they'll earn more?*

A You can't. A good adviser will not be swayed by commission. On the other hand, an adviser who charges no fees but never recommended commission-paying products could not survive. This is not just a conflict faced by independent advisers. Tied outlets are paid commission too and company reps may get commission or sales-related bonuses. While only an independent adviser would be in a position to recommend one company rather than another to earn higher commission, all types of adviser and salesperson potentially could recommend a sale when none is warranted, in order to get the commission. Sadly, there is evidence that this has sometimes happened.

To help remedy the situation, from January 1995 all advisers and salespeople will have to tell you, at the time of the deal, the amount of commission they will earn by making a sale to you. (At present, this information is available only after the deal or, earlier, only on request.) It is hoped that customers will develop a feel for commission levels and will be prepared to challenge a recommendation that looks as if it might have been influenced by commission.

To avoid the problem, you could go to an adviser who does not keep commissions and charges fees instead. You can get a list of fee-based advisers in your area by contacting the Money Management National Register of Fee-based Independent Advisers – see Addresses section.

Q *There is such a lot in the newspaper about bad investment advice and people losing money because of it. How can I tell if an adviser is any good?*

A There is no foolproof way, but a good adviser will:

- be authorised to carry on investment business
- tell you his or her status (tied or independent) and what kind of service he or she can offer
- ask enough questions to find out about your family and financial circumstances, your investment aims and your attitude towards risk
- consider the range of investments suitable for you, even if they are not ones which would earn the adviser commission
- discuss with you the reasons for the recommendations.

Q *What does being 'authorised' mean?*

A Financial advisers and many other investment businesses are regulated under the Financial Services Act 1986. The Act makes it a criminal offence for anyone to carry on an investment business without being authorised by an appropriate regulatory body (see Box). The regulatory body is responsible for ensuring that its members are fit and proper to be in the business and that they conduct their affairs in accordance with the various rules made under the Act. The chief regulatory body – the **Securities and Investments Board (SIB)** – keeps a register of all authorised firms which you can consult (see page 277) to check out any firm with which you are about to do business. If you suspect that a firm is not authorised, report it to either SIB or the police and do not do any business with it.

WHO'S WHO UNDER THE FINANCIAL SERVICES ACT

The Chancellor of the Exchequer is the government minister with overall responsibility for financial services.

The Securities and Investments Board (SIB) is the chief regulating body. A few investment businesses, e.g. most building societies, are authorised directly by SIB. But most of SIB's day-to-day functions are delegated to the **Self Regulating Organisations (SROs)** and the **Recognised Professional Bodies (RPBs)**.

The Self Regulating Organisations
Financial Intermediaries, Managers and Brokers Association (FIMBRA) authorises most independent investment advisers who deal direct with the public.

Securities and Futures Association (SFA) authorises stockbrokers, market makers, dealers in financial futures and so on.

Life Assurance and Unit Trust Regulatory Organisation (LAUTRO) authorises unit trusts and oversees the marketing activities of unit trusts and life insurance companies. (Life companies are authorised by the Department of Trade and Industry.)

Investment Management Regulatory Organisation (IMRO) regulates the managers who run unit trusts, pension funds, life company funds and so on, as well as professional advisers to them.

Personal Investment Authority (PIA) is a proposed new SRO for the retail investment industry (i.e. life insurance, unit trusts, advice to non-professional investors and so on). Following recognition by SIB, it is expected to replace FIMBRA and LAUTRO.

The Recognised Professional Bodies
Members of certain professions – accountants, solicitors, actuaries and insurance brokers – can be authorised by their professional body provided investment business does not form the major part of their work. There are nine RPBs: Chartered Association of Certified Accountants, Institute of Actuaries, Institute of Chartered Accountants in England and Wales, Institute of Chartered Accountants in Ireland, Institute of Chartered Accountants of Scotland, Insurance Brokers Registration Council, The Law Society, Law Society of Northern Ireland, Law Society of Scotland.

Q *What sort of rules do investment firms have to stick to when they are giving advice?*

A The rule books are large and the detailed rules extensive. But two of the most important from the customer's point of view are these:

- **know the client** Advisers must take reasonable steps to gather enough information about you to enable them to build up a clear picture of your financial circumstances
- **best advice** The adviser must recommend to you the most suitable product to meet your needs and circumstances. For an independent adviser, this includes recommending the most suitable company. For a company rep or tied outlet, it includes telling you if there is no product they can sell you which would be suitable.

This does not mean that every adviser would give you identical advice – some judgements will be subjective.

Q *I've been made redundant and have had to stop payments to an insurance plan I was sold two years ago. I'd been relying on getting a lump sum from the plan, but now I'm told that there's no cash value at all and that I should have realised it was a long-term investment. Nobody told me this at the time the plan was started.*

A If you feel that you did not fully appreciate the long-term nature of the insurance, or ended up investing more than you could really afford, because of misleading or over-zealous selling, complain to the person or firm which sold you the policy. If that does not produce results, complain to the regulatory body named on the seller's literature.

CHAPTER 8

YOUR PENSION

PENSIONS and pensions advice have been cast in a bad light in recent times. But don't let this deter you from saving for retirement. The biggest risk you face is an impoverished old age. Don't rely just on a state pension – it simply will not be enough. If an employer's pension scheme is open to you, that will usually be your best choice. If not, you will need to look at personal plans. There are ways to top up your pension savings tax-efficiently, and pitfalls to beware of if you switch jobs or transfer your pension for some other reason. And, at the point of retirement, there are yet more decisions to take.

Pension basics

Q *Does everyone get a pension from the state when they retire?*

A Not necessarily. You build up the right to a state retirement pension by paying (or being credited with) enough National Insurance contributions of the right type during your **working life**. Working life is defined officially and usually means the tax years from the one in which you reach age 16 to the last complete tax year before you reach state pension age. The main state pension is **basic pension**. You need to have contributions for roughly a quarter of the years in your working life to get any basic pension at all. And you need contributions for roughly nine-tenths of your working life in order to get the full pension which, in 1994–5, is £57.60 a week for a single person and £92.10 for a married couple.

Q *I worked for a while before I got married, but I haven't worked since. Will I be able to get any state pension when I retire next year?*

A It sounds as if you probably will not have enough years of National Insurance contributions to qualify for a state basic pension based on your own National Insurance record. But, provided your husband has paid or been credited with enough contributions, you should be able to get a pension based on his record. The basic pension for a 'dependent' wife is paid at about six-tenths of the rate the husband gets – in 1994–5, a maximum of £34.50 a week. Provided your husband is already getting state pension, the extra pension will be paid direct to you, when you reach state pension age next year, and will count as your income for tax purposes. If your husband will not have reached state pension age by then, you will have to wait until he does before you can receive your pension. Note that if a husband has already reached state pension age but his wife has not, the extra pension will not be payable if the wife has earnings above a certain level or is receiving another state benefit and, if it is payable, it is given to the husband, not the wife.

Q *I thought that women retired earlier than men. But a friend said that they now retire at the same age. Is that right?*

A The state pension age for men is 65 and at present the state pension age for women is 60. But for women born on or after 6 April 1950, the pension age is being gradually raised until it reaches 65 for all women born on or after 6 March 1955. Note that you become eligible for your state pension once you reach the *pension* age. This does not have to be the age at which you retire – this could be earlier or later.

Q *Isn't there an 'additional state pension' and is this the same thing as a 'SERPS pension'?*

A Yes, you can get an **additional pension** from the state which is provided under the **state earnings-related pension scheme (SERPS)**. Only employees are eligible for this scheme and the pension you eventually get is linked to your earnings throughout your working life between a minimum and maximum level (on which you pay

National Insurance contributions). The scheme aims eventually to give you a pension roughly equal to one-fifth of those earnings, and would be about £74 a week *at most* in 1994–5 money. But many people will get less than this because their earnings are lower than the maximum. Gaps in your work, e.g. because of unemployment, will also reduce your SERPS pension, as will periods when your earnings are below the minimum level.

Q *I've been told that I can 'contract out' of SERPS. What does this mean?*

A **Contracting out** means that, instead of building up SERPS pension over any period you can instead build up a pension through an employer's pension scheme or a personal pension plan. If you contract out through an employer's pension scheme, you (and your employer) pay National Insurance contributions at a lower rate. Your employer guarantees either to provide you with a given pension at retirement (called the **guaranteed minimum pension** or **GMP**) or to invest a certain amount (the **rebate**) to provide you with pension benefits. If you contract out through a personal pension plan you carry on paying the same level of National Insurance contributions, but the DSS pays part of them (the **rebate**) straight back into your plan, where they are invested to provide you with pension benefits.

Q *Is it a good idea to contract out of SERPS?*

A If you are contracted out through an employer's pension scheme and the scheme will provide you with a GMP, you cannot under the current rules lose by contracting out and you may well end up with a better pension than SERPS would have provided. But if you are contracted out on a rebate basis, whether or not it is worthwhile depends on a number of factors. Broadly, if you are a woman in your late 30s or a man in your early 40s, say, you are probably better off being in SERPS (but do not leave an employer's pension scheme simply to contract back in – you would lose more in other benefits than you would gain). If you are younger, contracting out could be a good idea.

Q *Can I find out how much pension I'm going to get from the state when I retire?*

A Unless you are just about to reach state pension age, there is no way of knowing for sure how much you will get. But if you get in touch with the **Retirement Pension Forecast and Advice (RPFA) Service** run by the Department of Social Security (DSS) you can get a statement of how much entitlement you have built up so far and an estimate of how much you will get at retirement if you keep on paying your National Insurance contributions. To do this, get form BR19 from your local Benefits Agency (see Addresses section) and send it to the address on the form. Allow several weeks for a reply. The RPFA service will also advise you whether there are steps you could take to increase your eventual pension, e.g. by paying different National Insurance contributions.

Q *Which National Insurance contributions count towards state pensions?*

A The following types of National Insurance contributions *do* count towards the pensions stated:

- **Class 1** contributions paid by employees (and their employers) count towards the basic pension and may help you to get SERPS pension
- **Class 2** contributions paid by the self-employed count towards the basic pension
- **Class 3** contributions are voluntary and count towards the basic pension.

The following contributions do not count towards state pensions at all:

- **married women's reduced-rate Class 1** (also called the **small stamp**) paid by some married women and some widows who are expected to rely on their husband's contribution record for a pension
- **Class 4** contributions paid by the self-employed.

Q *Will time taken off work to bring up my family affect the state pension I'll eventually get?*

A Usually, no. If you have to stay at home to look after a child (or an invalid) you may be able to get **home responsibilities protection (HRP)**. Any year for which you get HRP is deducted from the total number of years you need to get a given level of basic pension. And, if you will reach state pension age on or after 6 April 1999, years with HRP are also ignored for the purpose of working out any SERPS pension. HRP does not apply to any years before 1978–9 and it is given for whole years only – so, for example, if you were not working for the first half of the year, but then became self-employed for the rest, none of that year would qualify for HRP.

You will get HRP automatically, without having to make a claim, if you are receiving **child benefit** (see page 23). Otherwise, claim through your local Benefits Agency.

Q *I think I have several gaps in my National Insurance record from periods when I was out of work and, more recently, when I travelled round the world for six months. Can I pay extra contributions now to fill the gaps?*

A Some of these periods when you were not working may not appear as gaps in your record because you might have been credited with contributions. You may get credits:

- if you are claiming certain state benefits, such as unemployment, maternity or sickness benefit
- if you are a man who is unemployed and within five years of state pension age, even if you do not 'sign on'
- for the years in which you have your sixteenth, seventeenth and eighteenth birthdays and are still at school
- if you were born on or after 6 April 1957, for the years in which you take part in an approved training course (this does not include university courses) and you were born on or after 6 April 1957.

To fill gaps within the last six years which are not covered by credits you may be able to pay **voluntary class 3** contributions. Contact your local Benefits Agency or other DSS office for advice.

Q *I'll get a state pension, so do I really need to make any extra savings as well?*

A In 1994–5, the basic state retirement pension (see page 243) is just £57.60 a week for a single person – not a lot to live on. Even if you will get **state earnings–related pension (SERPS)** (see page 244) too, you will still need more income if you are to enjoy a reasonable standard of living in retirement. There are three ways of boosting retirement income:

- carry on working – bear in mind that this may not be possible if your health fails or if no jobs are available
- rely on income from investments – money you have saved or inherited perhaps
- save up for your own pension through either a company scheme or a personal plan.

Q *I've contracted out of SERPS and taken out a rebate-only personal plan instead. I understood that the plan would give me more pension, but now I've read in the paper that people in my position should be making extra savings for retirement as well. Is that right?*

A By **contracting out** (see page 245) you have given up your state earnings-related pension in favour of a private pension – in your case, a rebate-only personal pension (see page 245). The pension you get from this plan will not be exactly the same as the SERPS pension you are giving up: if you are fairly young now, the private pension is likely to be bigger than the SERPS pension given up, but, if you are in your 40s or older, it may turn out to be less. Either way, though, your pension will be of *roughly* the same size as the SERPS pension would have been – in other words, not enough to support a comfortable retirement. You would be wise to make extra savings as well.

Q *Why do experts say that pension schemes and plans are the best way to save for retirement?*

A They are usually the best way because they benefit from special tax treatment:

- you get tax relief on your contributions at your highest rate of tax
- the invested contributions build up tax-free

- although the eventual pension counts as taxable income, you can take part of the proceeds of the scheme or plan as a tax-free lump sum.

Provided you are a taxpayer, these benefits are worth having. On the minus side, a pension scheme or plan locks your money away until you reach pension age: you cannot usually get it back earlier except if you have to retire because of ill health.

Employers' pension schemes

Q *I can join my company pension scheme. Would this be a good idea or would a personal pension plan be better?*

A Company schemes are often the best way of saving because:

- your employer contributes to the scheme on your behalf. (You often pay contributions too, depending on the rules of the scheme)
- a company scheme is likely to provide a whole package of benefits, including life insurance, pensions for a widow/widower and other dependants, and help if you become ill. Replacing all these through a personal plan would be expensive
- the running costs of a company scheme are usually lower than those of a personal plan, so more of the money paid in is used for pensions and other benefits.

Q *But are company pension schemes really safe? The Maxwell affair really made me worried.*

A The late Robert Maxwell stole over £400 million from his employees' pension schemes and a lot of that money may never be recovered. As a result, the government set up a committee to suggest ways in which pension scheme regulation should be strengthened and some changes in the law are now being proposed. You can help to ensure that your scheme is soundly run by reading all the information sent to you and asking questions. Things to look out for include:

- how is the pension fund invested? Expect most of it to be in shares of large, well-known companies

- does the pension fund lend to your employer? It is less risky for pensioners if it does not
- when the scheme was last valued, were there enough assets to meet all the pension promises? If not, what is your employer doing about it?
- has the auditor (who must check the yearly accounts of the scheme) raised any doubts about the accounts?

Your union or staff association should be able to take up points like these with the pension scheme trustees, or you can approach the trustees yourself.

Q *How much pension will I get from an employer's pension scheme?*

A Many employers' schemes – those which work on a **final-pay** basis – promise you a pension which is based on your pay at or near retirement. This has two big advantages:

- as your pension builds up, it keeps pace with increases in your earnings
- you have some idea in advance of how much your pension will be in relation to your earnings at retirement.

Most other employers' schemes work on a **money purchase** basis – in effect, you build up a personal fund of assets. The amount of pension you get depends on how much is paid in, how well your fund grows and how much pension the fund can 'buy' at retirement.

Some schemes are **hybrid** and offer you the better of the pension which can be bought on a money purchase basis and a pension worked out on a final-pay basis.

Q *Which is best – a final-pay pension scheme or a money purchase scheme?*

A On the whole, final-pay schemes are the better deal because they promise you a given level of pension. Your employer must make sure that there is enough money in the fund to meet the promise, so he bears most of the risks. With a money purchase scheme, you take the risks – if investment returns are poor, you will get a lower pension.

Final-pay schemes may not be so good if you have to leave before retirement because:

- you will get a **preserved pension** which will be based on pay at the time of leaving, which will generally be lower than at retirement
- the preserved pension will be increased only in line with prices up to a ceiling of 5 per cent a year between the time you leave and the time you retire. On average, prices do not rise as fast as earnings – though this may not be so in your particular case.

Q *My employer's scheme works on a final-pay basis. How much pension will I get?*

A This depends largely on three factors:

- your **final pay** – i.e. your pay at or near retirement
- the number of years you have belonged to the scheme
- the **accrual rate** for your scheme. This means the fraction of pay you will get as pension for each year in the scheme. Common accrual rates are one-sixtieth for each year or one-eightieth.

Table 8.1 shows how your pension might build up in a sixtieths scheme.

Table 8.1: How much pension would be payable for each £10,000 of 'final pay'

Years in scheme up to retirement	Sixtieths scheme	Eightieths scheme
	£	£
5	833	625
10	1,667	1,250
15	2,500	1,875
20	3,333	2,500
25	4,167	3,125
30	5,000	3,750
35	5,833	4,375
40	6,667	5,000

Owing to the generous tax treatment of pension schemes, the Inland Revenue also puts a ceiling on the overall pension you can get. This is two-thirds of your final pay – less if you have been in the scheme for under 20 years (or ten years with some schemes). For schemes set up after 14 March 1989 or a scheme you joined after 31 May 1989, there is also a cap on the earnings which can be used to calculate your pension. The cap is £76,800 in 1994–5 and is usually increased each year in line with prices.

The maximum pension allowed is lower if you take part of the proceeds as a tax-free lump sum.

Q *How much can I take from the scheme as a tax-free lump sum at retirement?*

A The Inland Revenue rules put a ceiling on the tax-free lump sum of one-and-a-half times your final pay – less if you have been in the scheme for under 20 years. If the earnings cap applies to you (see previous question), the biggest lump sum you can get in 1994–5 is 1.5 x £76,800 = £115,200.

Q *How much is it likely to cost me if I join my employer's pension scheme?*

A Some employers' schemes are **non-contributory** – in other words, you pay nothing and your employer foots the whole bill. Other schemes are **contributory** and the rules of the scheme will specify how much you pay. Usually, it will be a given percentage of your before-tax earnings – commonly, 5 per cent.

Inland Revenue rules put a ceiling on the amount you can pay and this is 15 per cent of your earnings. If the earnings cap applies to you (see above), then only earnings up to £76,800 count in 1994–5 – i.e. the most you could contribute would be £11,520.

Q *I've joined a very good company scheme but rather late in life, so there's no way I'll get a full pension from it. What's the best way to boost the income I'll get at retirement?*

A You can increase the amount of pension and other benefits – except the tax-free lump sum – you will get from a company scheme by paying in extra either through your employer's **additional voluntary contribution (AVC)** scheme or through a **free-standing AVC (FSAVC)** scheme, which is like a personal plan except that it can be used only to buy extra pension or other benefits in an employer's scheme. The Inland Revenue limit on contributions (see opposite) applies to normal contributions together with any AVCs.

FSAVCs and, usually AVCs too, build up on a money purchase basis and the resulting fund is used to buy extra benefits in the scheme. Some AVC schemes let you buy **added years** in a final-pay scheme, resulting in a higher pension and other benefits.

Q *How can I estimate what pension I'll get from my employer's scheme?*

A Most final-pay schemes provide regular **benefit statements** which show, *inter alia*, what pension you can expect at retirement if you stay in the scheme until then and if you left now. If your scheme does not provide statements automatically, you can ask for one: you are legally entitled to one statement a year on request. Money purchase schemes are required to provide a statement each year showing how much you have built up in the pension fund to date.

Q *I received a benefit statement from my pension scheme recently and I'm certain that the scheme hasn't credited me with all my pension. I went to talk to the scheme administrator, but he's adamant that there's no mistake. How can I make him reconsider?*

A If you are in dispute concerning an employer's pension scheme and you have tried resolving the matter with scheme officials to no avail, you could contact the **Occupational Pensions Advisory Service (OPAS)**. This is an independent body which can help you to understand the rules of your scheme and will negotiate with the officials if necessary. OPAS also deals with disputes concerning personal pension plans. If, after taking your case to OPAS, you are still not happy, you could take your case to the **Pensions Ombudsman**, who can act as an arbitrator and can order compensation if appropriate. See Addresses section for how to contact OPAS and the Ombudsman.

Personal pension plans

Q *My employer doesn't run a pension scheme. Can I take out a personal plan instead?*

A Yes. There are five main situations in which you are eligible to take out a personal pension plan:

- if you are a member of an employer's scheme but the personal plan is used only to **contract out** of the **state earnings-related pension scheme (SERPS)** – see page 245
- if you are a member of an employer's scheme but you have additional earnings – from freelance work, say – which are not covered by the scheme
- you are an employee but have chosen not to join your employer's pension scheme
- you are an employee and your employer does not run a pension scheme
- you are self-employed.

Q *I'm self-employed, so there's no company scheme open to me. An insurance agent has been trying to persuade me that I should take out a personal pension plan. But I have a good business and should be able to sell it eventually for a tidy sum, which will give my wife and me a good retirement. What use is a pension plan to someone like me?*

A If you run a business, such as a shop or office, which has valuable assets or which can be sold as a going concern, you might plan to sell up eventually and retire on the proceeds. However, this is a risky strategy, because:

- you might not find a buyer at the time you want to retire (or need to retire, say, for health reasons)
- you might get less for the business than you had hoped
- the business might fail, even before you reach retirement.
  Therefore, it is wise to make separate savings for retirement. Doing this through a personal pension plan has a number of advantages:

- you get tax relief on your contributions to the plan
- your pension fund builds up tax-free

- though the pension will be taxable, you can take part of the proceeds of the plan as a tax-free lump sum.

Q *How much pension can I expect from a personal pension plan?*

A All personal pension plans work on a **money purchase basis**. This means that you cannot know in advance how much pension you will get: it will depend on the amount paid in contributions, how long this has been invested, the rate of return on the invested contributions and **annuity rates** at the time you retire. An annuity is a lifetime income which you get in exchange for handing over a lump sum, such as a pension fund. The annuity rate at the time you make the switch usually fixes the income you will get for the rest of your life – either at a level amount, or at an amount which increases each year by, say, five per cent a year or in line with inflation.

Q *How is the tax relief on contributions to a personal plan paid?*

A If you are an employee, you deduct tax relief at the basic rate from the contributions you make and hand over a net sum to the pension company. The company then claims the amount deducted from the Inland Revenue and adds it to your plan. So, for example, if you pay £75 to the company, it claims £25 from the Revenue and £100 in total is paid into your plan. You get basic-rate relief in this way even if you are only a 20 per cent taxpayer. If you are a higher-rate taxpayer, you have to claim the extra relief, which will usually be paid through an alteration to your PAYE code (see page 52).

If you are self-employed, you make gross – i.e. before tax relief – contributions to your plan. You have to claim the tax relief from your tax office and it will usually be given either through your assessment or, sometimes, as a tax rebate.

Q *Is there any limit on the amount I can save through a personal pension plan?*

A Yes. There are two types of personal plan. With a modern plan, up to the age of 35, you can contribute up to 17.5 per cent of your **net**

relevant earnings to the plan. If you are self-employed these are your taxable profits; if you are an employee, these are your pay including the value of fringe benefits. Only earnings up to £76,800 count in the 1994–5 tax year – this limit is usually increased each year in line with price inflation. If you are older than 35, you can invest more – see Table 8.2.

If you have an older-style plan – sometimes called a **retirement annuity contract** or **section 226 plan** – the limits are as shown in Table 8.3.

Table 8.2: Tax relief limits on contributions to modern personal pension plans

Your age at the start of the tax year	Contribution limit as a percentage of your earnings
Up to 35	17.5%
36–45	20%
46–50	25%
51–55	30%
56–60	35%
61–74	40%
75 and over	you can no longer contribute

Table 8.3: Tax relief limits on contributions to older-style personal pension plans

Your age at the start of the tax year	Contribution limit as a percentage of your earnings
Up to 50	17.5%
51–55	20%
56–60	22.5%
61–74	27.5%
75 and over	you can no longer contribute

Q *I'm a bit wary about starting a personal pension plan, because my profits vary so much from year to year. Do I have to commit myself to saving a regular sum?*

A No. You can choose whether to save a regular amount or to invest lump sums as and when you can afford to. The main advantage of regular saving is that it provides a discipline, making it more likely that you will save enough for the pension you want. But there are often penalties if you have to stop a regular payment plan early, so you are right to be wary given your variable income.

Q *I've been told I can invest more than the normal limit if I use the carry-forward rules. What are these?*

A They are special rules which let you carry forward unused contribution limit from the previous six years, provided you have completely used up the current year's limit. You always carry forward from the earliest years first and you get tax relief at the *current* year's tax rate. See Box for an example of how the rules work in practice.

Note that the money you put into your pension plan does not actually have to be part of your net relevant earnings provided you have the necessary contribution limit available. The carry-forward rules can therefore be very useful, allowing you to top up your pension savings if, say, you inherit some money.

EXAMPLE: HOW THE CARRY-FORWARD RULES WORK

Joe (aged 50) landed a good contract in the 1993–4 tax year which nearly doubled his usual earnings. As a result, he was able to put £6,500 into his (old-style) personal pension plan. This took him over the tax relief limit for 1993–4, but he was able to bring forward relief from earlier years as shown in the table:

Tax year	Joe's earnings £	Contribution tax relief limit £	Joe's contributions £	Unused relief £	Relief remaining after 1993–4 £
1987–8	8,200	1,435	800	635	0
1988–9	8,600	1,505	800	705	0
1989–90	9,200	1,610	1,000	610	0
1990–1	9,000	1,575	1,000	575	0
1991–2	9,600	1,680	1,500	180	0
1992–3	11,800	2,065	1,000	1,065	350
1993–4	17,600	3,080	6,500	0	0

As the Table shows, the £6,500 contribution uses up all the tax relief limit for 1993–4 and for the years 1987–8 to 1991–2. It also uses up £715 of the relief left over from 1992–3. After making the contribution, Joe still has unused relief of £350 left in the 1992–3 tax year which can continue to be carried forward.

Q *After years at home with the children, I now have a part-time job. I don't earn a lot – just £3,000 a year – but I'd like to save some of this for when I retire. Can I take out a pension plan?*

A If the £3,000 is all your income, you are a non-taxpayer. This means it is not worth your investing in a pension scheme or plan because you will not get any benefit from the tax reliefs. (See page 208 for alternative ways of saving.) Bear in mind, though, that even though your earnings are currently too low for you to pay tax, you will still have a small contribution limit (the relevant percentage of your £3,000 net relevant earnings). You can carry this forward for up to six years and it may be worth using later, if you become a taxpayer.

Q *What's the time limit for making pension contributions for last year?*

A If you have not yet made your contributions for last year, then you can pay them this year and elect to **carry back** the contributions to last year. Normally you can carry back contributions only one tax year, but if you had no relevant earnings last year you can carry them back two years. To use the carry-back rule, you do not have to have used up the current tax year's contribution limit first, and you get tax relief at last year's tax rates. You must make a carry-back election no later than 5 July following the end of the tax year in which you pay the contributions.

The carry-back rules are especially useful for people who are self-employed because:

- if your accounts take some time to make up, you might not be sure how much you can contribute until after the end of the tax year

- you get tax relief straight away on carried-back contributions. With normal contributions you have to wait until you receive an assessment for the year.

Q *Can I combine the carry-forward and carry-back rules?*

A Yes, you can, and in this way you can use up contribution limit from up to *seven* years ago rather than six. For example, suppose in 1994–5 you pay a contribution and elect for it to be carried back to 1993–4. You can go back six years from 1993–4 and use up unused limit from as far back as 1987–8.

Q *After a few bad years, my business is looking a bit healthier. I know I ought to be putting aside something for retirement now that we seem to have turned the corner, but I am very wary of tying up the money at present. What would you recommend me to do?*

A The main drawback to using a personal pension plan is that, once invested, your money is tied up in the plan until at least age 50 (the earliest you can start to draw a pension). This can be a real disincentive to save when business conditions are uncertain. While your wariness is understandable, putting off pension saving is not a good idea – Table 8.4 shows how a delay of a few years can drastically reduce the fund you will have available for your pension.

If you really cannot risk tying up your money in a pension plan right now, save in another way for the time being. For tax-efficiency, choose a personal equity plan (PEP) – see page 219. If you are within five years or so of retirement, you might consider a tax-exempt special savings account (TESSA) – see page 209.

Q *I've decided it's time to retire from my business and start drawing from my personal pension plan. But the insurance company has given me a much lower quote for my pension than I'd been expecting. Can I switch to another company?*

A Yes, with nearly all personal pension plans you have an **open market option**, which lets you switch to another company at the time you decide to start your pension. It makes sense to use this option, because some companies specialise in providing annuities and are more likely to offer higher rates than those who do not. Consider getting advice from an independent financial adviser or from Annuity Direct or the Annuity Bureau, both of which specialise in advice about the type of annuity to choose and the best rates available (see Addresses section).

Table 8.4: How your pension fund might grow

| | SIZE OF PENSION FUND BY AGE 65 | | | |
| | Regular premiums of £1,000 a year | | Single premium of £1,000 | |
Age you make or start contributions	Fund grows at 6% p.a.	Fund grows at 12% p.a.	Fund grows at 6% p.a.	Fund grows at 12% p.a.
	£	£	£	£
55	12,480	16,900	1,630	2,830
45	33,840	66,170	2,830	8,550
35	71,590	216,060	4,930	25,850
25	137,690	671,220	8,590	78,150

Source: *LAUTRO Projection Tables*, June 1993

Q *When I take my pension, is it better to choose an annuity which increases each year?*

A Table 8.5 shows the average life expectancy for men and women at various ages. You can see that depending on when you start your retirement, it might *on average* last 20 or 30 years – and, of course, some people live a lot longer. Even if inflation averaged a low rate – say, 3 per cent a year – throughout your whole retirement, each £1,000 of pension now would be worth only £750 after ten years, £550 after 20 years and £400 after 30 years in terms of what it could buy. An increasing annuity will help to protect the buying power of your pension as the years go by. However, as you might expect, an increasing annuity gives you less income at the start than a level annuity. You will have to weigh this against the advantage of having some inflation-proofing. If you are in poor health, it would probably be better to opt for the level annuity, but if your family is noted for its longevity an increasing annuity may turn up trumps.

Table 8.5: Average length of retirement

| | Average expected number of years in retirement | |
Retirement at	Women	Men
50	30	26
55	26	21
60	22	17
65	18	14
70	14	11
75	11	8

Source: Government Actuary's Department

Q *Could my personal pension plan provide a pension for my wife if I were to die, as well as just for me?*

A Yes. Sadly, many people are not as far-sighted as you and fail to provide any protection for a surviving spouse or partner. But it is possible to do this using a **joint life annuity**. This will carry on paying an income until *both* you and your wife or partner have died, rather than stopping simply when you die.

Another, though inferior, way to provide some protection is to choose a **guaranteed annuity**. This provides an income for your lifetime but also guarantees to pay out for a set period – usually five or ten years – regardless of whether you survive that long. The continuing annuity becomes part of your estate on death and can be left to anyone – your widow, widower or someone else – in your will.

The drawback with both these options is that the income you get will be lower than that from a straightforward annuity – see Table 8.6.

Q *When annuity rates are low, is it better to put off taking my pension and wait until rates get better?*

A If you can manage without your pension for a while, this might be a good idea, because a traditional annuity locks you into a pension based on rates at the time the pension starts. In other words, low annuity rates mean a low pension for life. Moreover, the amount you get under an annuity is based partly on the life expectancy for a person of your age, so the later you start your pension, the higher it will be. On the other hand, if you put off your·pension for a year, say, you will also have lost out on a year's income. You need to weigh that loss against what you hope to gain by waiting.

Table 8.6: How much pension from your plan?

Type of annuity	Annual income before tax for each £10,000 invested (best rates at 2 May 1994) £
Level annuity for man aged 65	1,167.60
Level annuity for man aged 70	1,375.92
Level annuity for woman aged 60	930.23
Level annuity for woman aged 65	1,029.96
Annuity increasing by 5% a year for man aged 70	977.64[1]
Annuity increasing by 5% a year for woman aged 70	782.64[1]
Joint life level annuity for man aged 65 and woman aged 60	909.48
Joint life level annuity for man aged 65 and woman aged 65	943.56
Level annuity guaranteed for five years for man aged 65	1,133.52
Level annuity guaranteed for five years for woman aged 60	925.57
Level annuity guaranteed for five years for man aged 65 and woman aged 60	909.48

Source: *Pensions Management*, June 1994
[1] Income in the first year.

Q *I couldn't afford to be without a pension once I'd retired. Is there any way, other than delaying the pension, that I could cover myself if annuity rates were low at the time I stopped work?*

A You could consider a flexible pension. A conventional annuity locks you into either a level pension or one which increases year by year at some pre-determined rate. But there are several alternatives:

- **phased retirement scheme** This type of scheme splits your pension fund into many segments. Each year, enough segments are converted into an annuity and the tax-free cash sum which pension plans can provide to make up your chosen amount of income. The rest of the segments are left invested to provide future years' pension. High charges mean these schemes usually suit only the relatively wealthy and 'young' retired

- **with-profits annuity** Your fund remains invested and has regular bonuses added which depend mainly on the performance of shares. The value of your fund cannot fall. If bonuses meet a target level, you get a level pension each year. If bonuses are better, your pension increases, but if bonuses are worse, your pension falls

- **unit-linked annuity** This is similar to a with-profits annuity, except that your fund is invested on a unit-linked basis (see page 228). Because the value of your fund can fall as well as rise and potential rises and falls in your pension are much greater, this option is riskier than a with-profits annuity and usually less popular

In late 1993 a **managed annuity** (also known as a **self-invested annuity**) was also launched. Under this type of scheme your pension fund remains invested usually on a unit-linked basis. You choose a level of pension which can be maintained if the fund grows at a target level. If growth is better, the fund increases; if growth is worse, the fund shrinks. The level of pension and the size of the fund are reviewed each year and the remaining fund can be converted into an annuity at any time. The scheme, which is suitable for funds of £100,000 or more, proved popular, but in March 1994 the Inland Revenue said that such managed annuities were not consistent with Revenue approval (and therefore tax reliefs) for pension schemes and plans. However, in June 1994 the government proposed changes to the law which would allow this type of flexible approach to pensions at some time in the future.

Though all these options are more risky than a conventional annuity, they look attractive when interest rates are low and the stock market is performing well.

Pension transfers

Q *I've had several jobs over the last fifteen years and have little bits of pension left behind in a number of schemes. Would it be better to transfer all these to one single scheme?*

A It is not possible to say on the information provided. You need to look at the pension you stand to get from each of the schemes and compare this with the pension you might get from the scheme or plan to which you are thinking of transferring. This is not easy, so consider getting some financial advice (see opposite). If you leave the pensions where they are, it is important that you keep in touch with the schemes, letting them know if you change your address. At retirement, if you have lost touch with a scheme or a personal pension plan provider, you can probably trace them through the Pensions Registry (see Addresses section).

Q *I've just switched jobs and I've got a pension in my old employer's scheme, which wasn't a terribly good one. I'd like to transfer it. What are my options?*

A When you have pension rights in an employer's scheme, you have several options. You can:

- leave the pension rights in the old employer's scheme until retirement
- transfer the rights to a new employer's scheme if it will accept the transfer
- transfer to a special **section 32 plan**: this is a personal plan but preserves some of the guarantees you may have had with the employer's scheme
- transfer to a personal pension plan: since these all work on a money purchase basis, you lose any guarantees you might have had under the old employer's scheme and could end up better or worse off.

Q *I've been wondering whether to transfer my pension from the scheme I was in when I was a nurse to a personal pension plan. Is this a good idea?*

A Not if you worked for the National Health Service (NHS). The NHS scheme is one of the best in Britain and will provide you with a better pension at retirement than you could get by transferring to a personal plan. Anyone who works in the public sector – teachers, local government employees, NHS employees, civil servants and so on – and anyone working for one of the privatised or formerly privatised industries is likely to be covered by a very good employer's pension scheme. If this applies to you, be very wary of opting out of the scheme or transferring benefits from it.

Q *I read in the press that a lot of people had been badly advised to transfer pension rights from old employers' schemes to personal pension plans. How can you tell if you're being given good transfer advice?*

A You can identify good pension transfer advice by these features:

- the adviser should carry out a thorough fact-find, asking you about your age, health, intended retirement age, career intentions, family commitments, existing financial arrangements and attitude towards risk
- the adviser must explain your options regarding pension rights with an old employer's scheme – i.e. to leave them where they are, or transfer them to another scheme or plan
- the adviser cannot give you sound transfer advice unless he (or she) knows what benefits you stand to give up, so he needs to know the pension rights you have with the old employer's scheme. He should ask you for your signed permission to allow him to contact the scheme for details, including your expected pension at retirement, your options for taking early retirement, the way the pension would increase during retirement, and so on
- if you can join a new employer's scheme, the adviser also needs to know what benefits that scheme would offer you. If you are unemployed but expect to get another job, sound advice would be to defer any transfer decision until you have a new employer (who may offer a pension scheme)
- having gathered all this information, the adviser is now in a position to compare the pension options. Under new rules from SIB, from 1 July 1994 the adviser must use a proper analysis system (which will have to conform to set standards from 1995 onwards) for comparing the benefits you would get by transferring with those you would get by staying in your employer scheme
- the adviser should give you a projection to illustrate the benefits you could get by transferring. Under the new SIB rules, the projection must mirror the benefits you could get by staying in the employer scheme – e.g. by providing for a widow's pension or guaranteed

increases in retirement, and so on. You can be given other projections as well

- the adviser should discuss the options and the results of the analysis with you, making clear the various risks involved with each course of action. Finally the adviser should make his recommendation to you. Under the new SIB rules, he will be required to give you a letter stating why the recommendation is suitable advice for you.

Firms which want to give pension transfer advice will, from November 1994, have to prove to their regulator that they can comply with the rules. Provided technical problems can be overcome, SIB intends at some time to introduce a 14-day cooling-off period during which anyone who acts on transfer advice can change their mind.

If your adviser did not – or does not – follow all the above steps, then the advice given is not satisfactory. This does not necessarily mean that the final recommendation is wrong, but it certainly should be checked, and you should report the adviser to the appropriate regulator.

Q *Having joined a really excellent employer's pension scheme, I decided to transfer the fund that's built up in my personal pension plan to the scheme. But the insurance company running the personal plan has messed up the transfer value. I know that there are some penalties for transferring, but the company simply seems to have got the figure wrong. What can I do?*

A First, you should take up the dispute with the insurance company and ask it to provide you with details of how the calculation has been made. If you are unable to come to an agreement, you could take your case to OPAS, which can help in disputes involving personal pension plans (see page 253).

On retirement

Q *I've reached 60 at last! But I've decided to carry on working so I don't really need my state pension just yet. I had intended to put it aside in the building society until later on, but someone suggested I might do better to put off my retirement. Is that right?*

A Under the current rules applying to state pension, you can delay starting your pension for up to five years. Your pension will then be increased by 7.5 per cent for each year of deferment (and pro rata for shorter periods), which means a maximum increase of 37.5 per cent when your pension eventually starts. Bearing in mind that pensions are increased each year in line with inflation, this is a substantial increase. For example, in 1994–5 the full single person's basic pension is £57.60 a week. If inflation averaged 3 per cent a year, this would have risen to £66.80 a week by the year 1999–2000. But, if you had delayed starting your pension until then you would get an increase of 37.5% x £66.80, so your increased basic pension would be £91.80 a week.

Could you get the same increase by saving your pension? Suppose an index-linked annuity at age 65 offered you £600 a year for every £10,000 invested. You would need to have built up a fund of about £22,000 to match the extra £1,300-a-year pension you would get in 1999–2000 by deferring retirement. Assuming your pension available for investment was £250 a month for five years, you would need a yearly return of nearly 16 per cent to build up that sum. On this basis, deferring your pension looks like a good deal, but you must weigh against this the chances that you will not survive long enough to enjoy the fruits of deferment – see next question.

Q *I've been considering deferring my pension. It seems to me that I'd have to live quite a long time to recoup the pension I forgo in the early years of retirement. How long would I have to survive?*

A You want to compare pension given up now with pension gained in future. Fortunately, because the state pension is increased by inflation each year, the comparison can be made quite easily in terms of today's money by simply ignoring the annual increases. Suppose you qualify for the full single person's basic pension of £57.60 a week, i.e. £2,995.20 a year – £3,005.20 including the tax-free Christmas bonus. If you gave up your pension for the full five years, you would give up 5 x £3,005.20 = £15,026 in total in today's money. This would earn you a 37.5 per cent increase in pension – i.e. an extra £21.60 a week, again in terms of today's money. You would need to survive 13⅓ years before the additional pension matched the pension you had given up.

The required survival period to break even is the same even if you defer your pension for a shorter period than one year.

A 65-year-old woman is likely to survive that long on average, but a 70-year-old man is not. However, a married man should also take into account that his wife is likely to live longer than him and would carry on benefiting from the increase in pension if her pension was related to his.

Given that you cannot know in advance whether your survival will be average, better than average or worse than average, you might prefer to defer the pension for less than the full five years or to draw it straight away and invest it if you do not need the income immediately.

Q *Can I just defer my SERPS pension and start drawing my basic pension now?*

A No, you must defer all your state pensions together – and if your wife's pension would be based on your contribution record, her pension must be deferred as well (and she too earns the same increase).

Q *I didn't realise that I could defer my pension. Now I've already started to draw it, can I change my mind?*

A Yes, you can decide to give up your pension even though you have already started to draw it. But once you restart your pension after a period of deferment, you cannot defer it again.

Q *I'm approaching 65 and will soon qualify for my state pension. Is it paid automatically once I reach my 65th birthday?*

A No, it is not paid automatically. You must claim your state pension. About four months before you reach state pension age, you should get a letter from the DSS with the appropriate claim form, BR1. If you have not heard anything by three months before your birthday, get in touch yourself with your local Benefits Agency (see Addresses section).

Q *How is the state pension paid?*

A You can choose either to be paid by order book – you cash one order at the post office each week – or to have the pension credited direct to your bank or building society account (see DSS leaflet NI105, *Payment Direct into Bank or Building Society Accounts*, available from Benefits Agencies, for more information).

Q *Can I still get my state pension if I retire abroad?*

A Yes, but you will not get the yearly increases to your pension unless you are living in a European Union country or one of the other countries with which Britain has an appropriate reciprocal agreement. See leaflets NI38, *Social Security Abroad*, and NI106, *Pensioners or Widows Going Abroad* (available from Benefits Agencies) for details. There are also leaflets about UK agreements with individual countries which you can obtain from the Overseas Branch of the DSS (see Addresses section).

Q *I'm pretty sure that I'm due a pension from a firm I worked for during my twenties. Needless to say, I lost touch with it years ago and they are no longer at the old address. How can I find out about the pension and claim it?*

A You could contact the **Pensions Registry**. This is a government body which holds details of employers' pension schemes and personal pension plan providers. It can help you trace 'lost' pensions. You will need to fill in form PR4, which you can get from the Registry or from OPAS (see Addresses section).

ADDRESSES

Advertising Standards Authority (ASA)
Brook House, 2–16 Torrington Place, London WC1E 7HN
Tel: 071–580 5555

Age Concern Insurance
Tel: 0883 346964

The Annuity Bureau Ltd
Tel: 071–620 4090

Annuity Direct
Tel: 071–375 1175

Association of British Insurers (ABI)
51 Gresham Street, London EC2V 7HQ
Tel: 071–600 3333

Association of Investment Trust Companies (AITC)
Park House (6th floor), 16 Finsbury Circus, London EC2M 7JJ
Tel: 071–588 5347

Association of Unit Trusts and Investment Funds (AUTIF)
65 Kingsway, London WC2B 6TD
Tel: 071–831 0898

Air Travel Organiser's Licence (ATOL)
Tel: 071–832 5620/6600

Association of British Travel Agents (ABTA)
Tel: 0891 202520 (calls charged at 49p a minute/ 39p a minute off-peak)

Association of Independent Tour Operators (AITO)
Tel: 081–744 9280

Association of Private Client Investment Managers and Stockbrokers
(APCIMS)
112 Middlesex Street, London E1 7HY
Tel: 0891 335521 (calls charged at 49p a minute/ 39p a minute off-peak)

Banking Ombudsman
70 Gray's Inn Road, London WC1X 8NB
Tel: 071–404 9944

Beale Dobie
Tel: Freephone Surrender

Benefits Agency
For your local office, see phone book under Social Security, Department of

British Bankers' Association
10 Lombard Street, London, EC3V 9EL
Tel: 071–623 4001

British Insurance and Investment Brokers Association (BIIBA)
14 Bevis Marks House, London EC3A 7NT
Tel: 071–623 9043

The Building Societies' Association
3 Savile Row, London, W1X 1AF
Tel: 071–437 0655

Building Societies Ombudsman
Grosvenor Gardens House, 35–37 Grosvenor Gardens, London
SW1X 7AW
Tel: 071–931 0044

Capital Taxes Office (England & Wales)
Minford House, Rockley Road, London W14 0DF

Capital Taxes Office (Northern Ireland)
Dorchester House, 52–58 Great Victoria Street, Belfast BT2 7BB

Capital Taxes Office (Scotland)
Mulberry House, 16 Picardy Place, Edinburgh EH1 3NF

CCN Systems Ltd
Consumer Affairs Department, PO Box 40, Nottingham NG7 2SS

Chartered Association of Certified Accountants
29 Lincoln's Inn Fields, London WC2A 3EE
Tel: 071–396 5700

Child Support Agency (CSA)
PO Box 55, Brierly Hill, West Midlands DY5 1YL
Tel: 0345 133 133 (9am-6pm weekdays, calls charged at local rate)

Citizens Advice Bureau
For local Bureau, see phone book, local newspapers or ask at your local council offices.

Confederation of Passenger Transport UK
Sardinia House, 52 Lincoln's Inn Fields, London WC2A 3LZ
Tel: 071–831 7546

Consumers' Association
(orders for books including *Starting Your Own Business, The Which? Guide to Divorce, The Which? Guide to Giving and Inheriting, The Which? Guide to Pensions, The Which? Guide to Renting and Letting, Which? Way to Save and Invest, Which? Way to Save Tax* and *Wills and Probate,* for the Action Pack *Make Your Will* and for *Taxcalc* software program and *Which?* subscriptions, including annual *Tax-saving Guide*) Castlemead, Gascoyne Way, Hertford X, SG14 1LH
Freephone (0800) 252100 (Access/Visa orders)

Council of Mortgage Lenders
3 Savile Row, London W1X 1AP
Tel: 071–437 0655

Credit Data and Marketing Services
CCA Department, Dove Mill, Dean Church Lane, Bolton, Lancashire
BL3 4ET

Department of Social Security (DSS)
For local offices, also called Benefits Agencies, see phone book under Social Security, Department of

DSS Overseas Branch
Benton Park Road, Newcastle-upon-Tyne NE98 1YX
Tel: 091–213 5000

DSS Freeline Social Security
This free telephone enquiry service is available in several languages: English 0800 666555; Chinese 0800 252451; Punjabi 0800 521360; Urdu 0800 289188; Welsh 0800 289011. Note also: Northern Ireland 0800 616757

DSS leaflets
From Benefits Agencies, some post offices and libraries or:
BA Distribution and Storage Centre, Manchester Road, Heywood,
Lancashire OL10 2PZ

Department of Trade and Industry
Consumer Affairs Division, 10–18 Victoria Street, London SW1H 0NN
Tel: 071–215 5000

Energy Action Grants Agency (EAGA)
PO Box 1NG, Newcastle upon Tyne NE99 2RP
For information about grants under the Home Energy Efficiency Scheme (HEES)
Freephone 0800 181667

Equifax Europe Ltd
Consumer Affairs Department, Spectrum House, 1A North Avenue,
Clydebank, Glasgow G81 2DR
Tel: 041–951 1253

Financial Intermediaries, Managers and Brokers Regulatory Association (FIMBRA)
Hertsmere House, Hertsmere Road, London E14 4AB
Tel: 071–538 8860/071–895 1229

H. E. Foster & Cranfield
Tel: 071–608 1941

Funeral Ombudsman Scheme (FOS)
The Office of the Funeral Ombudsman, Suite 3.3, 31 Southampton Row,
London WC1B 5HJ
Tel: 071–430 1112

Gas Consumers Council
Abford House, 15 Wilton Road, London SW1V 1LT
Tel: 071–931 0977

Health Advice for Travellers (free Department of Health leaflet)
Freephone 0800 555777

Home Energy Efficiency Scheme
See Energy Action Grants Agency

IFAP
(for a list of local independent financial advisers)
~~Tel: 0483 461461~~   0117/9711/117

Independent Schools Information Service (ISIS)
56 Buckingham Gate, London SW1E 6AE
Tel: 071–630 8793

Infolink Ltd
CCA Department, 38 Whitworth Street, Manchester M60 1QH

Institute of Actuaries
Staple Inn Hall, High Holborn, London WC1V 7QJ
Tel: 071–242 0106

Institute of Chartered Accountants in England and Wales
PO Box 433, Chartered Accountants' Hall, Moorgate Place, London
EC2P 2BJ
Tel: 071–920 8100

Institute of Chartered Accountants in Ireland
Chartered Accountants' House, 87–89 Pembroke Road, Dublin 4, Eire
Tel: 010 3531 680400

Institute of Chartered Accountants of Scotland
27 Queen Street, Edinburgh EH2 1LA
Tel: 031–225 5673

Insurance Brokers Registration Council
15 St Helen's Place, London EC3A 6DS
Tel: 071–588 4387

Insurance Ombudsman's Bureau
135 Park Street, London SE1 9EA
Tel: 071–928 7600

Investment Management Regulatory Organisation (IMRO)
Broadwalk House, 5 Appold Street, London EC2A 2LL
Tel: 071–628 6022

Investors Compensation Scheme
Gavrelle House, 2–14 Bunhill Row, London EC1Y 8RA
Tel: 071–628 8820

Job Centres
For local centre, see phone book under Employment, Department of

The Law Society
113 Chancery Lane, London WC2A 1PL
Tel: 071–242 1222

Law Society of Northern Ireland
Law Society House, 98 Victoria Street, Belfast BT1 3JZ
Tel: 0232 231614

Law Society of Scotland
Law Society Hall, 26 Drumsheugh Gardens, Edinburgh EH3 7YR
Tel: 031–226 7411

Life Assurance and Unit Trust Regulatory Organisation (LAUTRO)
Centre Point, 103 New Oxford Street, London WC1A 1QH
Tel: 071–379 0444

Mailing Preference Service (MPS)
Freepost 22, London W1E 7EZ

Money Management National Register of Independent Fee-based Advisers
c/o Matrix Data Ltd, Freepost 22 (SW1565), London W1E 7EZ
Tel: 0272 769444

National Debtline
Tel: 021–359 8501

Occupational Pensions Advisory Service (OPAS)
11 Belgrave Road, London SW1V 1RB
Tel: 071–233 8080

Occupational Pensions Board (OPB)
PO Box 1NN, Newcastle-upon-Tyne NE99 1NN
Tel: 091–225 6393/4

Office of Electricity Regulation (OFFER)
Hagley House, 83–85 Hagley Road, Edgbaston, Birmingham B16 8QG
Tel: 021–456 2100

Office of Fair Trading (OFT)
Field House, 15–25 Bream's Buildings, London EC4A 1PR
Tel: 071–242 2858

Office of Gas Supply (OFGAS)
Stockley House, 130 Wilton Road, London SW1V 1LQ
Tel: 071–828 0898

Passenger Shipping Association
9/10 Market Place, London W1N 7AG
Tel: 071 436 2449

Pensions Ombudsman
11 Belgrave Road, London SW1V 1RB
You must first let OPAS try to resolve your problem

Pensions Registry
See Registrar of Pension Schemes

Personal Insurance Arbitration Scheme (PIAS)
Chartered Institute of Arbitrators, 24 Angel Gate, City Road, London
EC1V 2RS
Tel: 071–837 4483

Personal Investment Authority (PIA)
3 Royal Exchange Building, London EC3V 3NL
Tel: 071–929 0072

Registrar of Pension Schemes
Occupational Pensions Board, PO Box 1NN, Newcastle-upon-Tyne
NE99 1NN
Tel: 091–225 6393

SAGA Insurance
Freephone 0800 414525

Securities and Futures Authority Ltd (SFA)
The Cotton Centre, Cottons Lane, London SE1 2QB
Tel: 071–378 9000

Securities and Investments Board (SIB)
Gavrelle House, 2–14 Bunhill Row, London EC1Y 8RA
Tel: 071–638 1240

SIB Register
Enquiries tel: 071–929 3652

Tax office
For local office, see phone book under Inland Revenue

The Timeshare Council
23 Buckingham Gate, London SW1E 6HB
Tel: 071–821 8845

Trading Standards Office
For your local office, see phone book under local council entry

Unemployment Benefit Office
For your local office, see phone book under Employment, Deparment of

VAT office
For your local office, see phone book under Customs & Excise

INDEX